Deliberation, Democracy, and the Media

CRITICAL MEDIA STUDIES:
INSTITUTIONS, POLITICS, AND CULTURE

Series Editor
Andrew Calabrese, University of Colorado at Boulder

Advisory Board
Patricia Aufderheide, American University • **Jean-Claude Burgelman**, Free University of Brussels • **Simone Chambers**, University of Colorado • **Nicholas Garnham**, University of Westminster • **Hanno Hardt**, University of Iowa • **Gay Hawkins**, University of New South Wales • **Maria Heller**, Eötvös Loránd University • **Robert Horwitz**, University of California at San Diego • **Douglas Kellner**, University of California at Los Angeles • **Gary Marx**, Massachusetts Institute of Technology • **Toby Miller**, New York University • **Vincent Mosco**, Carleton University • **Janice Peck**, University of Colorado • **Manjunath Pendakur**, University of Western Ontario • **Arvind Rajagopal**, New York University • **Kevin Robins**, Goldsmiths College • **Saskia Sassen**, University of Chicago • **Colin Sparks**, University of Westminster • **Slavko Splichal**, University of Ljubljana • **Thomas Streeter**, University of Vermont • **Liesbet van Zoonen**, University of Amsterdam • **Janet Wasko**, University of Oregon

Titles in the Series

Interactions: Critical Studies in Communication, Media, and Journalism, Hanno Hardt

Communication, Citizenship, and Social Policy: Rethinking the Limits of the Welfare State, edited by Andrew Calabrese and Jean-Claude Burgelman

Public Opinion: Developments and Controversies in the Twentieth Century, Slavko Splichal

Redeveloping Communication for Social Change: Theory, Practice, and Power, edited by Karin Gwinn Wilkins

Tabloid Tales: Global Debates over Media Standards, edited by Colin Sparks and John Tulloch

The Information Society in Europe: Work and Life in an Age of Globalization, edited by Ken Ducatel, Juliet Webster, and Werner Herrmann

Ferdinand Tönnies on Public Opinion: Selections and Analyses, edited, introduced, and translated by Hanno Hardt and Slavko Splichal

Deliberation, Democracy, and the Media, edited by Simone Chambers and Anne Costain

Deregulating Telecommunications: U.S. and Canadian Telecommunications, 1840–1997, Kevin G. Wilson

Forthcoming in the Series

Global Media Governance: A Beginner's Guide, by Seán Ó Siochrú and W. Bruce Girard

Continental Integration for Cyber-Capitalism, edited by Vincent Mosco and Dan Schiller

Deliberation, Democracy, and the Media

Edited by
Simone Chambers and Anne Costain

ROWMAN & LITTLEFIELD PUBLISHERS, INC.
Lanham • Boulder • New York • Oxford

ROWMAN & LITTLEFIELD PUBLISHERS, INC.

Published in the United States of America
by Rowman & Littlefield Publishers, Inc.
4720 Boston Way, Lanham, Maryland 20706
http://www.rowmanlittlefield.com

12 Hid's Copse Road
Cumnor Hill, Oxford OX2 9JJ, England

British Library Cataloguing in Publication Information Available

Library of Congress Cataloging-in-Publication Data

Deliberation, democracy, and the media / edited by Simone Chambers and Anne Costain.
    p. cm. — (Critical media studies)
    Includes bibliographical references and index.
    ISBN 0-8476-9810-6 (alk. paper) — ISBN 0-8476-9811-4 (pbk. : alk. paper)
    1. Freedom of speech. 2. Freedom of the press. 3. Liberty of conscience.
    4. Democracy. 5. Mass media—Political aspects. I. Chambers, Simone.
    II. Costain, Anne N., 1948–   III. Series.
JC591 .D45 2000
323.44—dc21

00-034201

Printed in the United States of America

⊗™ The paper used in this publication meets the minimum requirements of American National Standard for Information Sciences—Permanence of Paper for Printed Library Materials, ANSI/NISO Z39.48–1992.

Dedicated to

LeRoy Keller

Contents

Part 4: Media Representation of Social Movements

Part 5: Culture and Rhetoric

Acknowledgments

We owe great gratitude to LeRoy Keller, to whom this book is dedicated. He devoted his life to journalism and the free spread of ideas. As a young man, in the early years of the twentieth century, he and his mother lived in a house near the Boulder campus of the University of Colorado. At that time, there were few dormitories at the university, so most students rented rooms nearby. By taking in student boarders, the Kellers usually managed to pay Lee's tuition. The summer before his sophomore year, however, there was not enough money to send him back to school. He got a job in a hardware store in Denver to earn enough money to resume his studies. Three years afterward, he graduated. Many lessons might have been learned from such a life experience. For Lee, its meaning was clear. He wanted to be certain that highly motivated students attending a public university would be rewarded for their efforts by receiving the best education possible.

For Lee Keller, the foundation of knowledge is a freedom to think, question, and exchange ideas. In a conversation with one of his grandsons, who had recently been awarded a masters degree, Lee asked the young man about the roots of democratic freedom in America. Mr. Keller became concerned that his grandson had only a partial understanding of the Bill of Rights. He determined at that moment to make a gift to the University of Colorado to establish a First Amendment Center, which would support both teaching and scholarship.

LeRoy Keller died in January 1999, just months before the first "Media and Democratic Discourse" conference was held under the joint sponsorship of the LeRoy Keller Center for the Study of the First Amendment and the President's Fund for the Humanities, both of the University of Colorado. Lee enjoyed introducing himself to faculty associated with the Keller Center with the greeting, "I am the only Democrat, the only liberal, and the only atheist in my family. I want the Keller Center to work to make it easier for others to pursue their individual beliefs, as I have been able to do all my life." The book represents the collected scholarship from the conference, which was designed to reflect Lee's lifelong devotion to the news media and democratic freedoms. Bringing together scholars from the fields of law, journalism, political science, philosophy, communication, and sociology, there was no orthodox or privileged perspective. Lee would not have tolerated one. Rather, this book assembles the wisdom of many separate disciplines in addressing the question of how conflicts are communicated, debated, and sometimes even resolved in the public sphere under the intense light of a free press. As co-conveners of this conference, political scientists Simone Chambers and Anne Costain worried that the participants, coming from so many different fields, might create a tower of Babel, with each perspective proceeding from its own assumptions and in its own language. From the first hour of the conference, these concerns vanished in the shared passion for democratic dialogue and a common commitment to sustaining self-governing communities.

A number of people worked hard to put together the conference on which this book is based. Our thanks go first to the faculty at the University of Colorado, who serve as members of the governing board for the LeRoy Keller Center for Study of the First Amendment. We are grateful for both their creativity in designing this conference and their support in holding it. The Keller board consists of: Christian Davenport, political science; Douglas Costain, political science; Gerard Hauser, communication; Horst Mewes, political science; David Mapel, political science; and Karen Tracy, communication. Paul Gentile staffed the Center for two years and did an amazing job in communicating with participants and handling all the logistics of the conference. A number of other University of Colorado faculty, in addition to those presenting papers, served as chairs and discussants at the conference. We gratefully acknowledge the contributions of: Francis Beer, political science; Anne Laffoon, communication; Christian Davenport, political science; David Mapel, political science; Karen Tracy, communication; and Douglas Costain, political science. The President's Fund for the Humanities gave much needed financial support to help stage the conference.

Simone Chambers and Anne Costain also received a lot of help in preparing the book. Heidi Berggren, a graduate student in political science, gently prodded contributing authors to get their chapters in on time as well as copyediting and organizing most of the manuscript. Burt Rashbaum of the College of Arts and Sciences completed preparations for the edited book, working more swiftly than either of the editors could have anticipated. Brenda Hadenfeldt, editor at Rowman & Littlefield, not only attended the conference but patiently provided useful suggestions throughout the process as well. Andrew Calabrese participated in the conference and, as series editor, contributed meaningfully to the structure of the book.

Introduction

Simone Chambers and Anne Costain

Healthy democracies need a healthy public sphere where citizens (and elite) can exchange ideas, acquire knowledge and information, confront public problems, exercise public accountability, discuss policy options, challenge the powerful without fear of reprisals, and defend principles. More and more scholars are discussing this cluster of activities under the general heading of deliberation. Democratic deliberation, or the communicative processes whereby a democratic polity forms the opinions, interests, and preferences that will be expressed in acts of self-determination, is the seat of free citizenship. Voting, by itself, does not guarantee the free exercise of democratic self-determination. This is clear if we think of certain failures of democracy, for example, voting in the Supreme Soviet of the former Soviet Union. Few took such balloting as an example of democracy at work, but not because the votes were miscounted or fraud determined the outcome. This voting was suspect because certain background conditions were absent. These were conditions that could give us confidence that individuals had been able to develop and express their true interests and opinions.

What are the background conditions that can give us confidence that the exercise of democratic self-determination is authentic? At a minimum, we must insist on the guarantee of free speech, conscience, and press. First Amendment protections, however, are only the beginning of the wide range of issues that touch on what could be called the communicative prerequisites of democracy. Also relevant to maintaining a democratic public sphere are questions such as the following: Who speaks, and what idiom predominates? Who has access to what venues, and do we have sufficient knowledge of and control over new technologies that will shape the public spaces of democracy? How do market forces and power differentials affect the free exchange of ideas? What cultural trends are sweeping the public sphere and subtly altering the public topic of conversation? In investigating all these questions, the media looms large, for in mass societies face-to-face communication can be only a small part of the process of democratic deliberation. For the most part, public deliberation is mediated deliberation. Hence, this book is concerned with the intersection and mutual dependence of three concepts: deliberation, democracy, and the media.

The parts of the book are laid out thematically, gathering together contributions that share particular concerns about the conditions of democratic deliberation. In part 1, "Democratic Deliberation," philosopher James W. Nickel (chapter 1) and legal scholar Phil Weiser (chapter 2) investigate the relationship between First Amendment interpretation and public deliberation. Nickel is concerned with the way in which our definition of protected speech, particularly the emphasis on political speech, limits what we consider to be important types of speech. Democratic deliberation might be better served if we made the categories of speech we consider to be worthy of protection more inclusive. Weiser is also concerned with the way in which First Amendment doctrine shapes public deliberation. In particular, he investigates whether the advent of digital communication will offer the opportunity to revise existing policy regarding public access and content obligations on broadcasters. Weiser concludes by offering an alternative framework for interpreting the scope of First Amendment protection that both safeguards liberty at the same time as allowing for regulation that promotes deliberation.

Part 2, "Deliberative Equality and the Media," investigates obstacles in the way of achieving a truly free and equal public sphere. Alison M. Jaggar (chapter 3) is concerned with the way in which certain cultural identities may be excluded from full democratic participation. She calls for a new model of democracy that would be sensitive to difference, particularly difference in modes of communication, among citizens. James Bohman (chapter 4) also investigates inequalities in the public sphere. The differentials that worry him, however, concern the inequalities of knowledge and power between experts and ordinary citizens. The media has a special role to play in trying to ensure that democratic deliberation, while being informed by the knowledge of experts, is not dominated by their interests. Finally, Andrew Calabrese (chapter 5) balances the utopian possibilities of more universal values and information exchanges in the current communication age against the specter of unresponsive world government and submersion of minority perspectives flowing from these same developments.

In contrast to parts 1 and 2, where contributors discuss optimal conditions of democratic deliberation, part 3, "News Reporting and Coverage," hones in on current news coverage. Communication expert Roderick P. Hart (chapter 6) analyzes the language employed in electoral campaigns by print and television journalists. He finds little evidence of slanting the news in a partisan direction, favoring one party or candidate over another. However, he discovers a persistently negative tone to total coverage along with a great deal of reportorial opinion woven in with the news. The research of Shanto Iyengar (chapter 7) is more disturbing. He exposes racial "scripts" in most presentations of American crime news. Using audiences, he documents their recognition of the drama being played out in news stories and their quick jump to conclusions about the race and gender of criminals. Both chapter 6 and chapter 7 ask us to consider the power of the media in shaping the content and tone of deliberation.

Part 4, "Media Representation of Social Movements," looks at periods of social change and the social movements that often initiate that change. All three chapters in this part are interested in the way in which social actors are represented in the public sphere as well as the quality and content of debate concerning the appropriate response to social change. Doug McAdam (chapter 8) uses the case of the American civil rights movement to demonstrate that the media search for ways to represent to the public the challenges that these groups pose. At the same time, he reveals the strategic behavior of movements in working to shape this portrayal. Gerard A. Hauser (chapter 9) develops a sharp contrast between the representation of suffering bodies in Northern Ireland and in the United States. He emphasizes the subtle power inherent in the way in which stories are told. Although the mass media has long been criticized for its unsympathetic representation of suffering overseas and too emotional portrait of local suffering, Hauser exposes a different piece of the story. In this instance, the gender of the body seems to hold a key to how suffering is represented. The suffering of a young man in Northern Ireland, skillfully presented by an active social movement, is treated far more attentively by the American press than the individual suffering of many American women who are sexually tortured. Anne Costain and Heather Fraizer (chapter 10) probe the depiction of women's groups in America during a seventeen-year period starting in 1980. They find that even as the political force of the U.S. women's movement wanes after the defeat of the equal rights amendment to the U.S. Constitution, the media presence of its best organized groups persists. The media increasingly depicts these women's groups as mainstream political actors, voicing important social interests, and engaged in a sustained interaction with government institutions.

Part 5 examines cultural rhetoric. Mark Kingwell (chapter 11) and Simone Chambers (chapter 12) form a stark contrast in their respective discussions of the rhetoric of modernity and in particular their evaluation of the discourse of human rights. Kingwell acknowledges that modern discourse is dominated by the idiom of human rights but fears that the humanitarian content of that discourse is lost in bureaucratization on the one hand and is trivialized through global mass culture on the other. We have more success at spreading *Baywatch* than a concern for human rights. Or worse, we think that the globalization of *Baywatch* is the march of freedom. Despite his pessimistic evaluation of the emancipatory power of contemporary rhetoric, Kingwell ends on a positive note, calling on the power of the human imagination to make good the promises contained in human rights. Chambers is much more optimistic in her evaluation of the global rights discourse. She argues that the public and international debate about human rights has put those rights to a publicity test that strengthens their claim to universal validity. Free and open public debate, both in the international world as well as the domestic arena, is one of the most important safeguards we have against false universalization, that is, the attempt to promote particularist agendas by dressing them up in the sheep's clothing of universal values.

On balance, these chapters represent a faith that the power of reason and democratic principles will, over time, counter antidemocratic trends in a politically free but commercially constrained mass media. Even with this overarching optimistic perspective on speech and democracy, many of the chapters expose the pitfalls of trying to communicate through media, all of which possess their own frames of reference on the news. As editors of this book, we acknowledge that the future of free expression is threatened from many quarters. Yet we believe that the exchange of views from diverse perspectives constitutes its most dependable protection.

Part 1

Democratic Deliberation

1

Free Speech, Democratic Deliberation, and Valuing Types of Speech

James W. Nickel

One obvious purpose of protecting freedom of speech (or, more broadly, freedom of communication) is to ensure that it is possible for people to engage in the discussion and deliberation necessary for the successful use of democratic institutions. There is a link between the value of democratic deliberation and the value of free speech. Further, exploring this link helps us understand how some kinds of regulation of speech are compatible with freedom of speech. For example, a moderator who runs a political meeting so that people's comments are mostly uninterrupted and so that a wide range of perspectives are heard can make free speech more valuable. Alexander Meiklejohn famously used the idea of a town meeting to argue that freedom of speech should be viewed not as "unregulated talkativeness" but rather as a structured conversation in the service of intelligent democratic decision making (Meiklejohn 1948).

Some theorists, including Meiklejohn, have claimed not merely that promoting democratic deliberation is a goal of protecting freedom of speech but rather that it is *the* goal or the most important goal. They suggest that freedom of speech gets all or most of its justification from its contribution to democratic deliberation. On this view, the kinds of speech that have a prima facie claim to constitutional protection can be determined by identifying those kinds of speech that contribute to democratic deliberation. Different kinds of speech are different in the contributions, if any, that they make to democratic deliberation and thus can have lesser or greater degrees of claim to protected expression. Thus, talk about sports in a bar, about movies, about the state of the economy, about cooking, and about candidates for president will generate claims to protection of very different strengths.

Views that emphasize the link between freedom of speech and democratic deliberation provide an alternative to free speech absolutism (Sunstein 1993). Instead of claiming that infringements of free speech are never permissible or are permissible

3

only when the speech is highly likely to cause grave harm immediately, these theories claim that many kinds of regulation of speech are justifiable. Only political speech has the status that the absolutist claims for all speech.

In this chapter, I criticize two versions of the view that free speech is justified mainly by its contributions to democratic deliberation. I first offer some familiar criticisms of the strong version proposed by Meiklejohn. I then discuss and criticize a more qualified version recently offered by Cass Sunstein. Finally, I sketch an alternative view.

CRITICISMS OF AN EXCLUSIVE LINK TO DEMOCRATIC DELIBERATION

Linking expression to something valuable such as democratic deliberation helps explain why expression is valuable, but it does not explain why there is *a right* to freedom of expression (since this is a stronger notion than value). It also fails to explain why *everyone* has a claim to engage in expression (rather than merely those who are politically knowledgeable or competent), and it fails to explain why people sometimes have a right to express themselves politically at times and in manners such that their expression makes no contribution to intelligent political deliberation. However, these are generic problems with free-speech theories that focus on the good done by free expression. In criticizing Meiklejohn, I rather want to focus on problems about what freedom of speech should cover. I offer two familiar criticisms.

One criticism asks why we should privilege the goal of protecting democratic deliberation by claiming that it is the only goal of protecting freedom of speech. Surely there are other important goals as well. A glance at the U.S. Constitution suggests that it is not exclusively concerned with freedom to engage in and talk about politics. It is also concerned with freedom of religion, freedom to assemble, and the privacy of the home. Judge-made constitutional law includes freedom of movement, academic freedom, freedom to teach foreign languages, and reproductive freedom. The system of freedom that the Constitution establishes is not restricted to political freedoms. Speech that is part of other constitutionally protected areas of freedom, such as religion and association, is presumptively very important speech, and thus political speech is not the only high-priority area. Viewing the protection of democratic deliberation as the only or main goal of freedom of speech neglects these other high-priority areas.

A second and related criticism claims that if protecting speech that contributes to democratic deliberation were the only goal of protecting free speech, the scope of that protection would be too narrow. Only speech relevant to political matters would be protected. Speech in areas such as religion, social relations, sex, science, art, and commerce would be unprotected, and that result is pretty unattractive. One may attempt to avoid this criticism by saying, correctly, that some aspects of religion or science have political dimensions and thus that some sorts of religious and scientific speech will be protected. However, the idea that discussions of subjects such as evolution, sexuality, and contemporary art should be protected solely or even mainly because of their potential implications for what democratic political bodies should decide is very implausible.

DEMOCRATIC DELIBERATION AND THE MOST VALUABLE KINDS OF SPEECH

Cass Sunstein's book *Democracy and the Problem of Free Speech* offers a qualified version of Meiklejohn's idea. Sunstein sees freedom of speech as primarily, but not exclusively, concerned with protecting "a system of democratic deliberation."

Sunstein is well aware of the criticisms offered here of an exclusive link between freedom of speech and democratic deliberation, and he explicitly accommodates them. He says, "It would be especially obtuse to suggest that the free speech principle serves only political values" (Sunstein 1993, 129). Other First Amendment values that Sunstein accepts include "speaker autonomy," "listener autonomy," and "self-development" (146–147). Wisely, Sunstein is a pluralist about First Amendment values. He concedes that emphasizing the connection between free speech and democratic deliberation is just one good idea about the goals of the First Amendment.

Further, Sunstein mostly resists the temptation to play fast and loose with what we mean by political speech as a means of avoiding the criticism that Meiklejohn's approach is too narrow. He does not try to finesse objections by suggesting that almost any kind of speech is somehow political. He defines speech as political "when it is both intended and received as a contribution to public deliberation about some issue" (Sunstein 1993, 130).

Unfortunately, Sunstein is not fully content to say that Meiklejohn's theory just identifies one good idea about the purposes of the First Amendment. Although he allows that protecting the discourse necessary for democratic deliberation is not the only First Amendment value, he still wants to assert that it is the most important one. Political discourse is the top tier of free speech, while areas that are supported by autonomy and self-development alone are secondary, of lower priority. They belong in the "second tier of speech" (Sunstein 1993, 147). Only political speech "belongs at the First Amendment core" (146).

On this view, the value of a communicative act, and thus its appropriate degree of protection, can be judged by whether it has a political dimension. "Nearly all speech, and certainly much nonpolitical speech, deserves presumptive protection" (Sunstein 1993, 147). However, political speech deserves the most protection. "The free speech principle is centered above all on political thought" (252).

The two-tier system works like this. If a communication is in the top tier, then efforts to regulate it through content or viewpoint restriction must meet a very demanding standard of justification. It must be shown that the communication is harmful—where the harm is "likely, immediate, and grave" (Sunstein 1993, 122). If the communication is in the lower tier, then regulating it must be justified by showing that those efforts promote "a strong and legitimate government interest" (123). Thus, nonpolitical speech is relatively easy to regulate. This is not just an abstract possibility for Sunstein; he advocates considerable regulation of the broadcast media and at least some regulation of hate speech and violent pornography.[1]

Before offering some criticisms of Sunstein's theory, I want to make clear that my goal is not to defend free-speech absolutism. Some theorists who put personal autonomy on top reject any evaluation of communication except in terms of harm. They hold that all speech—good, bad, or ugly—has equal value for First Amendment purposes. They think that the only evaluative question we need to ask about a communication is whether it is seriously and immediately harmful. If it is, we may be justified in regulating it. However, if it is not harmful, we do not need to engage in any further evaluation of its value to know how protected it is. All nonharmful speech is equally—and highly—protected. On this issue, I am on Sunstein's side. I believe that different degrees of restriction can be appropriate for two equally harmful kinds of communicative acts, depending on their positive value.

I have three criticisms of Sunstein's theory. The first concerns his way of talking about "low-value" speech. Sometimes Sunstein seems to suggest that low-value speech is speech that merits regulation. For example, he says that "there are many other kinds of 'low-value' speech. Consider threats, attempted bribes, perjury, criminal conspiracy, price-fixing, criminal solicitation, unlicensed medical and legal advice, sexual and racial harassment" (Sunstein 1993, 11; see also 125). This suggests that low-value speech is speech that is immoral or illegal. However, Sunstein's real view is that all nonpolitical speech is low-value speech. On his view, a legitimate offer to purchase something has as little claim to constitutional protection as an offer of a bribe. Part of the problem here is that Sunstein systematically fails to make clear whether he is talking about (1) the value of a kind of speech apart from its costs or (2) its value when costs are factored in. If we are ranking the value of speech acts apart from their costs, then a two-tier scheme is unlikely to be useful since we will at least need to distinguish between speech that is (apart from its costs) very valuable, somewhat valuable, and of little or no value (e.g., a drunk at a bar muttering, "This beer is good!"). If we are doing the latter, then if—as seems likely—there is a continuous range of costs, running from low to high, factoring in these costs will transform a two- or three-tier scheme into a continuous range. To factor in costs, we need a continuous scale of value that runs from highest value down to no value and from there on down to negative value. Whether or not we factor in costs, a two-tier scheme for evaluating speech is simplistic.

A second criticism of Sunstein's view concerns his presupposition that we can rank the importance of speech by the use of broad categories such as "political" and "non-political." I doubt that this kind of ranking can be done with such a broad brush. I have already suggested that nonpolitical speech can be of the highest value, but it also is not clear that all forms of political speech are of the highest value. For example, suppose that a mayor and a contractor that does business with the city are talking about a kickback in exchange for continuation of a contract. This is political speech since it concerns the use of public funds, but as a discussion of a bribe it falls into a category that Sunstein classifies as low value. I think that with a little ingenuity we can find plenty of examples of high-value nonpolitical speech and low-value political speech.

My third criticism concerns Sunstein's claim that his view fits well with our considered judgments—personal and institutional—about what kinds of speech are important (Sunstein 1993, 133). I think that he is badly wrong about this. I will try to provide some counterexamples to the claim that only political speech is of the highest priority.

1. Suppose that a federal law prohibited evangelism on television for a widely despised religion that was totally focused on gaining access to heaven in the afterlife and thus had little relevance to the deliberations of democratic political bodies. This sort of religious discourse is not in Sunstein's top tier, and thus regulations of this sort should be relatively easy to justify. However, surely such a law would be an unconstitutional infringement of freedom of speech (and religion). Further, I submit that it would not be necessary to address the political implications of this evangelism in order to show the law's unconstitutionality.

2. Suppose that a local ordinance prohibited displays of erotic art and performances of rap music within the town boundaries. Suppose further that much of the art and music that would be prohibited by this ordinance would not be obscene or pornographic. Artistic expression is not in Sunstein's top tier, and thus regulations of this sort should be relatively easy to justify. However, again such a law would surely be an unconstitutional infringement of freedom of expression, and I would again submit that it would not be necessary to address the political implications (if any) of erotic art and rap music in order to establish the unconstitutionality of the ordinance.

3. Suppose that a state law prohibited the free public distribution of publications giving instruction about techniques for gaining sexual satisfaction. Discussion of sexual matters is not in Sunstein's top tier, and thus a law prohibiting this sort of written discussion of sexual matters should be relatively easy to justify. However, I submit that such a law would be an unconstitutional infringement of freedom of expression, and it would not be necessary to show the political implications of discussions of sexual techniques in order to show that this law is unconstitutional.

A SKETCH OF AN ALTERNATIVE VIEW

Meiklejohn's theory starts with the great value of successful democracy, claims that freedom of (political) speech is indispensable to successful democracy, and concludes that freedom of speech shares the great value of successful democracy. In this section, I suggest that this sort of argument can be applied to many other social and political institutions that are of great value, yielding conclusions about the great value of the kinds of speech that they involve. For example, having a successful economy that supports a high level of human well-being is of great value, and being able to discuss economic matters such as how to arrange production, obtain materials, and sell and distribute products is indispensable to having a successful economy. Thus, freedom of (economic) speech shares the great value of having a successful economy (Sunstein 1993, 53–92, 209–240).

This pattern of argument can be generalized to many areas of human activity that are of great value to individuals and society. I believe that these areas include—in addition to politics and economics—our intellectual life, including science, technology, religion, literature, and scholarship; our cultural and artistic life, including things such as painting, music, and cooking; and our social life, including things such as friendship, romance, sex, marriage, family, social gatherings, and the activities of all sorts of nongovernmental organizations. These are areas of life that are noncontroversially valuable (at least in general terms); they cannot proceed successfully unless people are free to communicate with others about them; and thus freedom of speech in these areas shares the great value of the areas themselves.

Another way of putting the same point is to focus on the roles that most people find to be of great value in their lives or that are indispensable to living their lives. Meiklejohn and Sunstein focus on the role of democratic citizen and the freedom of speech that it requires. People's roles as citizens and voters are very important in judging the importance or value of their communicative acts. However, so are other roles that go with the previously mentioned activities. There is the role of economic agent, where this includes being a worker, manager of resources, householder, and consumer. There is the role of learner, thinker, and inquirer; there is the role of cultural participant, where this includes learning about, arranging, and engaging in valued cultural activities; and there is the role of social being, where this includes learning about, arranging, and engaging in valued social activities. I submit that our theories of free speech have as much reason to take seriously these roles, and the speech they require, as the role of citizen and the speech it requires.

Another part of my alternative view is that we can partially judge the value of speech within these areas by asking about its centrality to the activity. One test of this is whether the communicative act is indispensable or highly useful to the activity. It is of lesser value if it is not indispensable or if it is only slightly useful. Information about what foods are healthy to eat is highly useful to almost everyone's role as a householder and consumer; information about how to use nylon net for various household jobs is much less so. Being able to talk about fundamental beliefs and attitudes is indispensable to people's roles as intellectual and moral beings; freedom to shout nonsensical sentences is rather less useful. By using this test, it is possible to avoid the mistake, criticized earlier, of trying to rank the importance of communicative acts by whether or they fall into some broad category.

I do not deny the autonomy theorist's point that one can choose to make the shouting of nonsensical sentences a central part of one's life—into something that is an important personal good. However, insofar as we need a public evaluation of communicative acts to decide how far to go in supporting and protecting those acts, the test of indispensability and usefulness to human activities and institutions that are of great value offers an attractive perspective.

NOTES

1. For a defense of the importance of economic liberties within a liberal egalitarian framework, see James W. Nickel, "Economic Liberties," in *The Idea of a Political Liberalism,* ed. Victoria Davion and Clark Wolf (Lanham, Md.: Rowman & Littlefield, 2000).

2

Promoting Informed Deliberation and a First Amendment Doctrine for a Digital Age: Toward a New Regulatory Regime for Broadcast Regulation

Phil Weiser

Changes in established doctrines, as Thomas Kuhn taught us, never come easily (Kuhn 1970). Only after repeated challenges to the status quo do long-standing practices give way to a new regime. And so it goes in broadcast regulation. For years, academics,[1] judges,[2] and even commissioners on the Federal Communications Commission (FCC)[3] have assailed the notion that First Amendment standards should be relaxed when it comes to evaluating the constitutionality of obligations imposed on broadcasters because access to spectrum is "scarce." Assuming that this criticism eventually has its intended effect, government officials will be forced to develop a new justification for the imposition of public interest obligations on broadcasters, such as the proposed requirement that they provide free airtime to political candidates.

The imminent arrival of the digital age may well provide the opportunity and even the necessary impetus to revisit the established regime of broadcast regulation. Although Congress toyed with the idea of modifying the regulatory framework governing broadcasters to address the advent of digital broadcasting in the Telecommunications Act of 1996, it declined to do so. Nonetheless, Congress, the FCC, or the courts are likely to ultimately decide that changes in the marketplace and in technology make it infeasible and/or undesirable to treat broadcasting differently from other communications technologies for First Amendment purposes.

Faced with a significant likelihood that the existing paradigm of broadcast regulation will eventually be discarded or invalidated, policymakers would do well to begin considering what an alternate regime of broadcasting regulation would look like. This chapter heads in that direction, setting out a new framework for justifying public interest policies, such as those focused on fostering political discussion and debate, for a digital age in which broadcast, cable, and Internet forms of communication can all be supplied in ever-increasing abundance. In particular, it suggests that broadcasters should be conveyed a license for use of the spectrum subject to an easement for public use that would provide the government with an opportunity to subsidize speech directly as opposed to taking the questionable First Amendment step of requiring broadcasters to engage in particular forms of speech.

THE PUBLIC INTEREST MANDATE AND THE RED LION

In the Communications Act of 1934, Congress authorized the FCC to promulgate regulations "from time to time, as public convenience, interest, or necessity require[d]" to govern the assignment of licenses to use the broadcast spectrum (1934, sec. 303). In its mandate to the FCC to license the use of broadcast spectrum, Congress stated that the spectrum belonged to the public and was to be held by individual licensees in trust for the public (Communications Act of 1934, sec. 301). To ensure that the programming aired by broadcast stations was consistent with the public interest, the FCC reserved to itself the right to regulate the content of broadcast television to, among other things, foster the public interest in public debate and discussion on political issues. The Supreme Court long ago upheld the legality of this regime, concluding in *NBC v. United States* (319 U.S. 190, 215 [1943]) that the FCC retains the authority to regulate content because its public interest mandate requires not only that it serve as a "traffic cop" to police interference between competing uses of spectrum but also that it "determin[e] the composition of that traffic."

Among the obligations imposed on broadcasters, the "fairness doctrine" has drawn particular scorn from the broadcasting industry and long stood as the symbol of the FCC's policy of promoting free and open debate. This doctrine provided that broadcasters were required to cover public issues and to present both sides when so doing. As a corollary to this doctrine, individuals who were attacked by broadcasters were afforded the opportunity to request airtime to respond to television coverage that attacked them personally. Although the fairness doctrine existed for some time, it was not until 1969 that the Supreme Court considered, in the *Red Lion* case, whether it violated the First Amendment's freedom-of-speech guarantee (*Red Lion Broadcasting Co. v. FCC*, 395 U.S. 367 [1969]).

In the *Red Lion* case, the Supreme Court concluded that the scarce nature of spectrum justified government regulation of the content aired on broadcast television pursuant to the Communications Act of 1934's public interest standard. The Court's understanding of "spectrum" led it to conclude that because there could be only a limited number of broadcast stations, that television was a medium "not open to all" (*Red Lion Broadcasting Co. v. FCC,* 392), and that, based on technology then in place, "scarcity is not entirely a thing of the past" (*Red Lion Broadcasting Co. v. FCC,* 396). On the basis of this premise, the Court determined that "[t]here is nothing in the First Amendment which prevents the Government from requiring a licensee to share his frequency with others and to conduct himself as a proxy or fiduciary with obligations to present those views and voices which would otherwise, by necessity, be barred from the airways" (*Red Lion Broadcasting Co. v. FCC*, 389). Finally, the Court concluded that it was "speculative" to worry that an enforced right of reply against broadcast stations would lead to "self-censorship and their coverage of controversial public issues will be eliminated or at least rendered wholly ineffective" (*Red Lion Broadcasting Co. v. FCC*, 393).

WHITHER THE *RED LION* REGIME?

It is difficult to overstate the intense criticism that *Red Lion*'s scarcity rationale has endured over the years.[4] The criticism tends to focus along one of two lines: technological changes or privatization of spectrum. With respect to technological change, there is an increasing tension between a First Amendment doctrine that proclaims that "differences in the characteristics of new media justify differences in the First Amendment standards applied to them" (*Red Lion Broadcasting Co. v. FCC*, 386) and the phenomenon of the convergence between existing technologies. As for privatization, the traditional rationale for content regulation has come under pressure as spectrum is increasingly recognized as a property right that is auctioned off to the highest bidder.

The questions regarding whether broadcasting should be subject to a more relaxed First Amendment standard began soon after *Red Lion* was decided. Just four years after upholding public access rights to broadcast television, the Supreme Court pointed out the danger of allowing for a similar approach to newspapers in a case involving the *Miami Herald*'s First Amendment challenge to Florida's "right of reply" law. In that case, the Court rejected—in sharp contrast to *Red Lion*[5]—the argument that such a law was necessary to address the influence of a powerful newspaper such as the *Miami Herald*. In so doing, the Court downplayed the concentration in the newspaper industry and pointed to the role of print journalism during our nation's founding, when "[a] true marketplace of ideas existed in which there was relatively easy access to the channels of communication" (*Miami Herald Publishing Co. v. Tornillo*, 418 U.S. 241, 248 [1974]). Moreover, the Court suggested that the touchstone of whether a government-imposed restriction on a newspaper violated the First Amendment was whether it "constituted the compulsion exerted by government on a newspaper to print that which it would not otherwise print" (*Miami Herald Publishing Co. v. Tornillo*, 256). In short, the Court concluded as to newspapers that a "government imposed right of access inescapably 'dampens the vigor and limits the variety of public debate'" (*Miami Herald Publishing Co. v. Tornillo*, 257).[6]

By concluding that the threat of self-censorship as a result of mandated access was real (and not "speculative," as suggested by *Red Lion*), the *Miami Herald* case suggested that broadcasting must be different from other media because spectrum (as opposed to the commodities used to produce newspapers) is scarce, thereby requiring the FCC to select among competing uses. In essence, this theory justifies a regime of licensing and content regulation for broadcast spectrum on the ground that a property rights and free-market model are unworkable. By moving clearly in the direction of property rights in spectrum,[7] however, the FCC has undermined this traditional justification for content regulation by enabling the market for spectrum to function like that of other commodities, such as those necessary to print newspapers.[8] Moreover, the emergence of new broadcast stations (and networks), the development of cable television, and the deployment of digital technology (with its ability to increase capacity fivefold) all make the concern over scarce spectrum increasingly questionable; at present, almost two-thirds of all American homes receive cable, and almost all others could order it if they so chose.[9] (Indeed, the increasing levels of concentration in newspaper ownership may provide a greater justification for an access right approach to newspapers than broadcasters based on the need to inform the public about political issues.[10])

Consistent with the barrage of criticism leveled at *Red Lion,* most commentators would agree that its scarcity rationale is "little more than fable" in today's world (Benkler 1999, 367). Moreover, it is very questionable whether the scarcity rationale ever made sense, as scarcity is an economic fact for every marketplace, not simply for broadcasting.[11] Nonetheless, despite the changes in technology and in the marketplace, the Court has thus far declined to abandon *Red Lion* even while acknowledging the emergence of "increasing criticism" (*Turner Broadcasting, Inc. v. FCC,* 512 U.S. 622, 638 [1994]). In fact, lower courts have even applied *Red Lion*'s rationale to new technologies, such as direct broadcast satellite, concluding that scarcity in spectrum justifies a lesser level of scrutiny in that context as well.[12]

Whether and when *Red Lion* will officially be buried is up for grabs. The FCC has discarded the fairness doctrine to the trash bin of history, but *Red Lion* still stands as good law for the proposition that broadcasting is different for First Amendment purposes.[13] However, in the wake of the convergence of different communication technologies and spectrum privatization, the FCC has yet to offer a satisfying answer for what separates broadcast from print journalism when it comes to regulation designed to foster public debate and discussion. For that reason, a number of commentators have concluded that *Red Lion*'s "conceptual and empirical underpinnings are so vulnerable . . . that it must be regarded as unstable and thus not necessarily 'good law.'"[14]

THE SEARCH FOR A NEW FRAMEWORK

The Achilles' heel of the *Red Lion* framework is that it justifies government regulation of speech on the basis of the increasingly questionable justification that there is too little spectrum to allow for multiple speakers. With the proliferation of means of communication and the privatization of spectrum, however, policymakers must find a new justification for enforcing public access rights or risk judicial invalidation of them. One attractive alternate justification would be to uphold the imposition of public interest obligations when the government decides to reserve spectrum at the time it assigns spectrum—that it could otherwise exact a rent for—for public use (as opposed to regulating the speech of private parties in a manner that restricts their editorial discretion).

The Reservation of Spectrum for Public Use

The reservation of spectrum justification gives center stage to and reformulates an important undercurrent in *Red Lion*: that government gives broadcasters licenses for free on the condition that they comply with certain public interest obligations. In *CBS v. FCC*, the Supreme Court made this point quite succinctly: "a licensed broadcaster is 'granted' the free and exclusive use of a limited and valuable part of the public domain; when he accepts that franchise it is burdened by enforceable public obligations" (453 U.S. 367, 395 [1981]).[15] Unfortunately, the Court's conception of what is often called the "quid pro quo" justification has tended to gloss over the significant First Amendment concern that, under the current regime, the "quid"—that is, free spectrum—is used to justify the imposition of the "quo"—that is, later obligations—that can interfere with the editorial discretion of the broadcasters.

Under the current regulatory regime, the public interest obligations are left inchoate and undefined by an opaque public interest mandate. As a result, broadcasters can justifiably complain that their speech is chilled—in the same manner that editorial discretion was affected in the *Miami Herald* case—because certain access rights may be imposed on the basis of editorial decisions. To avoid this situation, the government should make clear at the time the license is granted that it is subject to specific obligations that encumber the license assigned to the broadcaster, thereby ending the long-standing reliance on undefined obligations as a justification for more lenient First Amendment scrutiny.[16]

By adopting a regime in which the government reserves spectrum as an easement to be used by the public, courts would not need to water down the *Miami Herald* principle to preserve the viability of public interest policies. While it is open to debate whether the broadcast industry would view such a development as in its self-interest,[17] it seems clear that this reform would harmonize communications regulation and anticipate a First Amendment doctrine based on reality, not fable. To be sure, the effort to define the appropriate level of public interest obligations would spark a vibrant debate, but only by defining these obligations in a clear manner can the public be confident that it is obtaining true value for the grant of free spectrum.[18]

Benefits of the Proposed New Framework

The framework outlined previously would both put the imposition of public interest obligations on a sounder constitutional ground as well as have a number of salutary benefits. On constitutional grounds, the quid pro quo justification inherent in the current regime essentially excuses the FCC from the *Miami Herald* principle when it comes to broadcasters because it gives them a valuable benefit (i.e., a free license). This state of affairs is on shaky constitutional terrain, however, as it may transgress the unconstitutional conditions doctrine, which provides that "government may not grant a benefit on the condition that the beneficiary surrender a constitutional right, even if the government may withhold that benefit altogether" (Sullivan 1989, 1415).[19] In contrast, the approach of reserving spectrum for public use at the time that the spectrum is awarded leaves the obligation on that portion of the spectrum as an easement that the government uses to speak, which is quite different conceptually from regulating another entity's speech.[20]

The distinction between government reserved spectrum and government mandated access rights underlies why the imposition of wide-ranging access rights and obligations imposed on broadcasters, cablecasters, or satellite compaines are constitutional, whereas such a regime applied to newspapers or Internet content providers would be invalidated on First Amendment grounds. As to the first group of speakers, government provides critical resources in return for which it can exact a commitment that spectrum be dedicated to the public use, whereas in the second group, government cannot lay claim to any supply relationship that would justify such an exaction.[21] Put simply, when the government conveys some critical property that facilitates communication, it is constitutional for it to require the communicator to leave an easement available for public use; and this easement concept, I would suggest, can provide the appropriate justification for and understanding of access rights imposed on certain media to facilitate improved political debate and discussion.

The easement concept may also help us understand how some current First Amendment debates can be reframed to better justify current constitutional doctrine. For example, in the Supreme Court's recent decisions involving certain "must carry" obligations imposed on cable television systems, the Court struggled with the question of why it would be constitutional to impose this obligation on a cablecaster but not on a newspaper. In addressing this issue in *Turner Broadcasting v. FCC,* the Court explained that the cable company that gained permission to lay a cable to a home would, in all likelihood, not face competition, whereas a newspaper, even if dominant in its market, could not rest assured of such a fate. In dissent, Justice O'Connor suggested that government subsidies for certain types of speech, for example, would be a more appropriate means of supporting diverse viewpoints than the access right scheme imposed by the must-carry rules (*Turner Broadcasting v. FCC,* 684). However, if the channel capacity reserved by the must-carry rules constitutes an easement provided in return for access to valuable government-owned rights of way, the must-carry rules can be seen as government subsidization of speech that would withstand First Amendment scrutiny.[22]

By setting out the public interest obligations as an easement on otherwise unencumbered property, the FCC would act more like a conveyer of property than a regulator. In so doing, it would grapple more directly with the challenge of how to support "an electronic public sphere" that best promoted the public interest in political debate and discussion.[23] By reserving airtime as a subsidy for political speech (in the form of an easement on the license), the government would help create such a space,[24] as opposed to the present regime's reliance primarily on content regulation and the grace of broadcasters to act against their commercial self-interest.[25] Similarly, by setting out the obligations at the outset, the FCC would relinquish the public interest justification for adding undefined obligations during the course of a license. As a result, it would be forced to be more disciplined and systematic about determining what those obligations should be at the time spectrum licenses are assigned (or auctioned). Admittedly, it will not be easy to determine what the "easement" on the spectrum should be used to subsidize—public broadcasting, time for political candidates, children's educational programming, and so on—or how it should be administered—by the respective stations or by an independent government agency?[26] Nonetheless, the benefits of reforming an antiquated and unsound regulatory regime greatly outweigh the costs of taking on these challenges.

The Digital Opportunity

As a number of observers have pointed out, the transition to an age of digital television provides a unique opportunity to rethink and reform broadcast regulation. In particular, the allocation of new spectrum to the existing broadcast stations to facilitate the transition to digital television raises questions concerning what, if any, obligations should be imposed in return for the additional spectrum. As Reed Hundt, former chairman of the FCC, put it, this event presents "a rare opportunity. . . . We have a second chance to get television regulation right, to put real meaning into the public interest" (Hundt 1996, 529); and this opportunity also may provide the final death knell to talk of broadcast scarcity, as the transition to digital television will enable broadcasters to deliver five digital channels (which are superior to existing ones) over the same spectrum required by a single analog channel (Advisory Committee 1998).

How to manage the transition to digital broadcasting has already sparked some significant debate on how to regulate broadcast spectrum in a digital age. During the debates over the Telecommunications Act of 1996, certain members of Congress, including then–Senate Majority Leader Bob Dole, protested the conferral of new licenses to the existing broadcasters to enable them to transmit signals in both traditional analog format and the new digital format during the transition from analog to digital. (Unlike the transition to color televisions, analog television sets cannot decode digital signals, thus requiring a period in which both analog and digital signals are transmitted.) Critics of the FCC's plan (as left in place by the proposed bill) highlighted that the conferral of the licenses without payment, let alone during a long transition period, would be a "giveaway" that would leave the public without the funds that would be garnered by an auction of this spectrum (Goodman 1997, 533–535). Ultimately, the act passed without requiring the auction of spectrum or an expedited transition schedule, although it did make clear that the licenses would be given back to the FCC for auction at the end of the transition period (Communications Act 1934, sec. 336).

The award back to the FCC of the additional licenses used to broadcast in an analog format will mark the beginning of the digital era. Ironically, if the dawn of the digital era marks a transition to a property rights regime that recognizes a public easement on spectrum licenses for public interest obligations, that would represent a full circle in broadcast regulation. In the early era of broadcasting, a property rights regime was taking root through court decisions,[27] although any public interest regulations on programming had yet to be imposed. The story of this path not taken has often been told, with some commentators expressing chagrin that the government stepped in to take an active command-and-control approach to regulating spectrum.[28] Whether a property rights regime would have worked from the get-go is an open question, but the benefits of moving to one for broadcast regulation in a digital age seem quite clear.

In recognition of the opportunity presented by the dawn of the digital age, a commission appointed by President Clinton recently offered its recommendations of how to reform our regime of broadcast regulation (Advisory Committee 1998). This commission suggested some of the same approaches advocated with the new framework suggested in this chapter (subsidization of public broadcasting and a better definition of the required public interest obligations), but it declined to recommend a reform of *Red Lion*'s basic rationale and regime. Nonetheless, the report did highlight some of the important directions for reform of the current regime of broadcast regulation, including the need for government support of public forums and a more market-based regulatory regime.[29]

CONCLUSION

In examining the role of the media in promoting democratic deliberation, it is important to look for ways to promote public access to mass media while at the same time ensuring that First Amendment doctrine appropriately protects all speakers from government control. Supporters of the *Red Lion* regime often highlight the countervailing constitutional value of an educated public as a precondition to democratic deliberation.[30] While I am very sympathetic to the constitutional value of an educated and well-informed public,[31] I also believe that the *Red Lion* regime is an unsound and constitutionally unstable foundation on which to support such public interest goals. Indeed, I predict that moving from a command-and-control approach that regulates content to one by which the government reserves spectrum for public use—as a quasi-easement—will ultimately prove more effective than the current regime. While the current regime holds out the promise of public access rights, it ultimately falls short on this score because it depends on the regulation of private parties against their interest to do so. Thus, we should seize the opportunity presented by the dawn of the digital era and reform the regulation of broadcast television to assign (or auction) licenses that are encumbered by public easements at the outset, thereby ensuring a certain quantity of public interest programming as well as ending the content regulation that has been tolerated for broadcasting on the basis of *Red Lion*'s shaky constitutional foundation.

NOTES

1. See, for example, Krattenmaker and Powe (1995): "[T]he latest advances in telecommunications provide federal courts the opportunity to discard the inherently silly notion that freedom of speech depends on the configuration of the speaker's voicebox or mouthpiece" (1719).

2. See, for example, *Action for Children's Television v. FCC*, 58 F.3d 654, 671 (D.C. Cir. 1995) (Edwards, C. J.), cert. denied, 516 U.S. 1043 (1996): "[I]t is no longer responsible for courts to provide lesser First Amendment protection to broadcasting based on its alleged 'unique attributes.'"

3. See, for example, Powell (1998): "I do not believe that the growing convergence of technology will allow us to continue to maintain two First Amendment standards, one for broadcasting and one for every other communications medium."

4. See, for example, Ferris and Leahy (1989): "[C]ritics frequently argue that because of rapid innovation and technological change, the spectrum scarcity that gave rise to the public trustee concept of broadcast regulation is no longer relevant. Not only has the Commission licensed significantly more broadcast stations than it had twenty years ago, but the widespread availability of news and other information from many other sources ensures the public's exposure to a variety of viewpoints" (302).

5. *Red Lion Broadcasting Co. v. FCC*, 392. (In the absence of a mandated access right, "station owners and a few networks would have unfettered power to make time available to the highest bidder, to communicate only their own views on public issues, people and candidates, and to permit on the air only those with whom they agreed.")

6. Quoting *New York Times Co. v. Sullivan*, 376 U.S. 254, 279 (1964).

7. See, for example, Rosston and Steinberg (1997): "Using market-based spectrum policy to promote the public interest," an FCC working paper that "proposes a policy framework under which the Commission would generally rely on competitive market forces and allow spectrum that is of the greatest value to the public" (115).

8. As Judge Williams explained, "[a]lleviation of interference does not necessitate government content management; it requires, as do most problems of efficient use of resources, a system for allocation and protection of exclusive property rights" (*Time Warner*

Entertainment Co. v. FCC, 105 F.3d 723, 725 [D.C. Cir. 1997]; Williams, J., dissenting from the denial of rehearing en banc).

9. Balkin (1996), concluding that cable television makes the scarcity rationale "implausible" and that if the government was truly concerned about ending scarcity in spectrum, it could subsidize cheap cable television for those not receiving it (1134). One commentator put the point in more pragmatic terms:

> To the owners of the two hundred million television sets in America, any difference between broadcast and cable television is nonexistent, as both forms of television are transmitted to the home in the same way, and both are viewed on the same receiver. It is scarcely logical that broadcast and cable television should be treated differently for First Amendment purposes when they are virtually indistinguishable in the eyes of viewers. (Ryan 1998, 838–839)

10. BeVier (1998), noting that while "the number of broadcast channels has actually increased in recent years, the number of daily and weekly newspapers has steadily declined" (28).

11. As Judge Bork put it, "[T]he attempt to use a universal fact [physical scarcity] as a distinguishing principle necessarily leads to analytical confusion" (*Telecommunications Research and Action Ctr. v. FCC,* 801 F.2d 501, 508 [D.C. Cir. 1986], cert. denied, 482 U.S. 919 [1987]); see Logan (1997): "Although broadcast frequencies are no doubt scarce, so are other valuable resources, including those that go into publishing a newspaper" (1688).

12. See *Time Warner Entertainment Co. v. FCC,* 93 F.3d 957, 973–979 (D.C. Cir. 1996), upholding public interest obligations under *Red Lion*'s scarcity rationale.

13. Krattenmaker (1998): Although "the Supreme Court has not abandoned *Red Lion,* the FCC has abandoned the fairness doctrine and challenged most of the justifications asserted in the *Red Lion* opinion" (156).

14. "The scarcity argument upon which *Red Lion* was based has been so profoundly discredited—its conceptual underpinnings so thoroughly undermined, its empirical premises so utterly annihilated—that it provides scant support for the current disparity in First Amendment protection enjoyed by broadcasters and the print media" (BeVier 1998, 32–33); Although the regulatory regime for broadcast television "has been in place for more than seventy years, it rests on uneasy constitutional footing" (Logan 1997, 1688). "Even the Supreme Court has, however obliquely, raised doubts about the validity of the scarcity rationale, placing broadcast regulation on shaky constitutional ground" (Logan 1997, 1697); see also *Turner Broadcasting, Inc. v. FCC,* 637: "But the rationale for applying a less rigorous standard of the First Amendment scrutiny to broadcast regulation, whatever its validity in the cases elaborating it, does not apply in the context of cable regulation."

15. Quoting *Office of Communication of the United Church of Christ v. FCC,* 359 F.2d 994, 1003 (D.C. Cir. 1966).

16. For this reason, it is less justifiable to impose a subsidy on a license after it is granted, even if it is given free of charge. See *Time Warner Entertainment,* 105 F.3d at 728 (Williams, J., dissenting from denial of rehearing en banc) (noting that it was "troubling" that a number of providers of direct broadcast satellite that were subject to public interest obligations were notified of the obligations after receiving the slots for free).

17. On some accounts, the broadcast industry is quite content with a First Amendment doctrine that gives them less protection than other media. On this view, such a state of affairs protects the special benefits given to broadcasters (e.g., free spectrum, guaranteed carriage on cable television, and so on) by keeping in place a First Amendment doctrine that tolerates the imposition of undefined public interest requirements that would be declared invalid in other contexts. See, for example, Rubin (1998): "[B]roadcasters have leveraged their special First Amendment status, and the programming requirements placed on them, into advantageous government treatment" (692); see also Ferris and Leahy (1989): "If broadcasters were found to have full First Amendment rights, Congress would be justified in expecting compensation for broadcasters' use of the electromagnetic spectrum" (304).

18. See Rubin (1998): "Currently, with few exceptions, the public interest obligations are vague. This allows broadcasters to brag about doing plenty. There is no way, however, to measure what is being done or what the minimum acceptable level might be without clear obligations." (696); see also Hundt (1996), suggesting that the "high road" for reforming broadcast regulation would be to "translat[e] broadcasters' duty to serve the public interest into a few clear and concrete requirements that are understandable and enforceable" (530).

19. See Balkin (1996), noting that the theory that the benefit of free licenses justifies content regulation "proves too much" because the "government's conditions [on the license] may be unconstitutional conditions" (1135).

20. The Supreme Court has long recognized that, when acting as a subsidizer of certain types of speech—as opposed to a regulator—the government has considerably greater latitude. See *Rust v. Sullivan,* 500 U.S. 173, 178 (1991) (right to fund one type of reproductive planning over another); *Lewis Publ'g Co. v. Morgan,* 229 U.S. 288, 304 (1913) (upholding policy of government subsidy of carriage of newspaper through the mails, even though policy results in a "very great discrimination" against other material sent through the mails); see also *Time Warner Entertainment,* 105 F.3d at 735 (Williams, J., dissenting from denial of rehearing en banc) (recognizing that government subsidy argument might justify public interest obligations imposed on direct broadcast satellite providers); Price and Duffy (1997), suggesting that the imposition of public interest obligations could well be upheld under the "subsidy theory" (996, n. 81).

21. Ferris and Leahy (1989): "In return for their agreement to comply with FCC rules and regulations, broadcasters, unlike newspapers, receive substantial protections. They receive free and exclusive use of a valuable government resource that assures them a pathway into the home" (313).

22. In evaluating this alternate justification, it is worth noting that it is an open question whether the federal government can invoke access to local rights of way as a justification for obligations that it—and not the local franchising authorities who actually own the rights of way—impose on the cable companies.

23. See Grossman (1995), commenting that "[t]he new generation of telecommunications holds enormous potential to serve the needs of democracy," but it will take funds, difficult decisions, and a "determined and coherent national effort" to capitalize on the possibilities presented by recent technological advances (171).

24. Noah D. Zatz recently highlighted the importance of government subsidization of public forums to promote democratic deliberation:

> In the course of giving citizens access both to some of the material preconditions of speech (a place to stand and gather, use of land and air across

which to transmit visual, audible, and tangible communications) and to a social context by which an audience may be reached, public forums provide a range of free speech subsidies. In the absence of public forums and against the backdrop of a private property regime in which the state enforces law against theft and trespass, individuals and groups must purchase the means of exercising their right to free speech. (Zatz 1998, 161)

25. As noted earlier, the present regime's reliance on vaguely defined public interest obligations has often been criticized as ineffective. See note 14 supra; Grossman, note 23 supra (quoting former FCC Commissioner Glen Robinson as stating that broadcast regulation is a "charade—a wrestling match full of fake grunts but signifying nothing") (1995, 194). The late Chief Judge Bazelon was particularly critical of this regime, commenting,

> We reluctantly accepted content regulation in order to promote diversity. Yet we have not achieved significant diversity, and all we are left with is content regulation. This abysmal record alone would justify a reexamination of the First Amendment standards for telecommunications regulation. But recent events have not only cast doubt on the political assumptions behind regulation, they have also called into question the technological predicate of regulation—scarcity, (Bazelon 1979, 207)

26. In managing free time for political candidates, the FCC (or whatever entity is charged with this function) would confront the issue addressed by the Supreme Court in *Arkansas Educ. Television Comm'n v. Forbes:* which limitations on a political candidate's access to a state-sponsored media outlet violate the First Amendment under the public forum doctrine. See 118 S. Ct. 1633, 1638 (1998); see also *Time Warner Entertainment Co. v. FCC* (Williams, J., dissenting from rehearing en banc): "If spectrum regulation is to be analyzed as conditioned grants of government property, of course the analysis should mesh with the public forum doctrine" (727, n. 3). In the *Forbes* case, the Court concluded that by defining the criteria at the outset, the state-sponsored outlet will be subject to a lesser scrutiny, provided that it follows the specified criteria (1642–1644).

27. See, for example, *Tribune Co. v. Oak Leaves Broad. Station* (Ill. Cir. Ct. 1926), reprinted in 68 *Congressional Record* 215–219 (1926).

28. See, for example, Hazlett (1990, 135–165). For a good explanation of the benefits of a property rights regime in spectrum, see Spiller and Cardilli (1999, 53).

29. On the importance of electronic public forums, see, for example, Advisory Committee (1998): Forums for addressing political issues "should be designed not just to reduce some of the problems faced by candidates with limited resources, but also as a method to ensure that the broadcasting system, private as well as public, helps to promote democratic ideals" (57). On the benefits of a market-based approach, see, for example, page 44, noting its preference for economic incentives and self-regulation.

30. See, for example, Barron (1967): "I suggest that our constitutional law authorizes a carefully framed right of access statute which would forbid an arbitrary denial of space, hence securing an effective forum for the expression of divergent opinions" (1678). For a recent explanation of the importance of public access to the media, see Benkler (1999), noting that

centralized communications systems "are likely to exclude challenges to prevailing wisdom" and "translate unequal distribution of economic power into unequal distribution of powers to express ideas" (377–384).

31. See Weiser (1993), discussing the need for public forums and enriched political education as prerequisites to direct participation in constitutional politics (945–958).

Part 2

Deliberative Equality and the Media

3

Multicultural Democracy

Alison M. Jaggar

THE PROBLEM: CIVIC SOLIDARITY IN THE MULTICULTURAL STATE

Most contemporary answers to the question of how people can create a life together that is characterized by order, cohesion, justice, and freedom refer to the ideal of the democratic nation-state. This ideal envisions a politically sovereign nation of free and equal citizens and, for over four centuries, it has been invoked to justify struggles against oppression and colonialism, as well as to rationalize repression and genocide. In the past decade, the ideal of the nation-state has inspired groups on every continent to demand independence from states that include the former Yugoslavia and the former Soviet Union, Congo and Sudan, China, Indonesia, Canada, and even my own United Kingdom.

Despite the continuing popularity of the ideal, nation-states are under pressure from both without and within. The integration of the global economy undermines the autonomy of even the most powerful states, making sovereignty increasingly a fiction; at the same time, it disrupts traditional communities, accelerating the intermingling of peoples on the ground and creating so-called Russian doll phenomena in which "[e]very 'national territory,' however small, includes among its inhabitants members of other nations" (Tamir 1993, 58). These pressures create anxieties about the preservation of national identities and cultures, which are perceived as threatened from the outside by foreign domination and from the inside by foreign infiltration. Together, these developments generate a need to reevaluate the ideal of the nation-state. One aspect of this task is to rethink political sovereignty, but I do not take on this topic here. Instead, I address the second aspect of the task by investigating how cultural heterogeneity may be compatible with social stability and civic solidarity.

Despite the familiarity of the expression "nation-state," the ambiguity of each of its constituent terms, "nation" and "state," makes the ideal to which it refers quite indeterminate. Raymond Williams reports that "nation" originally meant a racial or ethnic group but that this meaning has now been overshadowed by its modern sense as a political formation (Williams 1976).[1] Contemporary English speakers often use "nation" and "state" almost synonymously despite the consequent redundancy of the expression "nation-state." British English does not distinguish consistently between nations as cultural entities and states as political entities; for example, even official British documents often use "nationality" interchangeably with "citizenship." The distinction between nations and states is further blurred in the United States by the facts that states are not sovereign and that the term "nation" is often used to refer to the sovereign entity constituted collectively by all the states. Jürgen Habermas helps to clarify such vague English usages by reminding us of the distinction between two significantly different conceptions of "nation." In the eighteenth-century social contract tradition, the nation is the *demos,* all those who voluntarily constitute themselves as a state by giving themselves a democratic constitution (Habermas 1998, 133). In the nineteenth century, by contrast, nations often came to be thought of in terms of *ethnos,* as prepolitical communities of shared descent organized around kinship ties or at least as communities with a shared history, traditions, and culture.

Increasing cultural heterogeneity within the boundaries of sovereign states is a matter of much greater concern to the "ethno-nationalists," who interpret "nation" as *ethnos,* than to the constitutionalists, who interpret it as *demos.* If a nation is a community constituted by a shared ancestry or cultural identity, then the dilution of blood or tradition is likely to undermine the civic solidarity necessary for political stability. If a nation is viewed as the product of a social contract, however, political stability is sufficiently guaranteed by citizens' commitment to democratic processes. Understanding "nation" as *demos* opens the possibility of a multicultural democracy, an expression that is oxymoronic when "nation" is construed as *ethnos.* However, just as the ideal of the nation-state is indeterminate, so too is the ideal of the multicultural state. In this chapter, I discuss three rather idealized conceptions of multicultural democracy and their associated conceptions of democratic discourse and multicultural citizenship. I argue that the third conception offers the best prospects for achieving social stability and civic solidarity.

TWO INADEQUATE MODELS OF MULTICULTURAL DEMOCRACY

Multicultural Democracy 1: Procedural Liberalism

Multicultural democracy 1 (MD1) is a direct descendent of the eighteenth-century constitutional tradition. Interpreting "nation" as "demos," it assumes that a fairly clear distinction can be made between politics and culture. It views politics as a culturally neutral set of institutionalized practices that establish a framework of justice within which people may pursue their varying conceptions of the good life. MD1 presumes a similar separation between people's universal identities as citizens and their more specific identities as members of distinct cultures. People's cultural or ethnic identities help to shape their conceptions of the good life but are secondary to their citizen identities, which are defined by their overriding commitment to maintaining a common political life, including a commitment to resolving conflicts among themselves peacefully through democratic means. This political commitment may be expressed through allegiance to such symbols as the queen or the flag, the Constitution or the Charter of Rights. MD1 proposes a kind of "procedural democracy" (Walzer 1992) that is neutral among conceptions of the good.

A major problem with MD1 is that, as many theorists have observed, a liberal framework is not neutral among all conceptions of the good. Steven C. Rockefeller calls liberalism "a fighting creed," associated with such values as freedom of inquiry, speech, and assembly (Rockefeller 1992), and liberalism's substantive commitments mean that conflict is inevitable between some liberal and some "ethnic" norms. Often such conflicts focus on women because cultural anxieties are frequently displaced onto the control of women's sexuality and labor, generating disputes over issues such as arranged marriage or women's participation in paid work or politics. Because of its substantive commitments, a liberal state can accept only attenuated versions of cultural diversity; it encourages members of minority groups to express their distinct cultures primarily in the private sphere, for example, through religious or dietary practices, but in the public sphere it allows them little more than symbolic expressions, such as distinctive dress or hairstyles. Even though individuals' cultural identities are typically unchosen, MD1 construes them rather on the model of lifestyle choices.

Because there is no way of defining once and for all what is implied by liberal principles such as freedom of religion or expression, conflicts over the boundaries between liberal principles and cultural practices erupt perennially within MD1. That such tests and challenges regularly emerge is not in itself an objection to MD1; on the contrary, frequent public discussion of the meaning of liberal principles is likely to deepen people's understanding of them and strengthen their commitment to them. However, the fairness and even coherence of this conception of multicultural democracy is brought into question when one observes that the outcomes of such conflicts tend to favor the dominant culture. To borrow an example from Charles Taylor, French authorities object to Muslim girls' wearing headscarves in French schools but raise no objection to Christian girls' wearing crosses. Similarly, even the mildest forms of female circumcision are outlawed in many European countries, but male circumcision is routinely practiced.

Procedural liberalism assumes that cultural bias may be eliminated by scrupulous fairness in considering cases, but this assumption is problematic. The problem is not simply that liberalism is nonneutral among cultural practices; rather, it is that no political formation can ever be culturally neutral (Lichtenberg 1997, 172). Even states that aspire to toleration of cultural diversity cannot manage without some minimal national culture. Charles Taylor calls nationalism the "motor of patriotism" and follows Ernest Gellner in arguing that modern statehood requires something like nationhood for economic reasons, especially the need for a mobile and educated workforce; Taylor further contends that some shared sense of nationhood is politically necessary in order to create the high level of solidarity required in welfare states (Taylor 1997). Will Kymlicka adds that a common culture is necessary for equality of opportunity:

> [M]odern political life has an inescapably national dimension to it. This is reflected in decisions regarding official languages, core curricula in education, and the requirements for acquiring citizenship, all of which involve diffusing a particular national culture throughout society and all of which seek to promote a particular national identity based on participation in that national culture. (Kymlicka 1997, 57)

Cultural bias in this sense affects even the democratic forms in which social conflicts are debated and adjudicated. The most obvious manifestation of such bias is that democratic deliberation must occur in some specific language, and language is not a neutral medium but rather is the congealed history of a culture. Many words have exact counterparts in other languages, but many do not, and languages also include idiomatic turns of phrase and culturally specific allusions. Even within a single natural language, there exist differences of dialect, idiom, and accent that operate to legitimate the speech of some and to delegitimate the speech of others, and those others include groups constituted not only by ethnicity but also by class and by gender.[2] Vocabulary and accent are not the only components of discursive style. Carol Cohn observes that the language of North American nuclear defense intellectuals and security affairs analysts is masculine both in habitually employing terms such as "wimp," "limp-dicked," "fag," and "pussy" and in adopting a calculative and dispassionate tone. Although this style purports to be rational and objective, discrediting compassion or horror as unacceptably "emotional," Cohn contends that in fact it validates culturally masculine emotions, such as aggression, competition, macho pride, and swagger. In the context of defense discourse, however, these are unlikely to be recognized as emotions and instead are "invisibly folded into 'self-evident,' so-called realist paradigms and analyses" (Cohn 1993, 242). Cohn argues that the culturally masculine style of North American military analysts shapes political decisions by branding certain strategic options as unmanly and so ruling them out of bounds. Cohn's work illustrates the fact that style is not just an "external" matter of how ideas are packaged but also shapes and limits those ideas. Her work also illustrates the fact that informal cultural norms may inhibit democratic participation by the members of subordinated groups, even where they possess a formal right to speak. Within masculine discourse, for example, options may be framed in a way foreign to the thinking of many women, who may find their participation limited to expressing assent or dissent.

Because all discourse inevitably privileges certain cultural styles, diverse and stratified societies always confront the likelihood that the members of some groups constituted by ethnicity, class, or gender will be forced to use an alien style when they seek to engage in democratic deliberation. Dominant languages may not contain sufficient discursive resources to express the perspectives of subordinated groups, with the result that, when the members of those groups press their claims, they may appear inarticulate, confused, or, in the worst case, even be unintelligible by nonmembers. In such situations, the perspectives associated with subordinated groups are not excluded from democratic deliberation de jure but are systematically excluded de facto. Privileging some forms of language undermines the credibility of some speakers and may even silence some entirely.

When multicultural democracy is construed as procedural liberalism, it is hard to see how it can generate civic solidarity or social cohesion. When democratic participation is understood only in a formal sense, it seems unlikely to produce solidarity and cohesion among diverse and culturally unequal citizens. Instead, it seems more likely to generate resentment and alienation among the members of those groups who find themselves not only outvoted but even unheard.

Multicultural Democracy 2: Groups as Political Atoms

One response to the problem that cultural inequality may systematically impede democratic participation by the members of subordinated groups has been proposed by Iris Marion Young. In order to counter the dominance of "the allegedly common public" and to "[equalize] the ability of oppressed groups to speak and be heard," Young (1990, 184) argues that a multicultural democracy should establish institutional mechanisms and public resources that will support group representation by providing for the self-organization of oppressed groups, group generation and analysis of policy proposals, and group veto power regarding policies that directly affect that group.[3] She believes that group representation will provide all social groups with the resources for meaningful participation in setting agendas, deliberating, deciding, and acting.

Young's proposal is valuable in focusing attention on the problem of the systematic political exclusion of some groups of citizens, and it is attractive in offering a direct group-based remedy for a form of group disadvantage that has often gone unnoticed. However, her proposal is also problematic because it relies on an overly simple conception of groups as internally homogeneous, clearly bounded, mutually exclusive, and characterized by quite determinate interests.

The flaws in this conception of groups first emerge in considering which groups are the appropriate candidates for group representation. Young suggests that political recognition be granted in virtue of a group's being oppressed and identifies five "faces" of oppression, namely, exploitation, marginalization, powerlessness, cultural imperialism, and systematic violence. However, Young's tests are quite vague and, on some plausible interpretations, could include the majority of, for example, the U.S. population.

A second problematic aspect of Young's conception of groups is revealed by the difficulty of determining which individuals belong to which groups. Individuals typically belong to more than one group, thus raising questions about whether they should be represented as members of groups defined by race/ethnicity, gender, age, class, or ability or some combination of these. Moreover, Young's proposal ignores what Naomi Zack calls microdiversity within individuals, namely, the fact that increasing numbers of people are members of more than one cultural tradition "enjoying what other theorists have called hybrid or *mestiza* or multiplicitous identities" (Anzaldua 1990; Zack 1993). Contests around the definition of membership may lead to policing group boundaries, challenging some individuals' "authenticity" or establishing racist definitions that rely on "blood" quanta.

In failing to address the inevitable diversity and divisions within groups as well as among them, Young's proposal also evades the politically crucial question of how to determine who speaks for a group. For example, the assumption that only women can represent women's views relies on a simplistic conception of gender identity that ignores the ways in which women differ from each other on multiple dimensions, such as class, race, age, sexuality, and marital status.[4] Group representation for other groups faces similar problems: ethnic and national groups are divided by, among other things, class and gender, just as economic classes are divided by, among other things, ethnicity, race, and gender. The members of oppressed groups may tend to share some common interests and perceptions, but they are also heterogeneous and sometimes deeply divided. Wilcox argues that group representation may even reinforce privilege within groups "by allowing the perspectives and interests of the more privileged members to dominate, while marginalizing those who are unable to make their voices heard" (Wilcox 1997, 23). Thus, group representation may end up replicating in a microcontext the problem that it was designed to solve in a macrocontext.

Young is certainly not oblivious to the heterogeneity and inequality that exist within most groups; on the contrary, it is precisely her awareness of these phenomena that leads her to warn against romanticized ideals of community (Young 1990, 226–236). Given this awareness, it is ironic that the logic of Young's proposal for group representation seems to require an essentialist and naturalized conception of groups as internally homogeneous, clearly bounded, mutually exclusive, and maintaining specific determinate interests. Such a conception is not only empirically inadequate; because it facilitates and reinforces adversarial ways of thinking about groups, it also makes civic solidarity inexplicable. Portraying people's identities as bound so tightly to their group affiliations suggests a model of multicultural democracy akin to that of interest group democracy. On such a model (MD2), it is difficult to understand how citizens can develop any deep allegiance to the polity or any noninstrumental concern for the larger social good. It is also difficult to imagine how democratic discourse might move beyond what Gloria Anzaldua calls "counterstance," "a duel of oppressor and oppressed," in which the oppressed "stand on the opposite river bank, shouting questions, challenging patriarchal, white conventions." As Anzaldua notes, "A counterstance locks one into a duel of oppressor and oppressed; locked in mortal combat, like the cop and the criminal, both are reduced to a common denominator of violence" (Anzaldua 1990, 378).

Multicultural Democracy 3: Composite Democracy

Young is certainly not the only political theorist to conceive of groups in reified and essentialist terms. Within the disciplines of international relations and ethnic studies, Valève P. Gagnon observes, it is commonplace for states and ethnicities, respectively, to be treated as entities that are seminatural, with interests taken to be fixed and uncontroversially identifiable. The state is treated as "an almost natural entity with objective and identifiable interests vis-à-vis other states" (Gagnon 1997, 48). Similarly,

> [e]thnic, national or religious groups are defined *a priori* as groups of people who share an essential sameness and thus a commonality of interest. People are members of a group because of what they "*are* . . . we tend to think of culturally defined groups peoples, nations, ethnic groups as somehow organically natural. (Gagnon 1997, 50)

Despite groups' seeming naturalness, their understandings of themselves and their history, traditions, and values are culturally constructed, evolving and often the object of direct and politically motivated manipulation. Even the appearances of naturalness and timelessness may be deliberate fabrications. Benedict Anderson has described the myths and practices used in the nineteenth century by builders of modern nation-states to create a sense of common national history and identity among disparate peoples (Anderson 1983). In a similar vein, Uma Narayan has observed that representations of the supposed contrasts between "Western culture" and the cultures of various Third World colonies were never simple descriptions; instead, they were "inevitably implicated in the *political and discursive struggles* that marked the colonial encounter, and [were] an important part of attempts to justify, and interrelated attempts to challenge, the legitimacy of colonial rule" (Narayan 1997, 15). For example, westerners could represent their culture as committed to the values of liberty and equality, disregarding Western practices of slavery and colonization; similarly, some Indian nationalists could insist that Indian culture saw women as "goddesses," disregarding the oppression of poor and lower-caste women and even of women in their own families. Reflecting on such examples, Narayan concludes that accounts of national traditions and national cultures "are always in fact *political notions*" used to prescribe which groups among the body of citizens are important, which ways of life deserve honor and respect, and how a particular nation should imagine its political future" (Narayan 1997, 21).

Narayan notes that the images of culture deployed in nationalist and colonial struggles in India were idealizations that often were at odds with reality; moreover, they were "totalizations" that "cast values and practices that pertained to *specific* privileged groups within the community as values of the 'culture' *as a whole.*" For example, "Indian culture" was often problematically equated with aspects of upper-caste Hindu culture, ignoring the actual cultural and religious diversity of the Indian population (Narayan 1997, 15). Narayan's view supports Gagnon's contention that naturalized conceptions of states and ethnicities are in fact disguised "normative visions"; they are "ideologized images" based on and reinforcing very specific structures of power" (Gagnon 1997, 51). Offering examples from the Cold War United States and Soviet Union, from India and Rwanda, and from the former Yugoslavia, Gagnon argues that such reified conceptualizations of states and ethnicities are of greatest benefit to particular parts of local elites who are facing threats from processes of change within their societies. For example, by setting external threats as the common defining characteristic of the group and thus privileging "national security," they delegitimize internal dissent and rationalize the suppression of open debate.

As an alternative to misleadingly reified conceptions of states, ethnicities, and nations, Gagnon proposes that "culturally defined groupness" be construed in terms of a shared system of communications or as a kind of language:

> People who share a common culture share a similar way of expressing similar sentiments or thoughts. Specific words, gestures and behaviors have a relatively common or shared meaning. If people sharing a culture also experience a common history, then these people also share a frame of reference in terms of the past. (Gagnon 1997, 56)

On Gagnon's view, what makes someone an American or a Serb is that she shares with other Americans or Serbs a specific system of communication, including a set of common references, and thus communicates in a characteristically American or Serbian way. The shared system of communication constitutes the frame of reference within which those who share a common culture discuss, struggle, and resolve conflicts. For Gagnon, then, culture is not a set of interests but rather the vehicle in which people "express and realize their very diverse values and interests" (Gagnon 1997, 57).

Gagnon's conception of "cultural groupness" has a number of advantages. It "does not discount the reality of an individual's identification with culturally defined groups; indeed, it helps explain the importance of such identification" (Gagnon 1997, 55). However, it is more empirically adequate than reified conceptions because it portrays cultures as heterogeneous, porous, and changeable, reflecting the facts that most territories are characterized by diversity, the overlapping of cultural groups, and the mixing of people. Gagnon believes that his analogy between cultures and natural languages offers a more productive way of thinking about cultural boundaries than that provided by reified conceptions. The boundaries between languages are not hard, and, in border regions, "there is often much mixing of languages, multi-lingualism, and intermarriage" (Gagnon 1997, 59), Thus,

> [i]f we think of groupness in communicatory terms, then borders are never totally closed, unchanging or impermeable, and never can be. Communication across cultural borders may be harder than within them, but it is always possible. And the borders themselves cannot be defined as walls or even as clear lines, but rather as regions, frontiers, places of contact, mixing, and transformation. People can learn new systems of communication, they can share different systems. Different cultures can influence each other. (Gagnon 1997, 60)

Gagnon's paper was presented at a conference in Belgrade in 1996, and its aim is clearly to undermine rigid and essentialist understandings of group identity. Despite the advantages of his conception, I find it inadequate in several respects. First, his concern to emphasize that cultures cannot be defined in terms of shared interests leads him to neglect the contingent likelihood that at least some commonalities of interest will exist within cultural groups, especially if the groups have been subjected to external oppression. Second, Gagnon's emphasis on language as a vehicle for expressing a multiplicity of ideas suggests that languages are vehicles in which one can drive virtually anywhere. As we have seen here, however, languages are not entirely transparent: they enable the articulation of some ideas but hamper the expression of others. As Wittgenstein famously observed, "The limits of my language are the limits of my world." Finally, Gagnon's account ignores the fact that, more often than not, cultural diversity is correlated with cultural dominance and subordination. It lacks any explicit acknowledgment of power differences among culturally defined groups, including among their systems of communication. Even if we agree to think of cultures on the analogy with languages, Gagnon fails to address the fact that some languages are privileged vis-à-vis others. In his concern to avoid reifying cultures and thus naturalizing political interests that in fact are contingent and contestable, Gagnon swings to the other extreme and misleadingly presents cultural membership as politically neutral and entirely innocent of power relations.

Despite these important omissions, Gagnon's suggestion that cultural identity be understood by analogy with linguistic competence is far superior to MD1's portrayal of cultural identities as personal lifestyle choices and to MD2's portrayal of them as all-encompassing or total identities. By borrowing Gagnon's metaphor of culture as language and supplementing it with an acknowledgment that, at any given stage of development, languages have finite resources and are likely to be in unequal relationships with each other, we can more easily understand some of the issues facing diverse societies that aspire to be truly democratic. We can also gain a clearer understanding of what is required of the citizens of such societies.

We have seen already that the possession of formally equal rights and liberties is often insufficient to ensure that the members of all groups are able to enjoy fully the privileges of citizenship and to exercise all its responsibilities. In heterogeneous and stratified societies, respect for some people's formal rights and liberties, including their right to democratic participation, may be systematically undermined by extralegal cultural factors. Since the 1960s, many so-called new social movements that have arisen in the United States and elsewhere have drawn attention to such culturally based inequalities, including democratic inequalities. Inspired by the struggle for African American civil rights in the United States, these movements have challenged cultural barriers to the full equality of women, of indigenous or aboriginal peoples, of ethnic minorities, of people who engage in stigmatized sexual practices, and of the physically and mentally disabled.

The goals of these movements are often characterized as struggles for cultural recognition.[5] Articulated originally by Hegel, the notion of recognition has recently been taken up by liberals such as John Rawls (Rawls 1993), communitarians such as Charles Taylor (Taylor 1992), and critical theorists such as Axel Honneth, the last of whom makes recognition the central value in his social theory (Honneth 1992, 1997). Honneth contends that people must acquire social identities that enable them to conceive of themselves as equal and at the same time unique members of society; he believes that they learn this through social forms of communication in which they are recognized as both equal and individual. Honneth argues that intersubjective recognition is indispensable to the proper formation of individual identity and that denial of recognition "is injurious because it impairs . . . persons in their positive understanding of self—an understanding acquired by intersubjective means" (Honneth 1992, 188–189). As Charles Taylor writes, "The projection of an inferior or demeaning image on another can actually distort and oppress, to the extent that the image is internalized" (Taylor 1992, 36). Nancy Fraser has emphasized that, in addition to their universal identities as citizens, moral agents, and legal persons and their personal identities as unique individuals, people also have particular but still collective identities as members of social groups (Fraser 1986, 1997). These collective identities are often central to individuals' conceptions of themselves. If healthy identity formation requires that people mutually recognize each other's worth and agency in virtue of their common humanity and unique particularity, it surely also requires that they recognize each other's membership in various specific social collectivities. Without adequate recognition of their specific collective—as well as individual and universal—identities, people may well come to deny or hate aspects of themselves, and this denial or hatred will infect all aspects of their lives, including their ability to engage in democratic participation.

Denial of cultural recognition is a form of collective injustice, and Young is right to argue that collective injustices require collective remedies. However, although it is easy to agree in principle that people's collective identities deserve recognition, it is much harder to determine what such recognition requires in practice. On the level of public institutions, recognizing cultural differences may take many forms short of formal political representation. It might include conducting official business and publishing official documents in more than one language. It might include establishing festivals or holidays celebrating personages or events that are significant in minority cultures or publishing postage stamps or currency commemorating them. It might also include practicing affirmative action in appointments to prestigious offices or positions, changing legal definitions (such as those defining family relationships or racialized demographic categories), and transforming school curricula to recognize the contributions made by members of minority cultures. My goal here is not to assess these or any other institutional proposals since I believe that the appropriateness of specific proposals can be determined only in particular contexts. Within these contexts, however, MD3 requires that the main guideline for assessing each proposal should be that proposal's potential to facilitate full and equal democratic participation by all citizens. In the next section, I indicate how cultural differences may be recognized on the level of democratic discourse.

CITIZENSHIP IN A COMPOSITE DEMOCRACY

The three idealized interpretations of multicultural democracy discussed previously are distinguished by their varying conceptions of culture and cultural identity. The differences between the three models are not necessarily reflected on the level of formal institutions; for example, only MD2 is characterized by formal group representation, but other institutional proposals seem compatible with any of the three, although each might justify such proposals differently.[6] The varying normative implications of each interpretation of multicultural democracy become more visible, however, when we examine the varying conceptions of civic responsibility and democratic discourse that each suggests.

On the (idealized) model of MD1, an individual's citizen identity is separate from and takes precedence over her cultural identity. Practicing her culture primarily within the private sphere, she can fulfill the basic obligations of citizenship by respecting the law, voting, and tolerating the practices of other citizens whose cultures are different from her own. On the (idealized) model of MD2, individuals' citizen and cultural identities are also separate from each other, but here the priorities are reversed; MD2 suggests that people's cultural rather than their citizen identities are the source of their primary loyalties. Thus, proponents of MD2 expect that the members of subordinated cultures, in addition to respecting the law and voting, will promote the interests of their own groups within the larger society. MD3's conception of cultural identity produces more integrated conceptions of citizenship and cultural membership than those associated with either MD1 or MD2. On this third conception, we will see that individuals must continually reassess and balance obligations originating in simultaneous allegiance to the state and to possibly multiple subcommunities. MD3 also generates a more complex and demanding conception of democratic discourse.

Reinventing Our Own Communities

I noted earlier that dominant languages might well be inadequate to express the perceptions and interests of subordinated groups. Developing new vocabularies is, by definition, a collective rather than an individual project, and I have recently argued that, in order to develop systematic alternatives to dominant ways of thinking, subordinated or stigmatized communities may sometimes need to close their discussions to outsiders (Jaggar 1998a). By agreeing on certain shared assumptions, subordinated groups can provide the intellectual space in which members are freed from pressure continually to defend their premises and instead may explore the implications of these premises. Moreover, when the ideas involved are challenging to the larger society, such communities provide emotional as well as intellectual support for their members. Patricia Hill Collins asserts that a "realm of relatively safe discourse, however narrow, is a necessary condition for Black women's resistance" (Collins 1990, 95).

Nancy Fraser describes such spaces as "subaltern counterpublics." She sees these as functioning on the one hand as spaces of withdrawal and regroupment and on the other as bases and training grounds for agitational activities directed toward wider publics. Fraser argues that, by these means, subaltern counterpublics are able "partially to offset, although not wholly to eradicate, the unjust participatory privileges enjoyed by members of dominant social groups in stratified societies" (Fraser 1997, 82). Citizenship within diverse and stratified societies thus requires acknowledging the political and epistemological necessity of temporarily closing minority communities of discourse. Because measures that appear at first sight to limit democracy may sometimes be necessary in order to expand it, one way in which citizens in a multicultural democracy may manifest their recognition of cultural difference is by respecting the counterpublics established by groups other than their own.

When the citizens of heterogeneous and stratified societies are members of subordinated groups, they should also participate actively in their own subaltern counterpublics—and this may not be easy. Theorists of multicultural democracy usually focus on the problem of how the members of minority groups might gain a voice within the larger polity and have paid relatively little attention to the processes occurring within subaltern counterpublics. What goes on within the counterpublics is often imagined as a smooth and even exhilarating process of emerging group consciousness and growing solidarity, as group members develop a shared awareness of their collective oppression and a language for articulating it. Such a romantic image is plausible, however, only when subordinated groups are assumed to be internally homogeneous and egalitarian. Once they are seen as internally heterogeneous and stratified, the responsibilities of group or community membership may be recognized as more challenging and sometimes more painful.

We saw earlier that representations of groups' identities and traditions typically promote the interests of some members at the expense of others. In Western societies, the working class has often been portrayed as white and male, ignoring the large numbers of male and female workers of color as well as of white women. Similarly, women have often been imagined as white, as mothers, or as heterosexual. Citizenship has been imagined in terms that are not only masculine but also heterosexual. Members who do not fit the dominant image of a group may find that their perspectives are ignored and their interests neglected.

If groups are not unitary, organic, and fixed but rather internally complex, culturally constructed, and ever-evolving, then the members of every community have the responsibility to make our voices heard in determining how our traditions are interpreted and our interests represented. In particular, we must challenge exclusionary or repressive interpretations of our own group's identity, including exclusionary or repressive representations of how our community is constituted. Such challenges will inevitably be unwelcome to many members of the group. Often they will be met with defensiveness, ridicule, or outright attack; those resistant to change may even contest the authenticity of the challengers' membership in the community. Feminists' challenges to practices established within their own communities are routinely portrayed as alien and subversive of cultural tradition. In India, as Narayan notes, feminism is condemned as "Western"; in the former Yugoslavia, it is dismissed as American; meanwhile, antifeminists in the United States assert that feminism is subversive of "American" family values and the "American" way of life. Homosexuality is also often regarded as a betrayal of national traditions. For example, Carla Trujillo writes that "[t]he vast majority of Chicano heterosexuals perceive Chicana lesbians as a threat to the community" (Trujillo 1991, 86; cf. Moraga 1983).

Feminists are constantly engaged in challenging the self-representations of their own communities, and the former Yugoslavia provides some recent and especially inspiring examples of feminist women heroically resisting conservative and militarist nationalisms. Dasa Duhacek describes how, during the recent wars, "[f]eminist activists from the nation-states at war . . . organized to meet, in order to share, discuss and perhaps overcome the border lines. It seemed as [though] women associated borders with the need to cross them . . . erasing and transgressing [them]" (Duhacek, in press, 10). She also reports that, from the very beginning of the war in Croatia, the Belgrade Women in Black

> stood in silent protest, holding unambiguous anti-war slogans in plain sight of downtown Belgrade. This highly charged political activity has been taking place *every* Wednesday, without fail, regardless of weather or the political climate for a period of five years, making it the only continuous protest against the war. . . . Their intent was a conscious act of subversion. (Duhacek, in press, 12)

The women's protests are met with insults, hostility, and sexualized slurs (Tesanovic 2000).

Narayan asserts that "bigoted and distorted nationalisms must be fought with feminist attempts to *reinvent* and *reimagine* the national community as more genuinely inclusive and democratic" (Narayan 1997, 36). Her words resonate with those of Stasa Zajovic, a leader of the Belgrade Women in Black, who writes,

> Self determination of the state has nothing to do with women's self determination; it means that I accept that the so-called national leaders speak in my name, in the name of the nation. The national militarists have appropriated our cultural heritage. I believe that we can redefine (it) so that we do not renounce our women's heritage, but retain a sense of belonging *based on choice, not on imposition.* (Zajovic 1994, 51)

Narayan's and Zajovic's words offer a striking contrast to Virginia Woolf's oft-quoted declaration that "in fact, as a woman, I have no country. As a woman, I want no country. As a woman, my country is the whole world" (Woolf 1938). Whereas Woolf explores the possibility that a woman may work against masculine militarism by dissociating herself from her nation, Zajovic's words imply a belief that neither the privileges nor the burdens of membership are easily shed.[7] Instead, they suggest that, when we inherit collective identities, we may well be responsible for reconstructing them.

When groups are acknowledged to be internally heterogeneous and stratified, they can no longer be regarded as unfailingly safe havens from a cold, impersonal, and often threatening world of strangers. Community members may speak a familiar language, but what they say may be unacceptable and even menacing to some members. Communities offer refuge from some dangers but are the source of others: the so-called women's community may be racist, the so-called black community may be sexist, and the so-called Latino community may be heterosexist. Just as women across the world find that their homes and families often pose more danger than the outer world, so dissenters may feel even more vulnerable in their own communities than in the larger society. It may be easier to face the disapproval of strangers than the censure of those among whom we feel we belong. Before our communities can provide a safe home for us, they may require extensive renovation.

Recognizing Difference in Multicultural Democratic Discourse

Within a multicultural democracy, debate within our own groups and communities must always be balanced by constructive engagement with the members of other groups and communities. Citizens of a multicultural democracy must learn how to speak and be heard across difference and dominance, and this requires developing a number of citizen virtues whose necessity becomes most apparent when groups are conceptualized by analogy with systems of communication existing in unequal relationships to each other. These citizen virtues include multicultural literacy, moral deference, and openness to reconfiguring our emotional constitutions. They represent additional aspects of what cultural recognition may involve on the level of democratic discourse.

Many authors write of the difficulties encountered by people seeking to communicate across difference and dominance. Laurence Thomas contends that people's ability to understand each other's experiences is limited by what he calls the emotional category configurations produced by systematic social injustices. For example, Thomas asserts that African Americans, who must endure the pains and humiliations of racism, experience an emotional vulnerability, anger and hostility, and even a bitterness and rancor that most white Americans cannot imagine, even if they have suffered occasional insults and affronts and even if those have come from someone in what Thomas calls a diminished social category. "[J]ust as a person does not know what it is like to be a bat by hanging upside down with closed eyes, [so] a person does not know what it is like to be a member of a diminished social category merely on account of having been affronted and insulted by a diminished social category person" (Thomas 1992–1993, 240). Thomas contends that, in an unjust society, there is no "vantage point from which any and every person can rationally grasp whatever morally significant experiences a person might have" (233).

In a now classic article, Maria Lugones and Elizabeth V. Spelman offer a similar description of the difficulties that Hispana women encounter in speaking with white/Anglo women in the United States:

> We and you do not talk the same language. When we talk to you we use your language: the language of your experience and of your theories. We try to use it to communicate our world of our experience. But since your language and your theories are inadequate in expressing our experiences, we only succeed in communicating our experience of exclusion. We cannot talk to you in our language because you do not understand it. (Lugones and Spelman 1983, 575)

Despite the difficulties of communicating across difference and dominance, none of these authors believes that such communication is impossible, and they suggest several strategies for succeeding in it. Thomas argues that, when people who have been marginalized and degraded speak of their own experience, listeners from privileged social classes should accord them "moral deference."

> The idea behind moral deference is not that a diminished social category person can never be wrong about the character of his own experiences. Surely he can since anyone can. Nor is it that silence is the only appropriate response to what another says when one lacks that individual's emotional category configuration. Rather, the idea is that there should be a presumption in favor of that person's account of her experiences. This presumption is warranted because the individual is speaking from a vantage point to which someone not belonging to her diminished social category group does not have access (Thomas 1992–1993, 244).

Lugones and Spelman suggest that U.S. white/Anglo women's deficiency in understanding Hispana women is due primarily to their ignorance of U.S. Latino cultures, not to their unfamiliarity with Spanish grammar. Lugones and Spelman do not argue that, in order to understand Hispana women, Anglo women must learn the Spanish language; instead, they focus on the need for white/Anglo women to learn the traditions, perspectives, and self-understandings of Latino communities:

> [I]f white/Anglo women are to understand our voices, they must understand our communities and us in them. . . . This learning calls for circumspection, for questioning of yourselves and your roles in your own culture. . . . This learning is then extremely hard because it requires openness (including openness to severe criticism of the white/Anglo world), sensitivity, concentration, self-questioning, circumspection. (Lugones and Spelman 1983, 581)

Learning Spanish may be valuable, but it is not sufficient for white/Anglo women to engage in meaningful communication with Hispana women; instead, it is simply a tool that white/Anglo women may use in overcoming their privileged ignorance of the perspectives of a subordinated culture. That Hispana women do not face comparable problems in understanding the Anglo women is not primarily because they are more likely to be bilingual but rather because, as members of a subordinated culture, they are forced to "travel" daily into the Anglo "world." "[W]hite/Anglo women are much less prepared for . . . dialogue with women of color than women of color are for dialogue with them in that women of color have had to learn white/Anglo ways, self-conceptions, and conceptions of them" (Lugones and Spelman 1983, 577).

Lugones and Spelman's work suggests that democratic discourse in a multicultural society requires citizens to develop what might be called multicultural literacy. Unlike U.S. mainstream versions of cultural literacy, multicultural literacy is not a knowledge of the self-interpretations of the dominant culture; instead, it requires understanding the characteristic experiences and self-conceptions of groups constituted by age, gender, class, and disablement as well as by ethnicity. For the members of dominant groups, multicultural literacy also includes a willingness to confront subordinated groups' perceptions of the dominant culture and the ways in which that culture continues to exploit subordinated groups and maintain its dominance.[8]

Developing multicultural literacy is one means by which citizens in a multicultural society recognize each other's specific collective identities. Such recognition does not mean treating speakers simply as representatives of their groups, as "typical" or "authentic" women or as disabled persons or African Americans. Instead, because different groups have distinct styles, perceptions, and concerns, recognizing speakers' collective identities means learning how to figure out the meanings of their words, even if they are delivered in a halting or unorthodox style or express ideas incompatible with dominant views. It means being open to the possibility that someone's words may offer valuable insights generated not independently of, much less despite, her group identity but actually in virtue of that identity. On this interpretation, the cultural recognition becomes an active project, quite unlike the more passive liberal virtue of respectful tolerance for alternative cultural styles and practices.

The concept of moral deference indicates another way in which cultural recognition is an active project. Moral deference is entirely different from accepting uncritically any utterance made by someone from a subordinated group. Thomas is clear that individuals from what he calls diminished social categories do not always provide the most reasonable account of their own experience; on the contrary, he notes, social deprivation may fill its victims so full of bitterness and rancor that they perceive even innocent interactions as offensive (Thomas 1992–1993, 244). The members of subordinated groups, like anyone else, may be insightful or insensitive, perceptive or unperceptive, naive or paranoid. For this reason, Thomas presents moral deference as presumption of a speaker's credibility that is defeasible or open to rebuttal. Someone practicing moral deference thus must engage in highly sensitive and difficult processes of weighing the credibility of people from subordinated social groups.

Moral deference is also active in a second sense. Thomas sees it as a means by which the members of more privileged social groups may begin acquiring the knowledge necessary for what he calls reconfiguring their emotional constitutions. This means

> rendering oneself open to another's concern, and to letting another's pain reconstitute one so much that one comes to have a new set of sensibilities—a new set of moral lenses if you will. Moral deference is rather like the moral equivalent of being nearsighted, putting on a pair of glasses for the first time, and discovering just how much out there one had been missing. (Thomas 1992–1993, 247)

Reeducating one's emotions is likely to be difficult and painful, but citizens who begin this process are better able to perceive and respond appropriately to systematic group injustices. For example, they may learn to feel outrage at racist insults and compassion for those subjected to them.[9] They may also learn how to bear witness to the moral pain of people who have suffered forms of oppression to which they have not been subjected, although Thomas asserts that such witnessing typically requires authorization by those who have been oppressed (Thomas 1992–1993, 245–246).

Within multicultural democratic discourse, recognizing the collective identities of others requires not only respecting their subaltern counterpublics but also developing such citizen virtues as multicultural literacy, moral deference, and openness to emotional realignment. Operationalizing cultural recognition in these ways presumes the falsity of the view that the experience of people from one social group is forever opaque or incomprehensible to people from other social groups. It also challenges the view that only members of a group may speak for that group, although this is a sensitive and complex issue.[10] Engaging in such practices of cultural recognition is necessary, although perhaps not sufficient, to enable people from subordinated or marginalized cultures to speak in their own distinctive accents and styles, draw on their own cultural narratives, and expect that their hearers will understand their vocabulary and allusions.[11] Democracy will always be imperfect, especially in heterogeneous and stratified societies, but recognizing cultural difference and dominance in these and other ways can increase democratic inclusiveness and equality for the members of all groups.

THE VALUE OF MULTICULTURAL DEMOCRACY

Social stability and civic solidarity are not necessarily undermined by cultural diversity: The real threats come instead from cultural insensitivity, injustice, domination, and imperialism. Many authors suggest that peoples come to perceive themselves as nations in response to shared histories of oppression. When citizenship and democratic discourse are conceived according to the model of MD3, civic solidarity in diverse societies appears more possible and more likely than it does on the models of either MD1 or MD2, neither of which shows how it is possible for citizens to develop common bonds across cultural differences. MD3 not only reminds us that groups are porous and overlapping, so that individuals are likely to enjoy multiple affiliations; it also suggests a way of construing people's specific cultural identities and their universal citizen identities that opens the possibility of those identities becoming integrated rather than separated, with neither subordinate to the other. This conception certainly does not eliminate the possibility of individuals experiencing conflicting loyalties, but it does suggest how such conflicts might be productively addressed. MD3's interpretation of cultural recognition suggests how democratic discourse may move beyond "counterstance," "a duel of oppressor and oppressed." When multicultural democratic discourse is understood in this way, it may enable deep understandings across cultural divides.[12]

MD3's conception of citizenship and democratic participation is valuable not only for the instrumental reason that it indicates how social instability may be avoided. We have seen that this model views cultural borders not as lines of division but rather as "frontiers, spaces of mingling. Instead of dividing they become bridges between other regions, between groups" (Gagnon 1997, 60). Cultures typically enrich each other, and, as Gagnon observes, "[d]iverse cultures, or regions of cultural diversity, have historically tended to provide the world with high levels of artistic and scientific creativity" (Gagnon 1997, 60). Multicultural societies construed on the model of MD3 are not only likely to promote artistic and scientific creativity; they are also able to offer a wider range of moral and political perspectives than monocultural societies. John Stuart Mill argued the benefits of individual diversity but failed to recognize that the best way of expanding individual diversity—as opposed to individual eccentricity—was to encourage cultural diversity. As states become increasingly multicultural and increasingly democratic, they broaden the horizons of all their citizens and thus enlarge their freedom.

NOTES

My thinking on this topic was sparked initially by a conversation with Colin Bourne. It developed in the course of several discussions in Belgrade with Gordana (Dasa) Duhacek, director of the Belgrade Women's Studies Centre. Dasa provided me with the hospitality of her home and also with indispensable resources unavailable outside the former Yugoslavia. As well as Colin and Dasa, I would like to thank David Kahane, who gave me the opportunity for writing by inviting me to speak on this topic at the meetings of the Canadian Philosophical Association in May 1998. David also provided generous comments and even hunted down an elusive reference. I received further helpful comments from Anne Costain, Frank Cunningham, Annette Dula, Chandran Kukathas, Shelley Wilcox, Iris Young, and an anonymous reviewer for the *Journal of Political Philosophy*. Finally, I have benefited from responsive audiences at the 1998 meetings of the Canadian Philosophical Association and the Radical Philosophy Association and at the Universities of New Mexico at Albuquerque, Colorado at Boulder, and Nevada at Reno.

1. In the former Yugoslavia, however, the term for "nation" still seems to retain more of what Williams identifies as its older Anglophone sense. In the former Yugoslavia, a nation was an ethnic group of a particular kind, namely, one with credible aspirations to political sovereignty. Yugoslavs marked the distinction between nations and other ethnic groups by using words that translated more or less directly as "peoples" and "peopleties," implying that peoples, or nations, had a respectable claim to political sovereignty but that peopleties, or ethnic groups, were appropriately political minorities.

2. The clearest examples for me concern class and gender. As a young woman, I was unable to articulate many vague and confused feelings and perceptions because the language necessary to do so had not yet been invented. The vocabulary I needed included such terms as "gender" (applied beyond grammar to social norms and identities); "sex role"; "sexism"; "sexual harassment"; "the double day"; "sexual objectification"; "heterosexism"; "the male gaze"; "marital, acquaintance, and date rape"; "emotional work"; "stalking"; "hostile environment"; and "displaced homemaker." In addition, there were many public contexts in which I was embarrassed to speak in my Yorkshire accent, which sounded very different not only from the "Queen's English" I heard on the BBC but also from the way that most "Oxford philosophers" spoke.

3. The policies of political gender parity established by some Nordic nations and New Zealand's system of reserving four Parliamentary seats for Maoris may be seen as examples of something like Young's proposal. However, in her book *Inclusion and Democracy* (2000), Young abandons the idea of group representation and seeks alternative means of guaranteeing democratic inclusion for the members of subordinated groups.

4. The diversity in women's social identities means that, although many or even most women may share some common interests, such as protection from domestic violence and acquaintance rape, different classes of women are likely also to have systematically divergent interests; for example, the interests of a poor woman who pays few direct taxes may lie in increased public transportation, whereas those of a more heavily taxed wealthy woman with her own car may lie in reducing public transportation services.

5. Some of the following discussion draws on Jaggar (1998a, b).

6. For example, proponents of MD1 might justify establishing public holidays in terms

of the value of equal toleration for all cultural practices compatible with liberal principles, whereas MD3 would justify them in terms of the value of democratic inclusiveness.

7. Thanks to Marcia Westkott for her reading of Woolf's views. Rosi Braidotti criticizes as ethnocentric the somewhat similar metaphor of exile used by some Western feminists in the 1970s. Braidotti writes, "In this end of century, where Europe as well as many other parts of the world is confronted by an unmanageable problem of refugees from the East and the South and migrations of populations away from war-torn homelands, exile is too serious and urgent an issue to be taken as a mere metaphor." She continues, "In other words, unless feminists are clear about our national frameworks and cultural differences, we run the paradoxical risk of becoming implicitly ethnocentric." She asks, "How sensitive are feminists in the host countries to those migrant women whose rights of citizenship are vastly inferior?" (Braidotti 1992, 8–9). I am grateful to Kamala Kempadoo for drawing Braidotti's article to my attention. For a recent discussion of feminism and nationalism, see West (1997).

8. Braidotti (1992, 10) invokes a similar image of "multiple literacies."

9. For some discussions of morally and politically appropriate emotion, see Jaggar (1989), Lorde (1984), McFall (1991), and Meyers (1997).

10. For an excellent discussion of the complexities of speaking for others, see Alcoff (1991–1992).

11. Similarly, if respect were accorded to the culturally feminine, women speakers would not face the familiar double bind in which they are patronized or taken less seriously when they use styles of language, gesture, and intonation culturally coded as feminine but, when they adopt culturally masculine styles of speech, are dismissed as "not real women," inauthentic, or unnatural.

12. The possibility of reaching such understandings may encourage some citizens to pursue the ideal of what Gloria Anzaldua calls "la conciencia de la mestiza." Mestiza consciousness is a characteristic "consciousness of the Borderlands," and one who has it is able to stand "on both shores at once and, at once, see through serpent and eagle eyes" (Anzaldua 1990, 378). Anzaldua's image is simultaneously inspiring and, for non-Chicanas, dangerous. Shane Phelan warns of the risk of cultural appropriation when the image of mestiza consciousness is employed outside its original Chicano context (Phelan 1994). Additionally, this image is misleading if it is read to suggest the possibility of transcending one's situated perspective, which in turn may justify short-circuiting democratic discourse. We have seen already that it is presumptuous for anyone to imagine that she can see through another's eyes or stand in her shoes, and for this reason the need for cautious, morally deferential, empathic, and power-aware conversations is never transcended (Jaggar 1993; cf. Young 1997). As long as we remain alert to its dangers, however, the dream of developing "a consciousness of the Borderlands" may serve as a heuristic for multicultural democratic discourse, offering an ideal of citizen consciousness that affiliates only critically with preexisting collectivities and that merges, expands, and transforms preexisting identities, creating new ways of being.

4

The Division of Labor in Democratic Discourse: Media, Experts, and Deliberative Democracy

James Bohman

Since Weber, many sociological critics have been skeptical of the prospects of democracy under modern social circumstances of complexity and pluralism. Spurred by globalization and the widely perceived failure of parliamentary systems to adopt effective social and economic policies, these skeptical voices have once again become prominent in debates about the future of democracy. There is little doubt that many forms of democracy face an uphill battle given current social circumstances. Participation based on the model of face-to-face assemblies and town meetings, for example, is inappropriate for large-scale and complex societies. Even if voting and representative institutions have evolved in response to these very circumstances, mere majority rule is often irrational, ineffective, and open to manipulation in the face of social and cultural conflicts. Theorists such as Robert Dahl call for another great transformation of democracy beyond the usual mechanisms of voting and representation. This transformation should be thought of specifically as a response to globalization and the effects of the electronic media on how we think of political debate and communication. Even if the older locations for democracy in the national state and the print-based public sphere are not fully eclipsed, some rethinking of democratic ideals and arrangements is needed not only to make them feasible but also to become more effective in governing and problem solving in these new circumstances.

Rather than focus entirely on how to implement democracy in the nation-state, it is now more important to analyze how other institutions, such as the media, may affect the conditions of political discussion, persuasion, and communication. Many new influences on democracy are the result of the cognitive and communicative division of labor that are the inevitable structural consequences of technology, media, and expertise. The cognitive division of labor in science produces expert knowledge, the content of which laypersons can hardly test or evaluate. As this division of labor begins to shape political relationships, citizens no longer seem to be the free and autonomous agents who can directly rule themselves and control their shared circumstances of common life; rather, they are ensnared in relations of epistemic dependence, which at the very least produce political situations in which asymmetric information is increasingly salient (Bohman 1999b). Similar consequences ensue from the fact that most political communication is now mediated. Rather than citizens addressing each other in face-to-face interaction, most such communication passes through various expert communicators who package exchanges and discussions for audiences that have little opportunity to contribute to or shape its course. This communicative division of labor threatens to undermine the quality of communication and even to introduce distortions and manipulation, especially since the goals of the mass media are typically not to promote democracy but rather to shape communication in order to achieve greater market share or to further the goals of their paying customers.

As this division of labor begins to reshape democratic possibilities, its influence is especially unfavorable to more demanding participatory conceptions, such as deliberative democracy, that attempt to make politics more rational (Bohman and Rehg 1997). In the face of the social conditions of pluralism, complexity, and inequality, proponents of deliberative democracy develop the critical and reformist dimensions of proposals that seek to broaden the potential for self-rule of citizens through the public use of reason. It is critical of conceptions of democracy that are based on mere self-interest or preference aggregation. It is reformist because in place of such a conception of democratic politics, it proposes that decisions be made through public deliberation, that is, through a process of reasoned argument and dialogue among free and equal citizens. It presupposes an informal public sphere and a vibrant civil society as well as formal institutions that are hospitable to deliberation in decision making. The social asymmetries inherent in the communicative and cognitive division of labor threaten to short-circuit the deliberative process, making it impossible for citizens to have equal opportunities to influence many decisions, to express opinions freely and effectively, and to have their reasons fully and fairly considered. Nonetheless, a conception of deliberative democracy appropriate to societies such as our own cannot simply ignore the benefits and indeed even the necessity of both forms of the division of labor. Thus, it must make the division of labor more democratic and open to public deliberation without thereby falling into a form of technocracy, namely, the rule and domination by those with epistemic and communicative advantages.

In this chapter, I argue that the division of labor can be made democratic and deliberative in two steps. First, I argue that expertise need not undermine public deliberation, even as it raises difficult questions of democratic accountability. Expertise presents a dilemma for deliberative democracy in that it produces epistemic improvement at the cost of democracy. The resolution of this dilemma lies in creating deliberative situations and institutions in which those affected by experts can evaluate the political credibility of experts and acquire influence over the terms of cooperation with them. The second step of the argument is to show that the potential dilemmas of mediated communication can be solved in the same way as the problem of expertise. Here the problem is to create the conditions for active interchange between expert communicators and those to whom their messages are addressed, even as the communication media structure this social interaction in ways that make such influence difficult to achieve. The problem is made more difficult to the extent that political communication itself becomes professionalized, that is, as the type and scope of information and relevant options become determined by media and political organizations, each with their own strategic goals and interests.

Under a more democratically organized division of cognitive labor, there is no need to trade off between democratic deliberation and expert effectiveness. The division of labor can be democratic as long as it fulfills two conditions: It must establish free and open interchange between experts and the lay public, and it must discover ways of resolving recurrent cooperative conflicts about the nature and distribution of social knowledge and opportunities to communicate. It can do so only if citizens are well informed, particularly with regard to the conditions of social inquiry and public communication. Once aware of the limits and pitfalls of such communicative and cognitive practices for democracy, citizens could use the reliance of these practices on consent and cooperation to make well-informed and reflective judgments about the norms governing them.

DEMOCRATIC INQUIRY AND COMMUNICATION

The way to begin thinking about the cognitive and communicative division of labor in democracy is to see that public deliberation guides social inquiry. As Hilary Putnam puts it, "[A]ll cooperative activity involves inquiry" (Putnam 1994, 174). The regulation of means and ends has more to do with determining what is acceptable to those participating in this large collective and cooperative enterprise than with approximating some ideal state of full causal knowledge. In contrast to the cooperative paradigm, consider Hempel's individualist picture of the masterful engineer who chooses the optimal solution to a problem of design. For this ideally rational actor, "the range of permissible solutions is clearly delimited, the relevant probabilities and utilities are precisely specified, and even the criteria of rationality to be employed (e.g., maximization of expected utilities) is explicitly stated" (Hempel 1965, 481). Such an engineer is in little need of cooperation, only acquiescence. Such a communicator would need only to employ the proper scientifically informed strategy to convince others of the worthiness of their goals.

Actual experts and communicators, however, do not meet Hempel's criteria. Although they may know more about their areas of inquiry than ordinary citizens, they fall short of these improbably well-defined and ideal conditions; apart from the problems of sheer computational complexity, they do not possess such determinate knowledge that it would be unreasonable for anyone to reject their advice about options and criteria. No actor or group of actors can stand proxy for the whole since the inputs of noncooperators would always remain uncontrollable and indeterminate regardless of how much (and very costly) social coercion is used. In a democracy, the problem of noncooperation cannot be solved by the masterful engineer. Citizens must have at least the reasonable expectation of influencing the deliberation about some decisions and thus must have the same expectation with regard to the inquiry that is the basis for cooperative activity. Similarly, citizens can discursively reject both the substance of any communication as well as an entire way of being addressed in mediated communication. In rejecting such a mode of address, they undermine the strategic expectation that it will be successful. In both cases, we see an opportunity for influence even in an asymmetrical social interaction. Consider first social inquiry.

Thinking of democracy as a form of cooperative inquiry asks us to shift our thinking about the usefulness of the best forms of social knowledge away from the dominant model of expert authority. Rather than approximating prior standards of "rationality" or "the scientific method," achieving complex and stable forms of knowledge is dependent on ongoing cooperation and thus on the collective effort to define ideal social conditions and acceptable courses of action. The need for mutual knowledge of the basis of future cooperation places normative constraints on those who participate in the enterprise, which, along with conditions of publicity, would at least filter out some forms of strategic behavior by experts whose asymmetrical information may offer them opportunities for self-interested and noncooperative behavior. While effective when institutionalized, such informal constraints are weak: They apply to the actions of experts and other cooperators as a whole and not to any specific actions or situations. Thus, there remains a considerable degree of uncertainty concerning the credibility of expert knowledge itself achieved even in the cooperative division of labor. Even if feasible, the reliance on coercive sanctions would undermine all the advantages of cooperative inquiry.

The view of the democratic division of labor espoused by John Dewey, in which everyone is an expert in some area or other, proposes an efficient distribution of the cognitive resources of a community or group while idealizing everyone's social interdependence. If *each* of the members has to know everything that the group as a whole knows and thus become the "omnicompetent individuals" criticized by Walter Lippmann, then they *all* know less than a group characterized by the epistemic division of labor (Dewey 1988, 334). The division of labor accommodates the cognitive limitations of individual agents and provides a way to overcome them to a certain degree by specialization. However, in order that all may know more than each member singly, agents must ideally cooperate by engaging in inquiry as a joint venture: For all to know more, independent actions of each of them is necessary, and these actions may not be monitored by the others without loss of knowledge or efficiency. The advantage of the division of labor is to make each social actor dependent on the actions of many others, so that the outcome of the collective enterprise depends on the necessary actions of others that cannot be immediately controlled or predicted with certainty. This situation requires trust of the sort that is quite pervasive in all cooperative enterprises and thus hardly unique to the cognitive division of labor (Williams 1988, 7). One problem is that this dependence on trust may turn into a monopoly on knowledge and thus an enormous advantage in gaining political influence.

Nonetheless, the case of experts makes special demands on cooperators in the cognitively organized group. What is unique to expertise is that others may not be in a position to monitor and scrutinize the expert even if there were the opportunity. Most experts may not be able to judge the results of experts outside their own subfields (Arrow 1985, 37–51). Thus, the epistemic division of labor creates pervasive asymmetries of competence and access to information. These asymmetries filter into many situations of ordinary life, from stepping on an elevator to taking prescription drugs. The problem is not only in access to information but also in interpreting it since most of us are "unable to render medical diagnoses, to test the purity of food and drugs before ingesting them, to conduct structural tests of skyscrapers before entering them, or to make safety checks of elevators, automobiles, or airplanes before embarking on them" (Shapiro 1987, 627). These tasks are left to the assessments of experts: Here labor is not divided by simply delegating a task that we could do ourselves at the cost of time but rather by giving over a task to others that we could not do at all. The proliferation of such agent/principal relationships in modern societies may actually work to undermine the putative advantages of the division of labor for democracy, creating a passive citizenry of principal/clients to agent/experts who are now responsible for regulatory control of vast areas of social life.

In diagnosing the potential for the "scientization of politics," Jürgen Habermas discusses three different models for the relation of scientific expertise to political decision making. The first two are hierarchical, with either experts or politicians at the top of the hierarchy: The technocratic model gives experts the task of elaborating the consequences of various techniques to arrive at optimal strategies for control; the nondeliberative model simply sees expert knowledge as instrumental for ends independently decided on by political leaders. Dewey's pragmatism provides a third interactive model and the only one to make the division of labor more deliberative and democratic. Here "the strict separation between the function of the expert and the politician is replaced by a critical interaction between them" (Habermas 1970, 66). More important, this critical interaction is mediated by the larger public who tests both values and ends in light of available techniques and also techniques and strategies in light of shared interests, norms, and values. Above all, the interactive model requires extensive and reciprocal communication between experts and the wider public, if the social tendencies toward technocracy and antirationalism are to be avoided. This communication has at least the same effect of the norm of publicity; that is, it filters reasons in such a way that only those that could be accepted by the public of all citizens can be expected to be effective in decision making. The problem is then to ensure that such communication can take place and that the implementation of expert knowledge depends on such mediation and accountability to the public. More is required for critical interaction than the education of the public by experts or even the capacity of the public to tell the truth to independently organized and constituted power.

The crux of the problem for democracy is that expert knowledge does not produce merely dependence (which is a feature of its very social character) but also deference: Science improves deliberation only if it produces epistemic gains that are different in kind from lay knowledge (even when supplemented with public discussion). Such differences between expert and lay knowledge make critical interaction between the two more difficult than Dewey imagined. Difficult, but not impossible. First of all, experts and laypersons share some background culture, including a background political culture. Furthermore, well-informed citizens can overcome their lack of internal knowledge of the expert's framework by acquiring reflexive knowledge about the origin and character of such social frameworks as a whole. As much as Dewey discusses the communication between expert knowledge and public opinion as the solution to the problem of the democratic division of labor, he never makes explicit how this could come about. Furthermore, he underestimates the logical, interpretive, and social difficulties of such communication, especially the problems of strategic manipulation that seems a constant possibility. Translation problems go both ways: Not only is it difficult to translate scientific knowledge so as to make it publicly accessible, but it is also difficult to translate practical questions and public problems back into the framework of expert discourses. If the public of laypersons is not simply to become politically incapacitated (as epistemic deference in technocracy requires), it must create the opportunity for "mobilizing counter-knowledge and for drawing on the pertinent forms of expertise to make *its own* translation" (Habermas 1996, 372). Such a translation permits citizens to contest expert policies on everyday life and thus to regain the opportunity for making judgments without deference.

It is important in this context to recall that the social distribution of knowledge is itself a solution to a problem: the limitations of resources and human cognition. Still, the pragmatic answer leaves entirely open how crises in expert authority are to be resolved, crises that have become increasingly more typical in an age in which the results of science are not always seen as collectively beneficial or, even when beneficial, are not widely available. Such crises signal the breakdown in communication mediated through the public sphere between experts and affected citizens. Healthy communication can be repaired only by creating situations of public dialogue in which the cooperative basis for the division of labor can be reestablished. Cooperators seek to redefine the practical relevance of experts' knowledge with regard to the needs, activities, and consent of the wider public. If experts do not incorporate such publicly accessible and acceptable definitions of their activities, the social basis for their own knowledge becomes increasingly uncertain. By defining expert activity through its social consequences, lay participants can shape the very knowledge that is produced and make it an accessible and thus a shared resource.

With varying degrees of success, social movements in the public sphere are now doing just that. In this context, the problem of cooperation requires maintaining credibility and legitimacy more than trust; it is creating communication across divergent frameworks and interests among experts and the lay public rather than embedding expertise in larger social contexts of informal interaction or civic engagement. Expert institutions are already embedded within their own patterns of informal social interaction; however, such interaction is often intramural and limited to the professional communities, the norms of which provide the cultural basis for scientific inquiry. The question for the democratic division of labor is not whether science is a "republic" (as Michael Polanyi once claimed) but how to establish credibility and authority across communities of inquiry, each with their own interests and intersecting but often conflicting criteria of relevance and judgment (Warren 1996).

The division of labor that is required whenever there is expert knowledge does have a larger social context: the context of science as a large-scale social enterprise involving more than simply professional scientists and experts. Science is effective not only because it can use the impersonal forces of nature and machines but also because it enlists the aid of many different groups and occupations, all of whom are necessary participants in a large collective project. Consider the large collective enterprise required to discover treatments for AIDS. Even if we restrict ourselves to considering only the development of drug treatments and leave aside the countless public health workers, educators, and others involved in solving this problem, much more is required than the work done in laboratories. We could view this activity as centralized and hierarchical, with experts dispensing their scarce information in exchange for the cooperation of the frightened public. To the extent to which actual research approximated this model, experts would meet with stiff resistance even in the research process itself. As in any large collective enterprise, there are many points at which the ongoing cooperation of many different people and groups of people is required for research to go forward. At each of these points, the credible threat of noncooperation forces a less hierarchical and authoritarian, more decentralized and democratic procedure. The democratization of expert authority requires more than just endorsing the efficiencies of the division of labor; it shifts our understanding of the community of researchers so as to include all those involved in the collective enterprise, which in many cases, of medical knowledge most importantly, includes the patients themselves (Latour 1987). Inclusion in the process of decision making of all those involved in collective enterprises establishes and enhances the critical scrutiny and the epistemic authority of experts, while their political authority is diffused and decentralized among the new agents added to the collective enterprise. While medical research and other cases of "applied science" offer the best cases for such authority, even the most theoretical scientific enterprise now demands large-scale social cooperation and thus potentially affects nonexpert participants.

AIDS activism in the United States presents a particularly rich example of this process of democratic inquiry. It is a case of the relation between an emergent public of those affected by AIDS and a set of institutions that were not initially responsive to them. However, the important point of the activism was not to challenge expertise or the division of labor; rather, it challenged the advantages of experts in defining the cooperative enterprise of producing knowledge about AIDS. These advantages have less to do with their asymmetrical information than with the greater access of experts to the appropriate forums for decision making and setting norms. Moreover, what is particularly interesting in this context is the way in which Act-Up and other organizations have successfully challenged experts on their own ground and not merely in the broader political arena (Epstein 1996, pt. 2). The public debates spurred by their activism had very much to do with epistemic criteria and experimental validity, such as the necessary measures of statistical significance for tests of drug safety (Epstein 1996, 243–250). The continued cooperation between researchers and their public depended, perhaps surprisingly, on deliberating about epistemic norms. Researchers defined their interests in terms of very high standards of validity, while the activists had a conflicting interest in lower standards of validity for the sake of wider and quicker availability of drugs. Thus, activists challenged the credibility of requiring the highest standards of statistical validity and in this way shifted issues of experimental design into the public domain. The fact that patients must cooperate in trials (e.g., by not taking other drugs or treatments simultaneously) gave activists the leverage of a credible threat sufficient to challenge the nonpublic agenda setting of medical research. In the end, this need for nonexpert cooperation and the need of experts to convince nonexperts of their claims for research funding gave activists their entry into various decision-making and funding bodies, making the collective enterprise and its institutions more responsive to this emergent public.

What sort of general political economy of expertise do these deliberations about the political consequences of the division of labor suggest? Certainly, we may say that trust as a "moral resource" was depleted by its disuse, or abuse in this case. More important, asymmetries of knowledge and information cease to set the terms of cooperation. The asymmetrical distribution of information among individuals who make up the collective enterprise has not disappeared by making it open to the political process. Nonetheless, through the decentralization of expert authority in the wider public, available knowledge has been redistributed in the aggregate. Expert knowledge is no longer exclusively in the expert domain; it has become defined in such a way that it is a resource shared by contestation of the legitimacy of epistemic authority. The more the nature and process of gaining such knowledge becomes a matter of democratic decision making, the more widely such knowledge will be distributed through deliberation and debate. The epistemic advantages of the division of labor do not necessarily violate the requirements of the democratic process if all cooperators have access to deliberation at every level, including deliberation about the division of labor itself, as well as about the norms and definitions involved in the activity of acquiring knowledge.

Knowledge has particular properties that make it a plausible candidate for a shared resource. Under the proper conditions of free and open communication, it can be a public good, that is, one that is in principle accessible and useful to all. It also has some features of what Albert Hirschman calls a moral resource in that it is not exhausted by use. The political problem is somehow to ensure that the public is able to gain access to the relevant forums in which definitions and terms are negotiated and discussed; these forums were initially closed to patient activists in our example. Challenges by the public to expert credibility or to expert definitions of the epistemic enterprise do more than make experts accountable; they make the knowledge so gained genuinely social and shared, even if differentially distributed. Even if this sort of public use of reason depended on the public leverage of nonexpert cooperators to change the character of scientific institutions, these movements exemplify the public use of reason needed to cross social and epistemic boundaries in functionally differentiated societies. In a public sphere in which the boundaries between expert and laypersons, or between agents and principals, are bridged and norms of cooperation negotiated, there is no need for hierarchy or deference to authority. Such a public sphere would provide democracy with the political space for inquiry, including inquiry into how to make inquiry democratic. This dependence on a robust public sphere raises a new problem of socially organized expertise: Expert communicators are needed for the highly mediated and asymmetrical forms of communication typical of modern societies.

MEDIATED COMMUNICATION, EXPERTISE, AND THE PUBLIC SPHERE

Just as in the case of the cognitive division of labor, feasible proposals for deliberative reform ought to begin by accepting the realistic premise that the communicative division of labor is demanded both by social circumstances, such as the sheer size of the body of citizens, and by the complexity of social problems. Put positively, mediated communication permits the highly diverse and widely dispersed audience needed for modern democracy. Deliberation is often improved not just by widening opportunities but also by what Dewey called the "subtle, delicate, vivid and responsive art of communication." This task is at least in part best fulfilled by professional communicators who disseminate the best available information and technologies to large audiences of citizens. Even with this dependence on such art and techniques of communication, the public need not simply be the object of techniques of persuasion. Rather than a "mass" of cultural dopes, mediated communication makes a "rational public" possible in the sense that "the public as a whole can generally form policy preferences that reflect the best available information" (Page 1996, 5). If we focus on the totality of political information available and a surprising tendency for the public to correct media biases and distortions as stories and opinions develop and change over time, it is possible to see how mediated communication can enhance the communication presupposed in public deliberation.

In complex, large-scale, and pluralistic societies, mediated communication is unavoidable if there are to be channels of communication that are broad enough to address the highly heterogeneous audience and to treat issues adequately that vary with regard to the epistemic demands on speakers in diverse locales. Because of their speed and breadth, the media necessary for these tasks are thus the electronic "mass" media. Informal mechanisms alone would be empirically and normatively insufficient for this task for the same reason: They are always limited in scope and thus cannot reach a broad enough audience; they tend to reinforce preexisting patterns of communication and permit exclusions on the basis of unequal opportunities for political influence in closed epistemic and expert communities. Both features demand that such communication can take place only in formal institutions, given the need for resources and for a wide scope of communication across existing patterns of interaction. At the same time, if these problems can be solved, then mediated deliberation can be highly successful as a means for promoting a division of political labor while at the same time producing cognitive diversity and mutual criticism. Possible mechanisms for democratically correcting problems created by the necessity of mediated political communication itself seems to be of only one sort: more public communication based on unrestricted free expression as the basis of the public use of reason, including the rights of association and expression that can be used to change the public sphere, to create new public spheres or to wrest them from expert control.

As with the relation of agent and principal, the problem here is to develop democratic modes of interaction between expert communicators and their audience in the public sphere. Citizens must resist the "mediazation of politics" on a par with its technization by experts. Once again, the challenge is twofold. First, the public must challenge the credibility of expert communicators especially in their capacities to set agendas and frames for discussing issues. Second, as in the case of cooperating with experts, the public must challenge the reception of their own public communication by the media themselves, especially insofar as they must also report, represent, and even define the "public opinion" of citizens who are strangers to each other. This self-referential aspect of public communication can be fulfilled only by interactions between the media and the public that challenge both the ways in which the public is addressed and how its opinion is represented. Mediated communication inhibits deliberation when the public is denied the opportunity to make such a challenge. In the American context, deliberation is inhibited "when officials of both parties and the mainstream media take a position similar to each other and opposed to the public" (Page 1996, 119). This tight linkage is not merely a contingent affair. It is part of the interaction between media, government, and audience that is typical of mediated political communication. Media outlets are dependent on government agencies for much of their information; and officials and candidates must use the media as their main channel for communication to the widest possible audience. These problems are severe enough that they turn the benefits of the communicative division of labor into restrictions on effective political communication. Moreover, such problems are exacerbated as the mediated interaction becomes dominant in modern political and public spheres, creating new forms of social interaction and political relationships that reorder in space and time and become structured in ways less and less like mutually responsive dialogue (Thompson 1995, 85).

The Millian solution aims at establishing a "marketplace of ideas" through diversity of channels of communication. It is inadequate since each of them could be structured by the same narrow patterns of influence; rather, what is needed is a robust interaction between the audience of citizens and the professional media over the nature and character of public opinion and the power that the media themselves exercise in virtue of defining this relationship and available forms and topics of communication. The communicative division of labor makes possible the exercise of power by means of communicative asymmetries in subtle and not-so-subtle forms of coercion, deception, and exclusion. This form of power does not take the media out of the public sphere; as long as they are within the public sphere and addressing themselves to a *public* as their audience, they are subject to the public's own definition of itself, to its own identity as a public rather than some aggregate audience in front of which political actors appear. Thus, the solution to the problem of the communicative division of labor for democracy lies, I submit, primarily in the hands of the public to whom mediated communication is addressed. That is, it is only if the audience of such media-structured communication sees itself not as mere consumers of messages but as a public who can contest such mediation and structuring of political communication when it undermines the very conditions of publicity that it is supposed to support and enhance. In a deliberative democracy, there must be constant interaction between the media as institutions and the public to whom its messages are addressed. In this interaction, it is the public who must hold the media accountable for the structural limitations on its form of mediation, just as it was the patients who had to initiate reflection on the practices of medical experimentation in the AIDS example by shifting the issue into the public sphere. It may seem like we are treading in a circle. In order for this shift to be possible, however, the public sphere must function well under the conditions of mediated communication, and the public sphere functions well only if there is a public with a robust sense of its responsibility for sustaining the publicity of mediated communication.

The relationship of communicator and audience is marked by asymmetries of information, agency, and control. First, the communicator as producer addresses and defines the public as less well informed, if not entirely lacking, in knowledge of some expert social practice. Second, the audience is often addressed as a gallery, as bystanders who merely observe the actions of others who independently define and exercise control over the situation. This characterization of the audience as gallery extends even to parliamentary institutions where politicians are defined as experts and agents. Moreover, a variety of scarce resources are needed for mass communication to a large audience (including the scarce resource of public attention itself). Media institutions must act as filters for the selection of topics and speakers. Whether by political actors or experts, structuring of political communication permits strategic manipulation of public attention to relevant problems. Given the media's tendency toward centralization and the variety of concerns and possible topics of public deliberation in a heterogeneous citizenry, however, some form of gatekeeping control is inevitable.

As in the case of agent/principal relationships, these producer/audience relations cry out for normative regulation to limit the structural differences in social power. Professional standards such as balance and objectivity may help in establishing a certain type of impartiality, including such ethical standards as balance and diversity. However important, these standards alone are insufficient to overcome the tendency of any institution to act according to established patterns of problem solving, such as considering a well-defined spectrum of political opinions and plausible problem-solving strategies. Coupled with the cost of the infrastructure of electronic mass media, these tendencies toward selectivity endow the media with tremendous political power, particularly in defining problems and setting agendas. Such media power is enhanced even more if the basis for media presentations of issues is itself the prepackaging of information prepared by other media professionals of parties, lobbyists, and interest groups. Indeed, because of this potentially closed circuit of influence, many have deemed media institutions "the fourth branch of government," more like the executive branch, which administers the flow of free and effective communication and with little or no democratic accountability and legal regulation. The goal of such accountability and regulation for political communication would be to enhance rather than limit the equal opportunity for influence that the public spheres of a democracy requires. This requires political contestation.

Two general solutions to this problem of the accountability of media institutions are often proposed. One might propose a kind of code of ethics and democratic goals to be pursued by media professionals (Gurevitch and Blumler 1990, 270–271), for example, as embodied in the civic journalism movement, or again we might think of a kind of "regulated media pluralism" (Thompson 1995, 240–243) in which, with Mill, we promote the greatest amount of pluralism in speakers and channels of mediated communication in hopes of epistemic gains. However, pluralism by itself does not solve the problem of competition for the limited resource of public attention, and the dependence of effective political communication "on winning and holding the attention of a heterogeneous audience can inhibit the media for committing themselves wholeheartedly to the democratic task" (Gurevitch and Blumler 1990, 271). Since communication is a two-way process, such proposals ignore perhaps a more important dimension than the regulation of political speech in a democracy: its public character. Publicity in this sense not only requires democratic norms that prohibit exclusions; rather, the central feature of publicity among citizens is that it minimally entails a certain kind of critical reflexivity (Bohman 1999a) in that a public must think about itself as a public and be concerned with the public character of its political communication.

How can a public preserve the public character of deliberation and with it the opportunity to influence political communication? In the first instance, it must be through interaction with those institutions for whom it is a public. Part of the contrast between a self-identified public and an aggregate audience such as a gallery or set of bystanders is that the former's activities and speech are organized around the rules and framework of institutions that define opportunities and occasions for public interaction; in turn, a public may attempt to redefine itself by expanding and defining new opportunities for institutionally defined conditions for deliberation. As Dewey points out, the public can reshape an institution indirectly by forming a new public with which the institution must interact (Dewey 1988, 243). In such a process, the communicative process organized around an institution is changed in a variety of ways: in their agendas, in their definitions of problems, in their problem-solving strategies, and so on (Bohman 1996, 200–201). This sort of change is precisely what happened in the case of Act-Up, who, as a public of clients of medical experts, redefined the relationship of patients to medical institutions and in this way changed the rules and procedures of these institutions. Similar interactions must also take place between the media and its public and in so doing break the closed circuit of political influence and widen the opportunities for deliberation of influence. Indeed, there are good empirical reasons to think that this is possible since the need for market share makes the media sensitive to "any sign of decided audience dislike or rejection of certain ways of addressing it" (Gurevitch and Blumler 1990, 283). This veto power goes beyond not being convinced on particular issues and may include the rejection of the removal of an issue from the public agenda, implicit definitions of the audience of communication (e.g., as interested only in who won the election, not the issues involved), and/or whole modes of communication, such as attack ads, racial code words such as *crime,* or uncivil speech. While the empirical record of such contestation is not as rich as in the case of bringing issues to bear, certain types of campaign advertising have certainly been rejected because of their unacceptable mode of address, such as George Bush's famous Willie Horton ad. There have also been any number of cases in which the public has rejected the dominant framework in which a problem is presented, and here Act-Up and the environmental movement provide numerous examples of reframing basic issues in such a way as to change the mode of public address from client to citizen. In this way, actors in civil society must take responsibility for sustaining the conditions of communication and maintaining its public character.

The public can reject a mode of being addressed by institutions in a variety of ways. It can do so more or less directly, such as insisting that something is a concern when media and political parties do not adequately grasp public opinion. As in the case of transformative interaction, the usual means is much more indirect. It is not often the case that institutional or communicative means of addressing the public are directly taken up; rather, they are filtered through some specific problem or grievance taken up in the public sphere by some group in civil society. As in the case of Act-Up, such a group seeks public attention for some problem in order to redefine it. Similarly, the public does not just change its relation to media institutions by vigilance and surveillance of them and their practices; rather, it changes the patterns of opportunities for influence in them by challenging other institutions and asymmetrical relationships directly and thus defining itself as an active public. Thus, it is the existence of such a dynamic civil society and the vibrant public sphere that opens up media institutions to public deliberation and breaks the definition of the audience defined by an asymmetrical relationship of information and power.

This self-definition widens the circle of influence over the means of communication. The audience, too, must be addressed as potential agents whose influence must be reckoned with, even if it is only an influence that may be activated by rejecting aspects of media-controlled communication: its setting of particular agendas, its definitions of problems, and the means by which the media attempts to constitute its own audience. It is then up to the public to exercise such a veto over the structural patterns of mediated interaction, not so much by noncooperation as by publicly articulating and defending its own self-interpretations, definitions of problems, and agendas. In this way, the public sphere is maintained through public contestations of asymmetries that gain public attention and give new definitions and frameworks for particular problems and situations. Through such contestation, the nonpublic process of mutual influence of government, corporations, and media can be moved into the public sphere for deliberation of citizens on an issue-by-issue basis without exhausting the scarce resource of public attention.

The robust character of such a view of the interaction between publics and institutions can be illustrated in two ways. First, it is important to see just how important such a public process of agenda setting and creating definitions of a situation is for the problem-solving capacity of a democracy. This first point can best be illustrated by an example. In 1966, a Detroit Edison nuclear reactor suffered a partial meltdown that could have produced the worst industrial accident in human history; it was deemed a mere "engineering mishap" in the press (Gamson 1988). Only eight years later, a much less significant accident at Three Mile Island was blamed precisely on the danger of experts unchecked by public accountability. The difference in interpretation has nothing to do with the facts of two events but with who shaped the means of interpretation; social movements and other actors in the public sphere had intervened in the process of interpretation of such events and opened up opportunities for influence on such momentous decisions. The media then must be receptive enough to surrender its definitional authority to the democratic public. Second, and more important, these and other examples point to the need for a broader definition of politics in understanding democratic discourse in societies characterized by scientific expertise and mediated communication. All forms of dependence with the potential for domination must be opened up to the possibilities of contestation, in which the definitions of the roles of patient and audience are recognized as political precisely because they distribute power and opportunities for influence. Once understood in terms of the politics of the distribution of power and influence, these potential forms of domination are opened up to a public process among equal citizens that can change the rules and assumptions that shape the institutions on which such asymmetries depend.

Such political transformations are possible only if the public sphere is maintained by the constant contestation of particular problems and the public definitions of the significance of issues. In this way, a public of citizens who enter the public sphere with their roles and personal histories intact expand the public sphere and the definition of politics in a time when parliamentary institutions are limited in their abilities to regulate social life democratically. In order for democratic deliberation to flourish today, it will have to take a form that will be able to exert influence over the communicative and the cognitive deliberation that affects so much of our everyday lives in a complex society. This situation demands a particular role for the social scientific participant in democratic discourse about the politics of knowledge and information.

CONCLUSION: NEO-PROGRESSIVISM, CRITICAL SOCIAL SCIENCE, AND DELIBERATIVE DEMOCRACY

What does this discussion of experts and media in the communicative and cognitive division of labor say about the possibilities for democratic reform? It might be possible to see such criticisms as suggesting a procedural form of politics, concerned merely with second-order issues of procedures and agenda setting. On this reading, the democratic commitments to equal opportunities for participation in political discourse leave them with no substantive political point of view, only the goals of constantly testing the consequences of alternative procedures, goals, and frameworks. Such an idea of linking democracy to inquiry hardly calls for the rule of experts. By taking issues of power within democracy and science more seriously than did its more elitist predecessors (Westbrook 1991, 455), the democratization of inquiry itself could become one of the main political goals of a neo-Progressive politics of democratic reform. Suitably modified to deal with difficulties of communication and the potential for conflicts, a deliberative account of the role of the epistemic division of labor properly combines Progressivism's emphasis on improving the rationality of decision making with radical democracy's emphasis on egalitarianism and decentralization of power. It does not simply criticize expertise as technocratic; rather, it also places expert knowledge in the context of public accountability and testing of credibility. It understands the excesses of the majoritarian democratic will while avoiding excessive political rationalism. Dewey's approach to the question of expertise already proposed a model of how this form of politics might work: He clearly saw the epistemic advantages of the social division of labor in democracy over the politics of mere discussion among a "homogeneous" public. Expertise and mediated interaction do not just economize on the costs of acquiring information; they are part of using the social distribution of knowledge cooperatively and democratically. In this way, a neo-Progressive politics seeks to identify new, formal and informal possibilities for further democratization outside the representative state, especially as power in complex societies is increasingly organized around practices of social inquiry and the managing of political communication in the public sphere.

Because this task depends on agents attaining reflective knowledge of their communicative and scientific practices, critical social science has a particularly important role in democratic inquiry (Bohman 1991, chap. 5). It does more than simply suggest, as did Progressivists, that a variety of social and theoretical perspectives are needed in order to solve problems and test public policy; rather, it entails a critical stance toward existing forms of the division of labor. Thus, critical social inquiry is needed to take the Progressivist insight into the role of inquiry in democracy one reflective step further, asking not just how inquiry is conducted and promulgated to the larger society but how inquirers themselves communicate, interact, and set the terms of cooperation with the public of scientific institutions (Bohman 1999b). To the extent that modern scientific institutions depend on the social cooperation of many actors, the authority and power of experts can be scrutinized and made democratically accountable (as it was in the case of AIDS activists' understanding of the social production of knowledge). In the case of media institutions, the dependence of the media on acceptance of the communicative situation leaves them open to the audience's rejection of their role as filter. In both cases, the process of democratization reveals the dependence of such institutions on the convictions of citizens that their procedures are open, proper, and fair.

As distinct from other purposes, the goal of such a critical reflection on the division of labor is not to control such social processes or even to influence the sorts of decisions that agents might make in any determinate sort of way; instead, its goal is "to initiate public processes of self-reflection" (Bohman 1996, chap. 5). Thus, critical potential of social science (and reflective political communication in the public sphere) can measure its success against the standard of attaining such a practical goal. In certain cases, the goal may be attained simply by addressing agents as members of a functioning public sphere; thus, the success of critical social inquiry may be measured by its practical consequences for improving the quality of discussion and debate in the public sphere. Such a standard is the same measure of success for the contributions of any reflective participant in the public sphere, particularly those who are concerned about its public character or the quality of public opinion formed within it. However, it may not always be the case that a well-functioning public sphere exists, and even if one exists, it may be difficult to initiate reflection on various social themes or self-reflection on aspects of the public sphere. Such cases are the subject matter of most critical theories, such as the theory of ideology, which seem to introduce new asymmetric features into critical social inquiry, leaving the critic once again in a position of epistemic superiority. This suggests the need for a practical mode of verification of critical claims in democratic inquiry. In its context of inquiry, critical social science treats social actors as knowledgeable social agents to which its claims are publicly addressed. Social scientific knowledge helps agents to see their circumstances differently, especially at that point when mounting problems indicate that some change is practically necessary. In this way, critics do not employ social inquiry for the sake of goals set prior to inquiry (Habermas 1973,

40–44). Just as technical knowledge depends on the social conditions for free and open critical examination necessary to validate its predictions, so too critical inquiry seeks to create the appropriate social conditions under which the audience itself may verify or falsify the criticism offered.

Once this reflexive public inquiry into democracy is initiated, a politics of institutional reform inspired by a new Progressivism could begin to identify both institutional and noninstitutional locations for further democratization, especially in limiting the emergence of power in complex societies organized around knowledge as a resource. When its definition and social organization becomes a subject matter for deliberation, knowledge is a resource that may be democratically shared and publicly verified through first- and second-order reflection. Under these conditions, critical social inquiry can have transformative consequences as the sort of inquiry necessary for a democratic division of labor. Even if the social roles of agents and principals are part of inquiry in complex societies, the terms of cooperation among them is the proper subject of democratic deliberation. Even if mediated interaction cannot be made fully symmetrical, it is still the case that circuits of influence may become broader and the definitions of the audience not one-sidedly imposed on it. The enduring hope of deliberative democracy is that any such epistemic and communicative improvements of democracy would be had only by making its cognitive and communicative practices and division of labor more egalitarian, cooperative, and accountable.

Deliberative democracy faces new challenges that exacerbate antidemocratic tendencies in the division of labor already present in any complex and pluralistic society (Bohman 1995). Globalization has now begun to undermine the effectiveness of even well-ordered democratic nation-states to regulate the destructive effects of market-driven processes. A closer examination of the social conditions that promote globalization reveals that the cognitive and communicative division of labor forms its infrastructure in the possibilities and speed of interaction through new information and communication technologies and the spread of scientific and technological practices and in the forms of social organization needed for societies that operate on the basis of shrinking space and time. The solutions to the problems that mediated communication and technological expertise pose for global democracy are the same as the ones that I have outlined here. The emergence of a transnational civil society and a global public sphere provides the countervailing global infrastructure for the same sort of contestation that is the basis for democratic accountability of the media and technoscience. Cosmopolitan democrats must foster the conditions for communication that make this contestation effective. Their goal is to support the political infrastructure needed to expand the possibilities of democratic politics to the global arena and to challenge the unequal opportunities for influence that exist in the financial and organizational basis for the spread of global hierarchies of power and asymmetries of knowledge. Such contestation may open up the space for deliberative politics in asymmetrical social relationships that underlie

globalization. This neo-Progressivist politics could further the goal of a more deliberative democracy by instituting and sustaining practices of public communication
and contestation in the social and political interstices of the global cognitive and
communicative division of labor.

5

The Means of Communication and the Discourse on Sovereignty

Andrew Calabrese

In the age of CNN, twenty-four-hour financial trading, and Amazon.com, there is a growing consensus, whether justified or not, that the limits of culture, commerce, and political action are defined less today by the territorial boundaries of the nation-state than they were in the past. Whether facile or not, talk of "globalization" is everywhere, although the idea of the twilight of sovereignty is not reducible to that of globalization. The roots of the discourse on what I have termed "post-sovereignty" arise not only through exogenous pressures from activities and identities beyond the territorial boundaries of the state. However, the pressures that are seen to be eroding the principles of sovereignty are also endogenous, as numerous accounts of weak or broken cultural foundations of multi-nation-states now illustrate.

The discourse of the end of sovereignty has many faces. It is a source of optimism, pessimism, and ambivalence. It has captured the popular imagination, and it can be found in the anxieties of national leaders about the mingling and collision of cultures and cultural products within and across their borders and about growing awareness that environmental threats bow to no flag. According to much of this discourse, national governments are becoming increasingly powerless in their battles against real or imagined cultural imperialism (and subimperialism, that is, cultural imperialism within states) and capital mobility as well as in their efforts to exercise political control effectively through surveillance and censorship (Tomlinson 1991). The end of sovereignty is a theme in political discussions about new pressures brought on by global regimes of trade and investment and by unprecedented levels of global criminal networks for drug trafficking, money laundering, and trade in human flesh (Castells 1996, 1997, 1998). It can also be found in the fact that social movements and nongovernmental organizations (NGOs) have recognized the need to match the scale of the problems they confront with appropriately scaled collective action.

The means of communication, particularly the Internet, have come to be viewed as foundations for the transgression and redefinition of the boundaries of political space among many who embrace "the twilight of sovereignty" as an emancipatory discourse. In a world of deterritorialized or virtual space, the argument goes, the limits of national governments are constantly being tested and increasingly found to be lacking. According to some emancipatory themes, new means of communication have paved the way to a world in which democratic freedoms are enhanced dramatically by the creative destruction of political limits imposed by sovereign states. In turn, the new communication and information technologies have become tools for political organization and the bases for strengthening the global exercise of the principle of publicity, thereby enhancing the prospects for the advancement of truly cosmopolitan democracy. Today, the well-established mass media and the "new media" of converging communication and information technologies have become the basis for optimism and ambivalence toward the prospects for revitalizing democracy at the national level and for enhancing the prospects for transnational, cosmopolitan democracy (Calabrese 1999b; Calabrese and Borchert 1996, 249–268).

Almost by definition, the cultural, economic, social, and political dimensions of sovereignty, or assertions about its decline, cannot be adequately explained from within the limited confines of a single academic discipline. My aim in this chapter is only to describe and evaluate particular themes in that discourse. In particular, I highlight the importance of debates about how social movements have been redefining the meaning of the political beyond the limits of institutional politics. Social theorists generally highlight the anti- or extrainstitutional nature of social movement politics, an emphasis that implicitly, and sometimes explicitly, challenges the idea of the nation-state and national governments as defining the limits of legitimate politics. Politics "from below" is how the domains of social movements sometimes are characterized. Increasingly, innovative uses of communication and information technologies are seen as essential to this politics. It is the relationship between social movements and the prospects for democratic collective action on the one hand and the means of communication on the other that are my chief concerns here.

I focus on the discourse on postsovereignty (and, implicitly, sovereignty) rather than on nationalism and postnational identity, although, of course, these subjects overlap considerably. With that caveat, I am concerned mainly with the political-administrative structures that define the meaning of sovereignty and with how these structures may be challenged by developments in the means of communication. That inquiry begins with a definition of "sovereignty," followed by a description of the discourse about how social and technological innovation in the means of communication are viewed as bringing the twilight of sovereignty.

THE SOVEREIGN STATE AS THE SPACE OF POLITICS

The idea of the sovereign state is often traced to the political philosophy of Jean Bodin, whose *The Six Books of the Commonweal,* first published in 1576, focused on the power of the sovereign (who holds supreme power over citizens) to make laws (Bodin 1962). While Bodin's views on sovereignty favored monarchy above aristocracy or democracy, modern definitions tend to be grounded in democracy. In David Held's treatment of sovereignty, he begins by describing the "inescapably anarchic" system of states that is articulated well by Thomas Hobbes. Held's model derives from the state system that has existed continuously since the time of the Peace of Westphalia in 1648. The Peace brought an end to the German phase of the Thirty Years' War and the Holy Roman Empire. This system lasted until 1945, through the end of World War II. Two of the chief features of the Westphalian model are the treatment of cross-border wrongs as private matters and the resolution of conflicts between and among states by the use of force (Held 1993, 29; 1995). Departing somewhat from the Westphalian model is the UN Charter model. The major innovation in the latter is the recognition of single persons in international law in the context of war crimes tribunals, the Universal Declaration of Human Rights, and other instruments. While there continued to be an emphasis on "political and strategic (state) affairs" (Held 1995, 33), greater emphasis was placed on the "general welfare of all those in the global system who are able to make their voices count," thus increasing the number of trans-state actors (e.g., United Nations, World Bank, International Monetary Fund, Food and Agricultural Organization, World Health Organization) (Held 1995, 34). Ultimately, Held argues, the UN Charter model does not break fundamentally from the Westphalian mode since it respects the primacy of sovereign states (Held 1995, 36).

While Held proposes a third model of global governance, premised on ideals of cosmopolitan democracy (discussed shortly), in practical terms the UN Charter model's version of sovereignty holds primacy today. In articulating what constitutes a contemporary sovereign state, Held cites four basic characteristics: territoriality, control of the means of violence, impersonal structures of power, and legitimacy (Held 1995, 48–49). These characteristics, particularly the first two (territoriality and control of the means of violence) are familiar from most contemporary definitions of sovereignty (Giddens 1990, 70–71). A state cannot be said to be sovereign if its territorial boundaries, and its right to defend them, are not recognized by the state system, and sovereign control of the means of violence includes control not only of military forces but also of domestic police forces and the administrative structures that are needed to run them. However, although territoriality and violence are necessary for the construction of sovereignty, they are not sufficient, for states also need legitimacy, which cannot be sustained indefinitely by force. Rather, legitimacy depends on means other than violence, such as communication.

For better and worse, the legitimacy of sovereignty depends at least in part on a common sense of national identity. In an emerging European system of sovereign states, the printed word played a great part in shaping such identities. Following the introduction of the movable-type printing press by Gutenberg in 1455, the spread of this technological innovation was rapid and its political impact significant. From this invention, Bibles no longer had to be produced by the hands of scribes, and thus they were now increasingly available not only to priests but also to a greater segment of the emerging bourgeoisie. Concurrent with this development came the secularization and spread of literacy, which helped speed along the Protestant Reformation. Indeed, Martin Luther once waxed rhapsodically, "Printing was God's highest act of grace" (Eisenstein 1968, 34). By many accounts, the "press of protest" on which Protestant reformers relied represented a marriage of technological and religious revolution.

Printing and literacy are historically and politically significant not only for their role in spreading the word of God but also for the forging of early modern European nation-states. By the end of the sixteenth century (roughly 150 years after Gutenberg), the market in Europe for texts published in Latin, the universal language of print, was more or less saturated. Gradually, publishers sought to create new markets for books by consolidating linguistically similar geographic areas into single markets for publications printed in standardized vernacular languages. Thus, through a slow process of defining the geographic boundaries of linguistically unified markets, national literatures and elements of national cultures came to be reinforced and territorialized (Febvre and Martin 1976). While no claim is being made here of which is cause and which is effect, as the printing press spread throughout Europe, the number of literate people grew, and what began as a strategy for developing new publishing markets became, in effect, a means of unifying the reading publics of national bourgeoisies. Literacy was profoundly important for the circulation of political ideas in the time just before and during the French Revolution. The availability of political newsletters and broadsheets was vital to the emergence and consolidation of political power by the French bourgeoisie (Censer and Popkin 1987; Eisenstein 1986; Habermas 1989; Popkin 1990).

The steady rise in literacy throughout Europe, the United States, and most of the world was due in part to various forms of state intervention. A common sense of national culture has been shaped not only by the homogenization of markets for newspapers and magazines but also later through the establishment of post, telegraph, and telephone systems and through national radio and television broadcasting systems. Notwithstanding various accommodations made in some countries for cultural minorities or struggles for cultural autonomy or revolutions in the name of national sovereignty by subnational groups, there is no denying that industrialized cultural production has served as a means of creating images, if not always realities, of national cultures. In social democratic Europe, "public service" radio and television in the post–World War II era was a step to preserve and maintain national cultural identities. Through charter or statutory protection from state editorial control, European public broadcasters have sought to serve as beacons of national culture up to the present, although their viability has been threatened increasingly by competition from domestic and foreign commercial sources. Indeed, variants of public service broadcasting—many relying on the British Broadcasting Corporation (BBC) as their model (some certainly more faithful than others)—now exist throughout the world, including Japan, Australia, Canada, and the postsocialist countries of Central and Eastern Europe.[2] Today, there are many examples that can be given of former totalitarian regimes that have moved toward creating public service broadcasting systems and of cases in which leaders simply have cosmetically created the appearance of having done so. To be sure, just as the idea of a "democratic government" seems to be infinitely malleable around the world, a parallel pattern can be found in the employment and meaning of the term "public service broadcasting."

In sum, since before the Peace of Westphalia, the idea of a national culture has been edified by the construction of national systems of communication. Furthermore, in the process of building such systems, the principle of national sovereignty has been supported. The means of communication function as a primary means of securing *legitimacy* of laws and governments.[3] However, it is not necessarily the case that legitimacy will be derived democratically. This is illustrated by the fact that the means of communication are so heavily and frequently used in ways that are antithetical to the principle of publicity. The goal of subjecting political power to public reason is often thwarted. As Norberto Bobbio notes, the Enlightenment principle of publicity originally was advanced to render visible the hidden power (*arcana imperii*) of the absolute monarch. Bobbio also notes that the principle has no less currency today:

> Similarly, the practice of concealment has never entirely disappeared because of the influence public power can exercise on the press, because of the monopolization of the means of mass communication, and above all because of the unscrupulous exercise of ideological power, the function of ideology being to veil the real motivations which act upon power (a public and legitimate form of the "noble lie" of Platonic origin or of the "permissible lie" of the theorists of *raison d'état*).[4]

Echoing Bobbio, John Keane notes that this condition has become chronic in modern democracies: "Unaccountable power has always been regarded as scandalous in democratic countries, and yet those countries are now faced by a permanent scandal" (Keane 1991, 95). More important, Keane (1991, 94, 113) writes that the motivation to conceal power is often justified in the name of national security, a form of concealment that is enhanced by the complicity of the mass media. Today, such efforts are challenged increasingly not only by movements within states but also by ones that extend beyond the reaches of territorial states. However, movements for democratic communication are not the only forces challenging state sovereignty.

Perhaps the most influential voice behind the idea that sovereignty is in decline comes from the political theory of market liberalism with its views on the modern welfare state. Market liberals argue that the welfare state does greater harm than good for society by discouraging independence, innovation, and initiative. Through excessive taxation, the welfare state created disincentives toward entrepreneurship and investment. Consequently, it cannot sustain the heavy financial burdens that it has created. The market liberal view is that the welfare state is uneconomic, unproductive, inefficient, ineffective, despotic, and restricting of individual freedom (Pierson 1998, 45–47).

The solution, market liberals have argued, is to roll back the welfare state and to open markets not only nationally but globally (Pierson 1998, 62–65; Teeple 1995). The means of communication are seen to be instrumental to this process of creating open, more perfect markets. Not only are the mass media—particularly television—seen by many of globalization's ideological defenders as bases for a new and harmonious "global culture," but the growing density of the telecommunications infrastructure that blankets the earth has created optimism about prospects for the friction-free movement of information and capital for trade and investment. In place of the territory-bound sovereign state is the deterritorialized and sovereign consumer who reigns freely across virtual space. In the political theory of the market liberal, consumer sovereignty is not reducible to economic functions, the buying and selling of goods and services. Rather, the consumer also is able to exercise political power on an ongoing basis through the plebiscite of the pocketbook. As one market liberal states, "Markets are voting machines; they function by taking referenda" (Wriston 1992, 45), and in so doing, the story goes, markets bring discipline, efficiency, and quality to the performance of the state. The means of communication are a necessary feature in this development. As another writes,

> By providing efficient, integrated global data connections, telecommunication companies now offer voters the ultimate shopping experience: shopping for better government. . . . In the past you had to vote with your feet. Now you can vote with your modem, too. The Web supplies an instant global storefront. . . . With cyber power all physical distances are roughly the same. And with this kind of global production system in place, a manufacturing company can move jobs and capital around like pieces on a chessboard, shopping continually for the best-priced labor—and the best labor laws. . . . Competition improves the quality of everything else; it will improve the quality of government, too. (Huber 1996, 142–147)

From this point of view, national sovereignty is an anachronism, given a world wired for electronic commerce and culture, one that respects no boundaries (de Sola Pool 1990).

Of course, the common sense about the inevitability of a global economy that is beyond the control of sovereign states is a social construction that generally is left unexamined. Conventional wisdom ignores the use of political will and coercive state power in the negotiations for global and regional trade regimes such as the General Agreement on Tariffs and Trade (GATT) and the North American Free Trade Agreement (NAFTA) or in the development of the International Monetary Fund's structural adjustment policies. Although these regimes clearly demonstrate that the political will exists among heads of state to construct and implement universal policies of trade, investment, and property protection, it is not nearly as evident that equal will exists among those same leaders to create transnational regimes recognizing social needs, cultural differences, and human rights.

It is not that there has been a lack of effort to pursue visions of a postsovereign world that is governed by the principles of publicity, popular sovereignty, and respect for human rights rather than by the mobilization of capital and other democratically less accountable power. Such efforts rely increasingly on the same means of communication as are used by the forces to which they are opposed.

SOCIAL MOVEMENTS AND THE MEANS OF COMMUNICATION

For all its widely publicized deficiencies, the welfare state has been viewed by its defenders not only as providing a minimal safety net against market failure. It also has been seen as a force in the advancement of the effective exercise of citizenship rights (Bulmer and Rees 1996). However, this position is a matter of considerable dispute across the political spectrum, from market liberals and communitarians to feminists, Marxists, and postmodernists (Calabrese 1997, 9–14; Offe 1985). Of course, it is not necessary to romanticize the welfare state in order to recognize that its fundamental contradictions have included enabling the making of social citizenship, as Claus Offe has demonstrated. Offe challenges the widely held view, often attributed to T. H. Marshall, that social citizenship is a deliberate design feature in the Keynesian welfare state. Rather, Offe makes a more compelling case that the capitalist welfare state should be understood as "a pre-condition for the commodification of labour power" (Offe 1985, 263). By absorbing some of the costs and risks of social reproduction—such as health systems, schools, and housing authorities—the welfare state not only makes a contented and productive labor force possible but, in the process, also "decommodifies" labor. This is done by generating within labor competencies that are not specifically geared to the demands of market rationality but are, in fact, potentially useful in the exercise of political freedom (Offe 1985, 264). In other words, welfare ends up both functioning to reproduce the social conditions necessary for the smooth functioning of a capitalist economy— a factor of production that Offe sees as irreversible (because it is a necessary cost in reducing political and economic conflict)—and undermining capitalism by creating the (partly decommodified) conditions for autonomous social and political movements to exist (Offe 1985, 265).

Offe's thinking about this contradictory tendency within welfare states to subsidize the competencies of movements that challenge their authority is reflected in a similar line of reasoning advanced more recently by Ulrich Beck:

> One can even say, the more successfully political rights were fought for, pushed through and concretely realized in this century, the more emphatically the primacy of the political system was called into question, and the more fictitious became the simultaneously claimed concentration of decision-making at the top of the political and parliamentary system. (Beck 1992, 191)

The social forces that have called "the primacy of the political system" into question are described by Beck as "sub-politics," which emerge through the "unbinding" of the political system and rising demands for a "new political culture" outside the limits of institutional politics (Beck 1992, 185). In describing what he terms "reflexive modernization," Beck charts a departure from the instrumental rationality of industrial society to the ambivalence of what he terms the "risk society." Reflexive modernization is defined as "self-confrontation with the effects of risk society that cannot be dealt with and assimilated in the system of industrial society—as measured by the latter's institutionalized standards."[5] This confrontation, and the liberation that results from it, is taking place within the general context of the industrial welfare states of the West (Beck 1994, 7), moving politics outside (although not necessarily against) the arenas of "duly authorized agents: parliament, political parties, trade unions, and so on" (Beck 1994, 17). Challenging "those who unambiguously equate politics to the state, the political system, formal responsibilities and full-time careers," Beck draws from the feminist wisdom that the personal is political and observes that "the political constellation of industrial society is becoming unpolitical, while what was unpolitical in industrialism is becoming political" (Beck 1994, 18).

While Beck does not suggest that the state has been rendered irrelevant in light of the growth of reflexive subpolitics, he does see the state as taking on a new role that requires it to be more tolerant of ambivalence and more responsive to politics "from below" (Beck 1994, 23, 38–41). Beck describes a transformation of the state as it shifts from "the authoritarian and action state" to "the negotiation state," the latter of which "arranges stages and conversations and directs the show" (Beck 1994, 39). Elsewhere, in defining the practical meaning of "authoritarianism," he argues against the model of the political leader who operates on the assumption that being elected is the only or final test of democratic accountability. "If this were so, we would be living in a dictatorship that elects its dictator, but not in a democracy" (Beck 1992, 233).

Beck is not the first social theorist to offer an articulate account of the contemporary "unbinding" of the political system and the emergence of subpolitics, although his theme of the borderlessness of risk—best exemplified in his detailed reflections on politics of ecological risk—is of particular value in considering the relationship between sovereignty and subpolitics. In that regard, he treats the mass media as one of the "central forums of sub-politics" (Beck 1992, 195), a view that is tempered by his recognition that "media publicity can obviously never anticipate the political decision; and it remains for its part connected into the economic, legal and political presuppositions and concentrations of capital in the news business" (Beck 1992, 198). However, an issue that is underdeveloped in Beck's account is that of the *scale of politics,* specifically in terms of its relation to the means of communication. If the scale of the social problem or risk is transnational, then the corresponding space of appropriate political action must also have the flexibility to be transnational (Calabrese and Burke 1992, 56–57). Arguing this point with reference to communication systems, Nicholas Garnham states, "[T]he problem is to construct systems of democratic accountability integrated with media systems of *matching scale* that occupy the same social space as that over which economic or political decisions will impact" (Garnham 1992, 371; emphasis added).

Beck sees the means of communication as necessary tools of publicity in reflexive subpolitics, but he does not address the issue of scale raised previously. Specifically, he does not attend to the use of new and old means of communication in *transnational* subpolitics. While Beck's concerns lie elsewhere, those for whom these issues are more central include Manuel Castells and Alberto Melucci, the latter of whom has made a particularly valuable contribution to an understanding of the relationship between social movements and the means of communication (Calabrese 1999b; Castells 1997; Melucci 1996). Not unlike Beck, who makes a theme of the claim that we are witnessing the transformation from one epoch to another—from unambiguous modernity to ambivalent, reflexive modernity (Beck 1994, 17)—and that an essential characteristic of subpolitics is their "irreducible ambivalences" (Beck 1994, 12), Melucci sees ambivalence as an intrinsic characteristic of the impact of the new means of communication on contemporary social movements:

> On the one hand, there can be observed a concentration of power, with very few core centres that control the world in terms of the world-wide transmission and distribution of ideas, languages, programmes, and the like; on the other hand, we can see emerging symptoms of resistance to this trend, manifest in, for example, the action of hackers, information pirates, self-managed networks, and so on. (Melucci 1996, 194)

In observing this ambivalence, Melucci argues that transformations in information technology and the processing of information contribute both to concern over the destabilization of political space and to optimism about opening up of new political spaces in unpredictable and uncontrollable ways (Melucci 1996, 195). However, he suffers no illusion about the power of the concentrated world media system, which he refers to as "the manufacturer of master codes at the world scale" (Melucci 1996, 179), or about "the deprivation over the constitution of meaning" (182). Under these dubious conditions, we might ask whether movements are able to see and realize any emancipatory potential in the uses of the new means of communication, particularly in recognition of the fact that these communicative structures have been developed to further expand the circulation of capital and extend the commodification of culture. Lest we romanticize the emancipatory potential of the new social movements or their use of the latest means of communication, as David Harvey notes in a sobering observation, "movements of opposition to the disruptions of home, community, territory, and nation by the restless flow of capital" fight under circumstances not of their own choosing. "In so doing, they necessarily open themselves to the dissolving power of money."[6] A fundamental practical question that arises in response is whether, given that knowledge, such movements actually are in a position to opt out of opposing such disruptions. In this light, oppositional movements face a choice between the Scylla of commodification, cooptation, and embourgeoisment and the Charybdis of paralysis. It is surely a cause for ambivalence among sympathetic observers and participants alike and one for which there is no wisdom in seeking an immutable and undialectical moral high ground.

The relationship between the means of communication and social movements is very much an open one, but it is not a novel one. As a number of studies have illustrated, movement actors have made two primary uses of the media, namely, (1) in efforts to gain access to "mainstream" media in order to publicize oppositional politics and gain wider sympathies to their causes, not unlike what is suggested by Beck,[7] and (2) in efforts to sustain networks of those already committed to the movement. In the latter category, there are numerous examples of employment of so-called alternative or radical media that have served, either by design or by default, mainly as means of communication within a movement, functioning in the process to further organization and coordination.[8] While much of the literature on alternative media focuses on print, film, video, and even radio, since the early 1980s there also has been a steady stream of research and speculation about the uses of computer-mediated communication in the service of progressive politics (Athanasiou 1985; Goldhaber 1983; Haight, Rubinyi, and Zornosa 1983). Recently, attention to this latter trend, which began well before the explosion in popular use of the Internet in the mid-1990s, has led to optimistic speculation about a new dawn of progressive, transnational politics (Herod, Tuathail, and Roberts 1998; Lee 1997; Waterman 1996, 1998). Given the historical tendency in welfare states for organized labor politics to be restricted to national corporatist negotiations, involving representatives of the state, corporations, and trade unions, a particularly welcoming view seems to have been taken toward visions of a new, "labor internationalism" that can rely on the Internet as a means of organization, coordination, and publicity.[9] Much of this discourse treats the Internet as a revolutionary tool for direct action politics because of the enhanced prospects for globalizing the scale of political action across a wide array of movements. Because of such activity, the Internet is viewed increasingly as an essential infrastructure to support the ideas of a global civil society and a cosmopolitan democracy, the subject to which I now briefly turn.

GOVERNANCE WITHOUT GOVERNMENT?

According to Derek Heater, the cosmopolitan idea of governance, "either as an alternative to state citizenship or as a complement to it," has existed in Western thought since the ancient Greeks (Heater 1990, 8). One of the most inspiring expressions of it can be found in Immanuel Kant's *Perpetual Peace and Other Essays,* published in 1795, in which he wrote that "the idea of cosmopolitan right is not fantastic and exaggerated, but rather an amendment to the unwritten code of national and international rights, necessary to the public rights of men in general" (Kant 1983, 119). Foreshadowing much of contemporary discourse about media and globalization, in 1887 Ferdinand Tönnies suggested that the ultimate aim of the press could be "to abolish the multiplicity of states and substitute for it a single world republic co-extensive with the world market, which would be ruled by thinkers, scholars, and writers and could dispense with the means of coercion other than those of a psychological nature" (Tönnies 1957, 221).

More recently, David Held has advanced a normative model of international governance that he calls "cosmopolitan democracy." This model emphasizes global interconnectedness through commercial arrangements, networks of transport and communication, and international relations:

> What is new about the modern global system is the spread of globalization through new dimensions of activity—technological, organization, administrative and legal, among others—each with its own logic and dynamic of change; and the chronic intensification of patterns of interconnectedness mediated by such phenomena as the modern communications industry and new information technology. Politics unfolds today, with all its customary uncertainty and indeterminateness, against the background of a world shaped and permeated by the movement of goods and capital, the flow of communication, the interchange of cultures and the passage of people. (Held 1993, 39)

The cosmopolitan model that Held calls for explicitly recognizes issues fundamental to liberal democratic thought, particularly in the form of impediments to human need and dignity. By casting his arguments in terms of the harm principle, he argues for "empowering rights" (contra "citizenship rights"), which transcend the nation-state and are designed to cultivate and support civic competence in a variety of ways, not least of which is the creation of media and cultural cooperatives. As to how such a scheme will be funded and sustained, Held does not venture.

Such thinking has attracted criticism on a variety of grounds, including the argument that politics cannot exist without a state[10] and that the idea of a "world constitutional state and a transnational democracy capable of promoting peace, guaranteeing rights and protecting the environment" is a somewhat facile "globalist ideology" (Dryzek 1999, 30–51; Zolo 1997, 130). While opposing the idea of a world state and arguing that the "doctrine of the withering of the state . . . must be decisively opposed," Danilo Zolo (1997, 133) refers to the idea of cosmopolitan citizenship as "empty rhetoric." Furthermore, he has no greater optimism toward the idea of a global civil society, citing the expulsion of immigrants and "the negation of their status as civil subjects" as more accurate reflections of the sentiments that prevail in the affluent Western societies from which the discourse of cosmopolitan democracy arises.[11] Zolo does not dismiss the feasibility of increasing capacities for "governance" through "international regimes" that are capable of coordinating responses to global problems by national, transnational, and international actors. However, he argues, such coordination does not rest on the notion of drastically reducing the complexity of the world political environment, which is what he claims is done by Held and others who are focused on visions not of governance but of government (Zolo 1997, 134, 138).

In contrast to Zolo, Michael Walzer does hold a vision of a global civil society. With regard to questions of governance, while recognizing the reasonable grounds for euphoria about the rebirth of civil society from the ashes of totalitarian states, he warns against "the antipolitical tendencies that commonly accompany the celebration of civil society," which he presents as a justification for the continued presence of state power as a moderating force (Walzer 1991, 301). In his view, the "radically unequal power relationships" that civil society can generate can only be challenged by state power. However, because of its capacity to function transnationally, "civil society also challenges state power," an observation that Walzer uses to justify an appropriate scale of institutional response. He then argues that the best means to constrain multinational corporations lies in "collective security, in alliances with other states that give economic regulation some international effect" (Walzer 1991, 302). This vision bears resemblance to Zolo's notion of governance through international regimes, although it is not clear whether it is opposed to or in favor of Held's notion of a more formalized set of standing bodies for global government or aspects thereof. Although we do not seem to have anything close to a "world government," and I do not wish to suggest that one is desirable, we *are* witness today to ever greater levels of the trans-state coordination and institutionalization of governance functions in the arenas of trade and investment and in military affairs.[12]

Following the 1993 ratification of GATT and the establishment of the World Trade Organization (WTO), the WTO's director-general, Renato Ruggiero, said in a speech, "We are writing the constitution for a single global economy (Ruggiero 1996). Although we might not wish to characterize them as efforts in global state making, developments in the WTO and in other transnational institutions are reflective of gradual process, both administrative and discursive, that Michel Foucault termed "governmentalization."[13] Whether we wish to refer to the outcome of this process as governance or government, the reality is that standing institutions that are gaining in authority and enforcement capabilities have taken on the appearances and functions of government institutions. Such institutions as the WTO and the World Intellectual Property Organization (WIPO)[14] are concerned precisely with global government in circumscribed arenas, and they are indeed expressions of political will and the capacity for enforcement. In light of the undemocratic and exclusionary practices through which such institutions are governed, it would appear that a necessary, if not the only or best, means for monitoring the activities of such institutions will be increasingly through a global civil society, as the following example illustrates.

HIDING POWER IN TRANSNATIONAL GOVERNANCE

The rhetoric of the political irrelevance of the state is a powerful means to legitimate market liberalism's economic policies. From this perspective, the state is too weak to sustain domestic social welfare policies while at the same time it is absolutely essential as an instrument to create and sustain transnational regimes of trade, investment, and property relations. Hardly rendering the state irrelevant, in practice, market liberalism requires the backing of state violence to see to its requirements for labor discipline and other forms of "political stability." The highly interventionist quest for harsh state-imposed sanctions and enforcement mechanisms against violators of the principles of the proposed "Multilateral Agreement on Investment" (MAI)[15] shows how low the bottom line of market liberal practice can sink.

The Uruguay Round of the GATT talks, which resulted in the establishment of the WTO along with new developments in other international governing bodies focused on global trade (such as the WIPO), have led to even more intensified efforts to establish a stable and growing regime of international trade and investment. Opposition by a variety of groups has accompanied these efforts. Most prominent among them have been human rights, environmental, and labor groups. Recent attempts spearheaded by the Organization for Economic Cooperation and Development (OECD) to ratify the MAI were abandoned after the negotiations that were under way became public. The agreement has gotten very little press attention in the United States, but it has provoked considerable collective action in many other countries, particularly Canada, New Zealand, and France.

The MAI was abandoned in December 1998 after the French government refused to participate—responding to pressures from France's cultural industries (Taglieri 1999). Although the MAI had been under negotiation in Paris since 1995, the treaty, which is considered to be 90 percent complete, did not become politicized until a year later. Then, a photocopy of it was obtained by activists and later circulated around the world via the Internet. The MAI has been called "stealth MAI" by its critics because of the secrecy under which negotiations were conducted and because of the strong emphasis on corporate investment rights, minus any emphasis on corporate responsibilities (Public Citizen, Friends of the Earth, Sierra Club 1998). Leadership efforts by the United States to push forward the MAI ended after the release of the text worldwide by a number of citizens groups. This followed the derailing of "fast track" trade negotiation authority to the Clinton administration, which would have permitted the president to sign such an agreement without congressional amendment. According to Lori Wallach, director of Public Citizen's Global Trade Watch (founded by Ralph Nader in 1971), the U.S. congressional committees with direct oversight authority over international trade and investment were never consulted or informed about the U.S. State and Treasury Departments' efforts to lead U.S. representation in MAI negotiations (Wallach 1998a, 1998b).

Among the main concerns by the MAI opponents is its language regarding "barriers to trade" and "expropriation and compensation." As the argument goes, it would be possible for foreign investors to sue a national government in an international tribunal (probably administered by the WTO) if they felt that the conditions of investment in the host country threatened (expropriated) future earnings and a judgment could be made that would force the government of that country to obtain compensation on behalf of the plaintiff. Examples of U.S. companies suing the Canadian government under NAFTA rules have been cited as precedent.

Concern about the MAI arose in the U.S. Congress in March 1998, when the House Committee on International Relations' Subcommittee of International Economic Policy and Trade held hearings on it. One of the issues raised in testimony is that the MAI threatens states' rights and U.S. sovereignty by making it possible for MAI rules to preempt state and federal laws, something that many European and Japanese investors wish to achieve. Detailed testimony by Georgetown law professor Robert Stumberg points out that the MAI effectively would work as an amendment to the U.S. Constitution and, in essence, aims to reinvent the terms of U.S. sovereignty, given the many ways in which it would reorder jurisdiction over domestic trade and investment (Stumberg 1998).

Opposition has arisen in non-OECD countries as well, where it is feared that the establishment of such an investment regime would threaten the sovereignty of all countries by forcing them to become MAI signatories in order to attract or retain foreign investment. Human rights and environmental groups, and major labor unions uniformly oppose the MAI because they fear that it will precipitate a multifaceted race to the bottom, requiring national governments to use force against their people in order to comply with MAI rules on behalf of mobile capital. On February 12, 1998, a "Joint NGO Statement" was released on behalf of more than 600 organizational signatories, including leading human rights, labor, environmental, and consumer groups from more than seventy countries. In addition to complaints about the secrecy and exclusiveness of participation in the MAI negotiations, the statement also notes that the MAI takes no account of the differences between investment needs in OECD and non-OECD countries and that the agreement conflicts with many existing international, national, and subnational laws and regulations in many arenas, all of which would potentially be subordinated to MAI discipline (Public Citizen 1998).

The implications of the MAI controversy are far-reaching, and the point of this brief overview is simply to highlight one particularly contentious issue in international law and policy that has become a catalyst for international collective action. The scale and speed of mobilization against the MAI would probably have been impossible had it not been for the use of the global Internet as a tool of coordination and publicity. As a result of the rapid diffusion of information about the MAI, civil action, including large-scale demonstrations, took place in several European countries, the United States, Canada, Australia, and elsewhere (Khor 1998). What is interesting is that rapid grassroots mobilization and publicity seriously undermined, at least for the time being, a major international trade and investment agreement. It is a story that gives heart to any vision of a democratic and cosmopolitan civil society and optimism toward the potential uses of the means of communication in transnational political action. Of course, the story is not over, and it should be noted that the general view of MAI advocates is that the question is not one of *if* but of *when* a treaty such as the MAI will be passed, which is most likely true. In December 1999, the WTO Ministerial Conference met in Seattle, and an MAI-like treaty was a major subject of deliberation as well as a catalyst for protest. Microsoft CEO Bill Gates has advocated to the U.S. Congress that President Clinton be granted "fast track" trade negotiating authority (which he has been denied twice since November 1997) in order to enable Clinton to sign an MAI without permitting Congress to amend the agreement later, as it normally can (Reuters 1999). Various advocacy organizations, most prominently Ralph Nader's Public Citizen group, have been lobbying against this development (Public Citizen 1999), but the free-traders have not given up on their efforts.

CONCLUSION

The case of the MAI offers a compelling basis for concluding that there is something that might be called a nascent global civil society and that the power of publicity by resourceful activists can have a significant effect on exposing what otherwise might be unaccountable government power, buried in arcane processes of transnational deal making. The MAI case also illustrates the continued importance of the state as a means of leverage both for and against democratic processes in transnational governance. On the one hand, the Clinton administration and national governments acted in secrecy to establish an investment regime that threatens to undermine a wide range of rights currently protected under sovereign laws. On the other hand, that secrecy was exposed by transnational civic action that relied on the means of communication for purposes of coordination and broader publicity, resulting ultimately in demands by legislatures and parliaments for greater accountability from their executives. This case illustrates how such transnational action makes use of resources both within and beyond the scope of state power. Perhaps we might conclude from this that a new form of transnational governance is emerging, namely, one that makes effective use of principles of publicity and democratic discourse, but that it hardly signifies the abandonment of national politics in the age of a nascent global civil society. However, it should be noted that the anti-MAI mobilization was in reaction to powerful developments to institutionalize (or "governmentalize") ways of thinking about a wide range of political and economic priorities and in the process to pose significant ecological risks and threats to human rights. Such developments do not by themselves provide sufficient grounds for concluding that sovereignty has ended, although it is clear that national governments are playing an increasingly important role in sharing powers of global governance, both for and against democracy.

Many of the major events that provoke transnational civic action are made possible by forms of unaccountable power that hide within the jurisdictional interstices among nation-states. One of the unique features of social movements that has been discussed in detail here is their uncontrollable and unpredictable capacities to create new political spaces, now increasingly global in scale, to publicly challenge such power. However, in idealizing this virtue, we should not be deluded. Processes are taking place by which significant aspects of sovereign power are gradually being transferred to and consolidated within regimes of transnational governance, if not always on a fully globalized basis. Such consolidation is supported by the coordinated capacities to enforce these policies and to suppress civil disobedience through violent means when necessary. In recognition of this fact, any utopian view that might arise about the means of communication providing a necessary infrastructure for a global civil society should be tempered by ambivalence.

NOTES

1. Together, these means of violence constitute a significant part of what Althusser labeled "repressive state apparatuses": "Repressive suggests that the State Apparatus in question 'functions by violence' at least ultimately (since repression, e.g., administrative repression, may take non-physical forms)" (Althusser 1971, 143).

2. The historical dominance of commercial (contra "public") broadcasting in the United States constitutes a unique example among Western democracies. Nevertheless, despite the existence of competing commercial broadcasting networks, a sense of national identity has been undergirded by efforts in the regulation of broadcasting, telegraphy, and telephony to support a regime of national commerce as well as a system that could serve the interests of national security and defense (Headrick 1991; Horwitz 1989). However, through active diplomatic pressure and coercion, the values underlying the U.S. commercial system have come to influence many national movements toward deregulation, privatization, and liberalization in telecommunications and the mass media. Of course, the United States has been the dominant force in the movement toward establishing liberalized multilateral trade and investment regimes in these industries, particularly through negotiations and agreements in the North American Free Trade Agreement, the General Agreement on Tariffs and Trade, and, more recently, the Multilateral Agreement on Investment.

3. Althusser includes the means of communication in what he refers to as "ideological state apparatuses," the control over which is an essential outcome of any effective struggle to gain control of state power (Althusser 1971, 146). Need one doubt that this is the case after witnessing numerous decisive struggles to gain control of the media in the toppling of several political regimes in recent history?

4. Bobbio (1989, 21). Bobbio also reflects on the surveillance of citizens through the use of computer databases: "The new prince can get to know far more about his subjects than most absolute monarchs of the past" (21).

5. Beck, Giddens, and Lash (1994, 6). Beck also uses the term "media and information society" to refer to the risk society (Beck 1992, 46).

6. Harvey (1989, 238). Another reason for caution and skepticism toward uncritical romanticism about the emancipatory potential of social movements is that we should always recognize that grassroots action is not necessarily morally defensible action. Many hateful causes are advanced by the use of the tools of communication that are touted by left utopians as new means of creating progressive grassroots politics. Such tools also are used in carefully

constructed top-down political campaigns that are designed to appear as authentic expressions of "grassroots" action. Sometimes referred to as "astroturf," alluding to the artificial grass used in indoor sports arenas, such campaigns are common tactics in well-funded political lobbying efforts.

7. A classic account of this type can be found in Todd Gitlin's vivid chronicle of the U.S. antiwar movement and the efforts of the Students for a Democratic Society (SDS) to gain media coverage (Gitlin 1980). A more novel example is Montgomery (1989), who provides case studies of efforts by various social groups to pressure prime time television programmers in the United States to modify their programs, for example, through threats of boycotts and bad publicity for commercial sponsors of programs that are considered to perpetuate harmful racial and gender stereotypes.

8. Two valuable examples that fit well into this category are Downing (1984) and Waugh (1984). Also significant are the quarterly *Alternative Press Index,* published since 1969 by the Alternative Media Center in College Park, Maryland, and the *Utne Reader,* a widely circulated Minneapolis-based bimonthly magazine that has served since 1987 as a sort of reader's digest of the alternative press.

9. Today, nearly all (if not all) major trade unions in Western countries have web sites and use other capabilities of the Internet, including chat rooms and list servers. Andrew Herod describes these new developments as the basis of "a trade union politics of networks and flows rather than of territorial blocs" (Herod et al., 1998, 187). Quoting from *Le Monde,* "Workers of all countries, click here." Herod notes the playful and serious aims to view these developments within the historical legacy of socialist internationalism (189).

10. Guéhenno (1995). Guéhenno, French ambassador to the European Union, asks, "If solidarity can no longer be locked to geography, if there is no longer a city, if there is no longer a nation, can there be politics" (17)?

11. Zolo (1997, 137–138). Zolo considers it naive of Held (and Richard Falk, who argues along similar lines) to think that NGOs "will gradually point the way towards planetary social integration and thereby constitute the premise for the construction of a world constitutional state and a transnational democracy capable of promoting peace, guaranteeing rights and protecting the environment" (130).

12. To be sure, there are other highly visible forms of trans-state governmental structures than the ones I have highlighted, for example, ones dealing with ecological and human rights issues. However, the extremes of crisis that seem to be required to provoke coordinated (but often nonroutine) responses in these arenas put them into a different category than the more administratively rationalized and sustained arenas of trade, investment, and military control.

13. In an essay titled "Governmentality," Foucault describes the process by which, in the eighteenth century, a gradual rationalization of political power through a science of government resulted "on the one hand, in the formation of a whole series of specific governmental apparatuses, and, on the other, in the development of a whole complex of *savoirs*" (Foucault 1991, 103). However, this shift is not simply reducible to the processes of institutionalizing political and economic control through administrative means, although it certainly includes such functions. In addition to "government of the state," Foucault's concept of "governmentality" applies as well to "government of oneself" and to "government of souls and lives" (87). More generally, he is concerned with the capillary forms and expressions of power, particularly as they are found in discursive practices in state and society. Expanding on this idea, Toby Miller describes culture as "governmental" in the sense that it is, for better

and for worse, "both a logic of artistic training, concerned with the appreciation of textual norms, and as system for distributing cultural competence" (Miller 1998, 264). With a similar view, Stuart Hall describes the idea of "governing by culture": "We are not necessarily speaking about arm-twisting coercion, undue influence, crude propaganda, false information or even questionable motives here. . . . All our conduct and actions are shaped, influenced and thus regulated normatively by cultural meanings. The regulation of culture and regulation *by* culture are thus intimately and profoundly related" (Hall 1997, 23).

14. The existence of the World Intellectual Property Organization (WIPO) long pre-dates the establishment of the WTO. WIPO's origins as an intergovernmental organization date back to the 1886 Berne Convention for the Protection of Literary and Artistic Works. Following a series of developments in the international protection of intellectual property, WIPO was established in 1974 as a UN agency. See World Intellectual Property Organization, General Information, at <http://www.wipo.org/eng/main.html>.

15. The full text of the draft treaty is available at <http://www.essential.org/monitor/mai/contents.mai>. See also Michelle Sforza, Nova, and Weisbrot (1999).

Part 3

News Reporting and Coverage

6

The Unheralded Functions of Campaign News

Roderick P. Hart

As the twenty-first century dawns, many Americans feel knowledgeable about the contemporary press.[1] "The news anchors are in league with one another," conservatives bellow, "using their smarmy grins and innuendos to savage what is good and true." "The media are tools of the oligarchies," the Left answers, "captives of the multinationals that manufacture all the cars, all the computers, all the television sets." "When politicians are in trouble on the campaign circuit," modern Machiavellians suggest, "they should run against the media." Many politicians do just that and then retreat to the friendly confines of the morning talk shows rather than do battle with feisty reporters in conventional press conferences.

Most of the opinion polls show that antipathy toward the news media has never been higher. The public has steadily lost faith in all institutions, these studies show, but the nation's press has become a special object of opprobrium. Perhaps familiarity breeds contempt. At the turn of the millennium, television anchors and even some print reporters (David Broder and Maureen Dowd come to mind) are now celebrities in their own right, persons who must bow to the inevitable dictum—that fame and fortune are fleeting.

However, are the popular charges lodged against the press truly warranted? Are media personnel lazy imitators of one another, as some wags claim? Are press reports consistently tilted in one direction or another? Has the news become increasingly shallow as its audience has grown? Is the news now an endless story about elites and less and less a story about how life can be made better for ordinary people? These are large questions, to be sure, and they cannot be answered definitively here, but the following pages do report a broad-based examination of the news text, asking questions that have been asked before (but answering them more empirically and asking some new questions as well). The focus here is on political news, but the findings may well generalize to all forms of reportage. At the very least, this chapter establishes that some of the conventional wisdom about the news may be overly conventional and hence not as wise as it might be.

PUBLIC PERCEPTIONS

The Pew Research Center for the People and the Press (1997) conducts periodic surveys of opinions about the press but rarely reports heartening results. One of their recent studies shows that only 15 percent of the American people have a "very favorable" opinion of network news, that viewership as a result is dropping, and that people generally see little fairness, accuracy, or helpfulness in the media. Other research (Kerbel 1994, 1) shows that broadcast news "presents the viewer with a singular, cynical image of presidential politics and the political system" and that it also equips viewers with significantly more negative emotions about politics than do alternative sources of information (Hibbing and Theiss-Morse 1998). Then there is the issue of bias: Noyes, Lichter, and Amundson (1993) show that George Bush received 20 percent fewer positive stories than did Bill Clinton in 1992, a fact that is met with a sizable yawn by most reporters since Mr. Bush did little to advance his own cause during that campaign. Still, charges of news bias are persistent. The American people know what they know, and, when it comes to the media, they are not pleased with what they know.

They need to know more. For one thing, they need to know that consuming political news builds "diffuse support" for the political system even though it can also turn voters against specific candidates and parties (Farnsworth 1997). They need to know that heavily reported stories are best remembered by the electorate, suggesting that the mass media have considerable influence even when reviled (Price and Czilli 1996); they need to know that news reports can significantly affect voters' evaluations of candidates' "viability," an outcome of considerable consequence in a crowded electoral field (Ansolabehere, Behr, and Iyengar 1991); and they need to know that the mass media have especially powerful effects among undecided or marginalized voters (Bartels 1993). In short, the American people need to think in more complicated ways about the mass media. Only by knowing what the news is can they help determine what it can become.

This chapter focuses on one of the most basic features of the news: its language. The assumption is that only by looking at the news microscopically, empirically, can we determine whether the brickbats most commonly thrown at it are thrown justifiably. To facilitate that analysis, a large and representative sample of news texts had to be assembled and then subjected to analysis. Thus, the data reported here result from the Campaign Mapping Project, a multiyear examination of how political discourse has changed during the last fifty years, a project funded by the Ford and Carnegie Foundations and pursued by Kathleen Hall Jamieson of the University of Pennsylvania and the author.

One of the purposes of the project was to examine the language used by political elites and to compare the language of the press to that of the American political establishment. Thus, the database contained a wide variety of campaign speeches and political advertisements as well as print and broadcast news. All these materials were produced during general election campaigns for the presidency from 1948 through 1996. At present, some 12,000 such text segments are housed in the database, a text segment being defined as (1) a 500-word passage from a political speech or print news article or (2) the entirety of a campaign ad or broadcast story.

This chapter focuses on the news texts in the database. The print coverage in the sample (*n* = 7,309) consisted of feature and nonfeature stories from the *New York Times, Washington Post, Christian Science Monitor, Atlanta Constitution, Chicago Tribune, Los Angeles Times,* as well as AP and UPI syndicate stories. Clearly, the attempt here was to get both "national" and regional papers in the mix since so much of politics is local, especially during presidential elections. The broadcast coverage was more modest (*n* = 1,219), consisting of nightly newscasts produced during the 1980, 1988, 1992, and 1996 campaigns by the news bureaus of ABC, CBS, NBC, CNN, and PBS.

To deal with such massive amounts of data, a capacious research tool was needed that could also deal with the complexity of political language. The technique chosen was a piece of software called DICTION (Hart 1997), a lexically based program that passes over a text with the assistance of some forty-seven dictionaries or word lists. DICTION's overall search corpus consists of 10,000 individual words, with no word being duplicated in its search routines. Because DICTION examines a text from so many different perspectives simultaneously, it permits an unusually comprehensive examination of a given passage.[2]

Lying at the heart of the program are its dictionaries, each of which produces its own set of scores. When dictionary scores are combined (after standardization), they contribute to five "additive variables" that give a parsimonious view of a text's main features. These components include the following:

1. Certainty: Language indicating resoluteness, inflexibility, and completeness and a tendency to speak ex cathedra
2. Optimism: Language endorsing some person, group, concept, or event or highlighting their positive entailments
3. Activity: Language featuring movement, change, the implementation of ideas, and the avoidance of inertia
4. Realism: Language describing tangible, immediate, recognizable matters that affect people's everyday lives
5. Commonality: Language highlighting the agreed-on values of a group and rejecting idiosyncratic modes of engagement.

Space limitations do not permit a complete exposition of the methods used here, but some of DICTION's strengths can be sketched:

1. Unlike other research techniques, DICTION forgets nothing, thereby exposing patterns of raw epistemic choice that would remain hidden to the case-specific scholar.
2. DICTION fully operationalizes the constructs it taps and does so in protean ways (the average dictionary contains over 300 words).
3. DICTION allows for extremely sophisticated construct building by tapping a variety of linguistic categories simultaneously.
4. DICTION is completely reductionistic and, in a sense, hypothesis resistant, thereby permitting constant reanalysis of a passage under conditions not originally foreseen by the researcher.
5. DICTION compares each text it processes to a database of previously analyzed texts, thereby permitting a passage to be located in semantic space precisely.
6. DICTION's word lists are especially useful for dealing with political materials.

For further discussion of the strengths and weaknesses of such content analytic programs, see Hart (in press).

After running all the political and media texts through DICTION, four basic functions of campaign news were discovered (or rediscovered). As in all such matters, the data reported here are open to multiple interpretation, as are the characterizations offered of the media's functionalities. Nonetheless, the data reflect rather favorably on the press and hence prompt a reexamination of that institution.

THE DISCIPLINARY FUNCTION

One of the news's most important functions is also its most controversial. Whether because of tradition, institutional pressure, or sheer malevolence, the U.S. press has come to see itself as the nation's monitor—a cranky, disciplinary schoolmaster overlooking a set of unruly charges. Looking at language cues alone, I found the news texts to be consistently more negative than those of politicians, a finding that will not be surprising to many.[3] Figure 6.1 shows the rather dramatic nature of those differences, and figure 6.2 shows that the "optimism gap" has not diminished across time.

Why are the media so pessimistic? Recent events come to mind—Vietnam, Watergate, Iran-Contra, Whitewater—but the simple fact is that the press has always reported what is going wrong, and the American people, by and large, do not like it when things go wrong. Studies continually show that many Americans would, if they could, place severe constraints on the Fourth Estate, even as they embrace its First Amendment protections. People become especially discomfited with the press during election seasons, when they churn out endless stories of campaign misdeeds and malignant political motives. Although many Americans lose their footing from

Figure 6.1   Optimism scores for message types

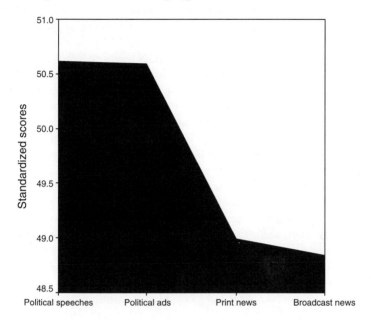

Figure 6.2   Optimism scores over time

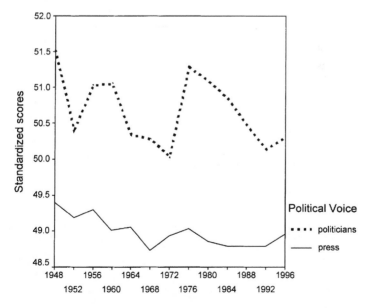

time to time, for example, it took but one stumble from a speaker's platform by Bob Dole during the 1996 campaign to produce a "news peg" for a month. Ordinary people seethe at such overreporting. They find it uncharitable in the extreme and find it lazy journalism as well.

Political news is also *reliably* negative. DICTION found no important differences among the seven print sources and five broadcast sources on Optimism. In addition, Optimism scores did not vary during the course of the campaign, they did not change from region to region, they were no higher in stories about incumbents than in stories about challengers, and both Democrats and Republicans received the same, sour coverage between 1948 and 1996. Using an entirely different set of measures, Lichter and Smith (1996) found a similar pessimism when they compared campaign reportage to the remarks of political candidates. To understand the press's negativity, however, one must distinguish between (1) partisan negativity and (2) universal negativity. That is, complaints about partisan negativity come and go. During the Monica Lewinsky scandal of the late 1990s, for example, one almost never heard Republicans complain about media bias even though that debacle produced some of the worst forms of pack journalism ever recorded. Similarly, when the press refused to pursue rumors of extramarital relations on the parts of George Bush in 1992 and Bob Dole in 1996, no hosannas were sung by Democrats.

The media also produce what Luke (1978) calls "artificial negativity" when it makes bad news out of nothingness or, at least, out of very little. Figure 6.3 pro-

Figure 6.3   Commonality scores by era

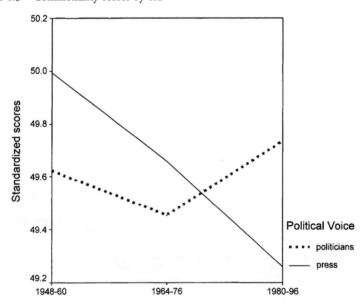

vides a vivid illustration of that tendency. The language of commonality—words that provide a sense of group concern and collective purpose—has dropped off a bit in press reports over the years, perhaps reflecting an increased fracturing of the American electorate.[4] When the twenty-five news reports with the lowest Commonality scores were extracted from the database, *every one* featured public opinion polls, a brand of reportage that has become a staple. Because polls are now so plentiful—in part because news organizations themselves are in the polling business—there are always enough data to support any claim the press wishes to make. So, for example, a news story titled "Clinton Has Edge in 3 Polls; But Figures Vary Widely" (AP-UPI Wire, October 30, 1992) has something for everyone: Clinton voters can take heart, but Bush voters need not despair. Four years earlier, a carefully phrased headline such as "Bush Makes up Ground" (*Los Angeles Times,* September 16, 1988) could stir up Republicans, while a story titled "The 1992 Campaign; Clinton Poll Lead Narrows" (*New York Times,* October 29, 1992) could motivate the faithful in both parties. Polls are now so omnipresent that metapolling has become a cottage industry ("In Judging Polls, What Counts Is When and How Who Is Asked What," *New York Times,* September 12, 1988). Even when the race has yet to be run, a race can be run in the newsroom ("Comparing the Post-convention Polls," *Los Angeles Times,* September 2, 1992).

Polling stories can also make local things national—"Poll in Minnesota Shows a Neck and Neck Race" (AP-UPI Wire, November 5, 1992)—and add nuance to a campaign that may have become bloated—"Poll Finds Most Americans Back Grants for Parental School Choice" (*Los Angeles Times,* September 7, 1992). Given the rhetorical attractions of polling stories, it is not surprising that they become increasingly popular over the course of a campaign. Such trend lines show how the media work to keep the campaign interesting, even though the candidates' own remarks showed no significant drop in Commonality during the campaign.[5] In defense of its negativity, the press would argue as follows: (1) The people of the United States have always disagreed with one another; (2) political campaigns naturally bring these disagreements to the surface; (3) the strength of the nation lies in its pluralism, not in a feigned homogeneity; (4) the press has a positive obligation to report on the nation's fault lines; and (5) it is the job of the politicians, not the press, to bring us together. Each of these propositions can be objected to, but they are not entirely unreasonable in a pluralistic democracy.

THE ENERGIZING FUNCTION

For the press, politics is a whirlwind of motion. Press coverage far outstripped political discourse on the language of Activity and did so consistently throughout the thirteen elections studied here.[6] These differences never really abated, suggesting a truly generic quality. In one sense that is not surprising since journalism is supposed to relate the events of the day. But the Activity found in news coverage far exceeds mere motor description. Rather, it creates a suggestive, involving narrative in which all action, both empirical and psychological, and all experience, including thought itself, have dramatic consequences. A rather breathless CBS news report from the 1996 campaign shows how carefully chosen language can give energy to an event that otherwise had none (emphasis added):

> Bob Dole is personally *ratcheting up* the attack on President Clinton's character and ethics. His campaign operatives *opened fire* on several fronts over the weekend including accusations about overseas contributions to the Clinton campaign. Today Dole himself *picked up* on that *line of attack*. . . .
>
> Campaign staffers also handed out a press release with five questions directed to President Clinton and Vice President Gore regarding campaign contributions from Indonesian banking interests. We were told Mr. Dole would raise this issue in his speech, but he didn't. However, at the airport, after a *quick strategy huddle*, he decided to *personally weigh in* on what he called the Clinton-Gore Indonesian connection relating to campaign contributions. . . .
>
> With the *gloves and coat off*, Mr. Dole basked under the Missouri sunshine before *heading off* to San Diego, where he's indicated he will say these same things to the president in Wednesday night's debate. . . .
>
> The Democratic Party's success at collecting huge campaign contributions from foreign sources has raised questions about the legality of its fund-raising operations and given the Republicans *an issue to jump on*. ("Analysis of the Dole Campaign," *CBS Evening News,* October 14, 1996)

Presumably because of such reportorial tendencies, candidates now build their campaign messages out of highly extractable sound bites, snippets that retain their dramatic punch even when shorn of their original context. What is an extractable sound bite? One with considerable linguistic Activity. For example, although George Bush was quoted only twice in one news clip (one that declared his 1992 campaign deeply troubled), it is significant that both extracts were chosen for their sense of dynamism: "2.7 percent is darn good growth and it *pulls the rug right out from under* Mr. Clinton, who is telling everybody how horrible everything is. And the economy of the United States led Europe, led Canada, led Japan, and *we grew* at 2.7 percent." After again declaring Mr. Bush's electoral chances grim, ABC's newscasters allowed the president one more chance on stage, and again he found the requisite verbal energy: "And we're *closing the gap*. And in seven days, we are *pulling ahead at the finish line* to win this election" ("President Bush on the 1992 Presidential Campaign," *ABC Evening News,* October 27, 1992; emphasis added).

Not all news is fashioned out of the same cloth, however. Print and broadcast news deals with distinctly different rhetorical challenges. The former must use language aggressively because it is picture starved, and the latter must use language economically because it has so little time to tell its story. Perhaps because of these latter pressures, television news has come under special scrutiny. Bartels (1997) reports, for example, that consumption of network news is systematically related to decreased regard for political candidates. In addition, he reports that watching television news tends to decrease viewers' abilities to correctly identify candidates' issue positions, especially during the last, crucial days of the fall campaign. Compounding these findings are those of Iyengar and Kinder (1987, 126), who report that "Americans believe by a wide margin that television—not magazines, radio, or newspapers—provides the most intelligent, complete, and impartial news coverage," thereby giving it special political authority.

The central feature of broadcast news is, of course, its pictures, which give the medium special command over viewers' perceptions. Pictures also give broadcast news its pace and variety, its psychological force, and its humanity. As a result, television news uses less Activity than does print news, as can be seen in figure 6.4.[7] Why? Ostensibly because pictures provide the action for viewers, thereby releasing the network reporter to attend to other matters. To *say* that the president boarded Air Force One is to waste time when the boarding can be easily shown. For print reporters, however, the absence of pictures taxes their prose significantly, requiring them to create a more complete verbal narrative. What can be shown (or implied) in a twenty-second video montage on television takes considerable effort in the newspaper:

> President Nixon will make his next campaign trip Monday when he will meet supporters from 11 Eastern states at the home of New York Gov. Nelson A. Rockefeller and take part in a motorcade and rally.

Figure 6.4   Activity and Realism scores by news type

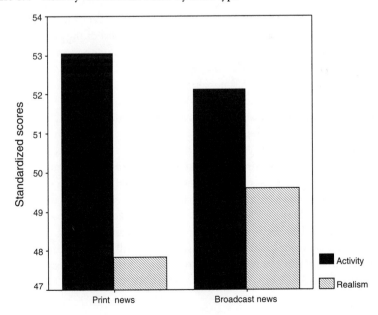

> The White House announced that the President will motorcade through ten com-
> munities in Westchester County, and then go to a reception at Rockefeller's home near
> Tarrytown.
>
> After the reception, to which campaign leaders from 11 states are invited, the Presi-
> dent will address an evening rally at the Nassau County Coliseum in Uniondale, L.I.
>
> With the election now less than three weeks away, Democratic efforts to force the
> President on to a stump campaign and to engage him in debate show no signs of suc-
> cess.
>
> No other campaign trips have been announced. The President is scheduled to go
> to Philadelphia Friday to sign the revenue-sharing bill in Independence Hall, but the
> White House describes that trip as "non-political." ("Nixon to Meet Rocky, Others
> in N.Y. Swing," *Washington Post,* October 18, 1972)

This sort of thematizing is rarely seen on television (except, perhaps, in its news
magazines or documentaries). In part that is because television uses a gaggle of voices
to tell its story while print coverage has a unitary authorial sense. The result, says
Iyengar (1991), is that television news becomes episodic, focusing on specific persons and events, not sociopolitical abstractions. Barnhurst and Steele (1997) report
that the episodic pace has picked up recently, with television now using more pictures with shorter exposure times than in the past. These decisions produce linguistic consequences: Television news is dramatically higher on Realism (see figure 6.4),
or, to frame it in the reverse, it is far less interpretive than print.[8] That is, television
eschews grand theory and works instead to maintain "flow"—the news anchor
introduces the acts and then steps aside. Perhaps because television news is so
underinterpreted, Chaffee and Frank (1996) find that those who watch it tend to
learn about the candidates *as people,* while newspaper readers gain more general
political knowledge. Similarly, television news is less critical of the political system
than are newspapers, perhaps because "the political system" (and most other abstractions) are so hard to depict for viewers (see Godek 1997).

The mass media commit no crime when using drama to make politics interesting. Some would argue that they actually do the nation a service when transferring
the energy of the campaign trail to viewers at home. A utilitarian might even claim
that any rhetoric that succeeds in increasing voter turnout is helpful in the long run.
As Hart, Smith-Howell, and Llewellyn (1996) argue, the news media may perform
a useful function when using dramaturgy to make governance interesting to the citizenry. At the same time, however, it must be remembered that drama requires spectators, while a democracy requires participants. Indeed, some researchers (Milburn
and McGrail 1992; Seago 1994) have found that dramatic news presentations can
actually *decrease* viewers' recall of political information and negatively impact their
overall political sophistication as well. In short, it is still too early to know which
kind of news is a blessing and which a curse, although it is not too early to worry
about such matters.

THE EXPLORATORY FUNCTION

Some years ago, Richard Weaver (1965, 182) discussed what he called the "spacious-ness" of political oratory in the nineteenth century, a time when issues of authority seemed settled and that allowed the orator to speak with a "declamatory quality" and assume that "he was speaking for corporate humanity." "Oratory of the broadly ruminative kind," said Weaver, "is acceptable only when we accredit someone with the ability to review our conduct, our destiny, and the causes of things in general." "If we reach a condition in which no man is believed to have this power," Weaver concluded, "we will accordingly be impatient with that kind of discourse" (183).

Weaver's predictions about impatience have come true, and the rhetorical quali-ties he identified have not waned. Politicians continue to look for "room" sufficient for their purposes. This is shown most dramatically by the sharp difference in Insis-tence scores between politicians and the press (see figure 6.5), a tendency that has not abated over the years.[9] The Insistence variable measures a speaker's tendency to become repetitive, to emphasize the same agenda time and time again.[10] Not sur-prisingly, politicians' low Insistence scores are their signal feature. That quality pro-duces the "openness" many find so frustrating in politics—the sudden renegotiations of just-completed compacts, the unsteady search for something agreeable to say, the impertinent amalgamations and transmogrifications. Low Insistence scores mean that politicians negotiate the intellectual terrain moment by moment.

Figure 6.5   Insistence scores by message type

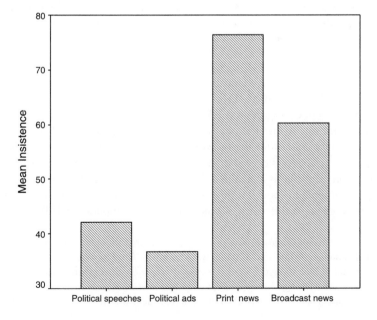

In contrast, and the contrast is stark, the press hammers home the same point again and again. News consumers become so accustomed to the unrelenting quality of the news that they fail to notice how such an effect is achieved. When cued for the language of Insistence, however, it becomes easier to see how rigorously the news sticks to its agenda (emphasis added):

> The *Commission* on Presidential *Debates* ruled Tuesday Reform Party nominee Ross *Perot* will not be allowed to participate in the *debates* with President Clinton and Republican presidential nominee Bob *Dole,* Cable News Network reported. The announcement is welcome news to the *Dole* campaign, which has said it did not want *Perot* included. "The unanimous decision today . . . to move forward on *debates* without the presence of third-party candidates was the right one," said former South Carolina Gov. Carroll Campbell, who has been representing the *Dole* campaign in ongoing *debate* negotiations with the *commission.* "The inclusion of any other participant in the *debates* sponsored by the *commission* would have violated the *commission's* own standard to include only third-party candidates who have proved they have a 'reasonable' chance to be elected president. None of the third-party candidates could make this claim," Campbell said. *Perot,* who won 19 percent of the vote during his first bid for the presidency in 1992, has so far failed to post poll numbers above single digits. *Dole,* who trails Clinton in the polls, hopes to make a strong showing in the *debates;* the first is scheduled for Sept. 25 in St. Louis. The *Dole* campaign opposed including *Perot* in the *debates* because it believed he would distract viewer attention away from the Kansas Republican. The *commission,* which has scheduled a press conference in Washington Tuesday to announce its ruling on *Perot,* still must decide how many *debates* to have, and when and where they will take place. The *Dole* campaign has said it would like six *debates*—four presidential and two vice presidential. The Reform Party has also scheduled a press conference in Washington Tuesday to respond to the *commission's* ruling. ("Perot Will Not Be Allowed in Debates," *Washington Post,* September 17, 1996)

Two things are noteworthy about the foregoing. One is that the story never departs from its quartet of issues—Perot, Dole, the debates, and the Commission— and the second is how long the text takes to get its work done. The text luxuriates in its topic, returning the reader time and again to its several concerns. In doing so, the story becomes tedious for the impatient reader. That, of course, is why politicians typically eschew Insistence and, instead, hit and run. A political advertisement by the Clinton campaign is illustrative. As can be seen in the following passage, the ad jumps from topic to topic but does so efficiently, with each phrase of each sentence acknowledging a different political constituency (emphasis added):

> Imagine if Dole and Gingrich were in charge. A hundred-thousand *more police.* The President's doing it; Dole and Gingrich would undo it. *Family and medical leave.* The President did it; Dole/Gingrich against. *College scholarships.* Strengthen education. The President did it; Dole wants to *eliminate the Department of Education* and undo it. *Banning cigarette ads* that target children. The President did it. Dole would undo it.

Dole/Gingrich. Wrong for our country. President Clinton. *Protecting our values.* ("Vote Clinton," Nationally televised commercial for the Clinton campaign, November 1, 1996)

Another manifestation of the exploratory function of the news can be found in its *interpretive* stance. As can be seen in figure 6.6, politicians refer to tangible realities far more often than the press; this is a marker of kind, not degree.[11] At first blush this may seem odd since one tends to think of the newspaper as a depository of facts and figures, a catalog of the day's events; and the parallel expectation is also attractive—that politicians bloviate. However, the trend lines here are obdurate: None of the twenty-one politicians studied came remotely close to the press on Realism.

Does this mean that the news media do not deal with the facts? No, it just means that people do not read an entire newspaper or watch a thirty-minute broadcast to find out what happened. They can do that in far less time. Instead, they want to know *what it means* that something happened. The *New York Times* does not offer all the facts that are fit to print; it offers all the *news* that is fit to print. It offers interpretations: the history and location of the World Trade Center, the philosophy of the Islamic fundamentalists, the logic behind the building's security system, the feelings of the bombing victims, and the relevant laws that apply to a capital crime. By definition, the news deals with the unexpected, the serendipitous. It takes but a minute to learn that something new has happened, but it takes much longer to

Figure 6.6   Realism scores by message source over time

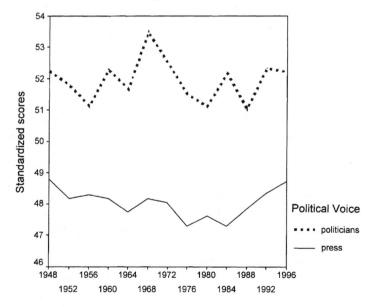

understand an event in its totality. The bombing of the World Trade Center is still discussed many years later because its meanings have not yet been exhausted.

It is this interpretive bias that sets journalists apart. It particularly sets them apart from politicians, who have a policy bias. The politician really only asks one question—What should we *do?*—while the journalist asks many questions. However, the press operates as it does for a reason: because the world refuses to interpret itself. Consider, for example, a thoroughly ordinary news story about a political debate. We have here a classic invitation for reportage: Three important people talked to one another for an hour and a half and then stopped talking. End of event. Then the journalism began, and it began with a headline: "Most Viewers Think Clinton Won Debate, Polls Say." Notice in the following story the paucity of facts. Notice that the victory was not Clinton's until someone *declared* it so:

> Polls taken after the third presidential debate suggest Ross Perot won some hearts and minds, and maybe a few votes, although more viewers thought Bill Clinton won the debate.
>
> In four sets of ratings put out by the networks Oct. 19, Governor Clinton came out on top in two polls, Mr. Perot in one, and they tied in the fourth. President Bush got the best rating from 1 in 4 voters in each poll.
>
> In an NBC News poll, 31 percent said the debate made them think more favorably of Mr. Bush, compared with 36 percent less favorably. Clinton's numbers were better: 36 percent more favorable, 29 percent less favorable. For Perot, 60 percent said they think more favorably of him, 12 percent less favorably.
>
> In a CNN–USA Today poll, 12 percent said the debate made them switch their preference, and for more than half the switch was to Perot. Re-interviewing voters who had been polled before the debate, Gallup found significant increases in their view of Perot as the best candidate to handle the economy and budget deficit. An ABC News poll measured preferences before and after the debate. Bush's support was unchanged at 29 percent; Clinton's dropped from 52 percent to 48 percent; and Perot's rose from 11 percent to 19 percent.
>
> ABC asked "who won?" and 36 percent said Clinton, 26 percent Perot, 21 percent Bush. Twelve percent called it a tie. "Who did the best job?" was the question posed by CBS, CNN–USA Today, and NBC. CBS got a Clinton-Perot tie at 30 percent, with 23 percent for Bush. CNN–USA Today came in with 37 percent for Perot, and 28 percent each for Bush and Clinton. Clinton had 35 percent, Perot got 30 percent, and Bush 23 percent in the NBC poll. ("Most Viewers Think Clinton Won Debate, Polls Say," *Christian Science Monitor,* October 21, 1992)

This article is at war with itself: Some say Clinton won, some Perot; going from 11 percent to 19 percent is not bad, but it is also not wonderful; Bush looks better in some polls but looks like a loser in others. That so many different surveys have been quoted here is itself an admission of defeat since, if one brawny fact had been found, the story could have been far shorter. However, in politics there are few brawny facts until election day, and so, despite the brave headline, the *Christian Science Monitor* is really only guessing here. The article bristles with numbers, but the numbers lead everywhere. At one point the reader is told that Clinton won the debate and at another that his percentage dropped—what is one to make of that? No bench scientist would know what to do with phrases such as "think more favorably" or "best candidate to handle the economy" or "won some hearts and minds." This is pure effluvia, but it is also what life provides.

Not everyone is happy with such reportorial tendencies. Research shows that "almost half of all reporting was punditry and analysis" and that "80% of the public felt that there was too much commentary in the coverage" (Committee of Concerned Journalists 1998). Numerous studies confirm those suspicions. Using very different methods than those used here, Steele and Barnhurst (1996) found a steady increase in opinionizing in broadcast news between 1968 and 1988, and that proved to be true for the print media as well (Barnhurst and Mutz 1997). (My findings show this to be roughly true as well.[12]) Other studies (Bartels 1997; Buchanan 1996) reveal that, in their rush toward commentary, the media fail to cover candidates' issue positions adequately. Also, the press is sometimes too creative in their interpretations. Mendelsohn (1998) reports, for example, that when a conservative wins an election, it is likely to be described as an "ideological mandate," while a victory by a political newcomer will be treated as a "personal mandate," not a philosophical one.

The media's interpretations are often misguided, but one must also consider life without the press: Facts without meanings, speculations without data. Journalists take the time to pause, to sift through the details of our lives, to make sense of them. The sense they make is sometimes wrong, as is true of all interpretive work, but that hardly means the quest should be abandoned. Sometimes the press becomes too caught up in its narratives, but such narratives are absolutely required if a large and diverse polity is to be reached. This makes journalism imperfect, but it is probably a necessary imperfection.

THE OBJECTIVITY FUNCTION

No discussion of the media's voice would be complete without asking whether that voice is honest. The question of media bias has been persistent, and it is still a major area of research. For many, however, there is no need for further study. Beginning some thirty years ago with Efron (1971), conservatives especially have decried the media's politics. Operating on the (correct) assumption that most journalists are registered Democrats, they conclude the inevitable—that the press's sole purpose is to undermine the Right. Such critics note that Richard Nixon's descent began at the hands of two journalists and that Gerald Ford's intelligence and George Bush's manliness were constantly the butt of media jokes. Lyndon Johnson, Jimmy Carter, and, recently, Bill Clinton might well disagree with this analysis, and even Ronald Reagan might attribute some of his Teflon qualities to his media-centric personality. However, anecdotes alone will never resolve this particular debate, for it is a war in which all parties have sufficient ammunition.

Scholars have broadened the discussion in recent years. Schiller (1989), most famously, has argued the opposite case: that the press has been captured by a set of interlocking directorates. Schiller cites case after case of where the press has held its fire when facing the avatars of capital. As Cook (1998) documents, the fact that newspapers and television networks are increasingly being folded into information conglomerates makes Schiller's concerns especially worrisome. Such scholars note that the genuinely radical voices of the Left are never really treated seriously in the mainstream press and that third-party and independent candidates never really have a national platform from which to air their views since money is often needed to buy an audience.

More controlled research is also equivocal. A study by Lowry and Shidler (1995) is typical: They find that Democratic and Republican candidates received the same number of sound bites during the 1992 presidential campaign but that the Republican sound bites were somewhat more negative—score one for both sides of the argument. Woodward (1994), on the other hand, found that over a twenty-year period, Democrats tended to get more press coverage during primaries but that Republicans got more during the general election—another draw. Many of these studies have focused on questions of proportionality, on which party has received the most media attention. However, for most people the real argument lies elsewhere, in the innuendos and snide interpretations reporters use to sway people's perceptions. These subtle kinds of bias are alleged to be more damaging because they are omnipresent, hard to discern, and pernicious.

DICTION is too crude an instrument to detect perniciousness, but some of my findings are relevant to the question of media bias. In exploring that question, the textual qualities most commonly thought to characterize the news—quantitative documentation, frequent topical references, use of a third-person voice, and an avoidance of overstatement—were fashioned into a Detachment Index and then a number of subanalyses made.[13] Detachment is not quite "objectivity," but it is as close as an instrument such as DICTION can get to that quality. By way of illustration, the text scoring lowest on Detachment in the database was a quotation from Daniel Webster, lovingly resurrected by a citizen of Wichita Falls, Texas, in a letter to the editor written during the 1964 presidential campaign:

> I am an American—These duties I share with my fellow citizens: It is my duty to obey my country's laws. It is my duty to vote, so my government may truly represent the will of the people. It is my duty to keep informed as to the honesty and ability of candidates for public office. It is my duty to pay such taxes as have been devised by representatives elected by me, to defray the cost of government.
>
> It is my duty to serve on juries when called on. It may sometimes become my duty to hold a public office for which I am suited, so my government may function efficiently. It is my duty to defend my country, if need should arise. It is my duty to abide

by the will of the majority, to stand behind my government, so my nation may be unified in time of crisis.

I am an American—I take pride in my country's Declaration of Independence. I am a believer in the American Creed. ("'Rights' vs. 'Duty,'" *Wichita Falls Record-News,* August 5, 1964)

In stark contrast is the text with the highest Detachment score, supplied, not surprisingly, by the Associated Press:

Here's a state-by-state (plus the District of Columbia) assessment of where the presidential race stood before Sunday's debate. The number of electoral votes in each state is in parentheses:

ALABAMA (9): Polls make it close, elevating Ross Perot's importance.

ALASKA (3): Surprising tossup in usual Republican stronghold.

ARIZONA (8): Surprising lead for Bill Clinton in state Democrats haven't won since 1948.

ARKANSAS (6): Clinton leads comfortably at home.

CALIFORNIA (54): Big Clinton edge in the biggest state.

COLORADO (8): Clinton ahead.

CONNECTICUT (8): Clinton leads in the polls.

DELAWARE (3): Surprising edge for Clinton.

DISTRICT OF COLUMBIA (3): Clinton way ahead [and so forth through the alphabet].

("The Polls," AP-UPI Wire, October 12, 1992)

Generally speaking, the most important results from the Detachment analysis are what was not found:

1. As can be seen in figure 6.7, there were no great differences in how the two parties were treated by the press in the thirteen presidential elections; if anything, Republicans were treated slightly better.
2. Third-party stories scored well above the mean for Detachment in 1980, 1992, and 1996, suggesting a respectful approach toward them on the part of the press.[14]
3. There were no pronounced differences in Detachment among the six newspapers in the sample—they tended to follow the same journalistic formula.
4. No important differences could be detected among the five broadcast sources either.
5. Detachment did not vary in meaningful ways across the campaign cycle (from the convention through election day).

While these data hardly settle the question of media bias, they are interesting nonetheless. The sanguine interpretation is that, over the long course, the press gives the candidates an even break. Less optimistically, one could conclude that bias cannot be isolated in word choice alone and that more sophisticated instruments are needed to detect it.

Figure 6.7   Detachment scores over time for story focus

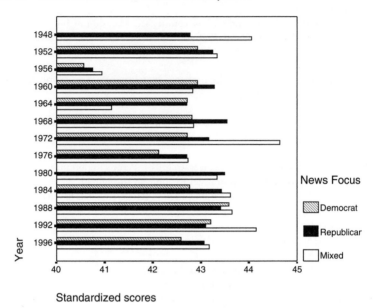

Standardized scores

More specific analyses showed that Detachment has actually gone up over the years for print coverage, suggesting that news norms are now being followed somewhat scrupulously by members of the press. These increases in Detachment held for *each* of the print sources studied here. In addition, when presidential elections became especially close, the media increased their Detachment, again suggesting deliberateness on the parts of journalists. Also, when prosperity indicators sagged in the United States (unemployment, economic worry, and a sense of uncertainty toward government), journalistic coverage became more detached, ostensibly an attempt to get judicious interpretations on the table when the nation most needed them. Finally, and at the risk of undermining the liberal-bias explanation, when stories focusing on Democratic front-runners were compared to ones featuring Republican front-runners, the "cheerleading theory" of press coverage failed. Republicans were treated with greater Detachment than were Democrats.[15]

Reporting, in short, seems a worthy enterprise, or at least much of it does. Even with the admittedly limited measure of Detachment employed here, none of the traditional sources of bias could be detected; and with the large number of texts examined in this study, those differences were given ample opportunity to present themselves. They failed to do so, and they failed do so consistently. These findings do not suggest that political news is perfect, but they are encouraging. The cloud darkens somewhat when the issue of modality is considered. Print news was *far* more detached than broadcast news and that is a fact of some consequence.[16] Optimistically, it may mean that television reporters need not be as careful with their language because they have highly concrete visual images to sustain their claims. More pessimistically, it may mean that broadcasters are more inclined than print reporters to appeal to the crowd, to play fast and loose with the facts, and to take unwarranted license with video materials. At the very least, these hypotheses deserve further testing.

CONCLUSION

There are data in this chapter to support anyone's theory of political news. Those who dislike the press will seize on the busy narratives described here and declare it facile. Those who hate journalists' negativity will argue for a more buoyant alternative. Those who object to the press's interpretations will call for a blander medium. In response, the press would argue that while a great many facts are always available, that is usually the problem—it takes *people* to sort through them and to draw prudent conclusions. Reporters feel that they are trained to do that, and, while they sometimes get things wrong, their track record is probably no worse than that of any other interpretive craft—stock brokerage, for example, or venture capitalism. Journalists call them as they see them, but because they make their calls in public, their mistakes are remembered more often than their rectitude. When one takes the grand view, however, the rectitude seems obvious.

However, these data pose questions, too: If the news were less dramatic, would voters still pay attention to it? If the news were more saccharine, would voters be forewarned when they needed to be forearmed? If the news were less interpretive, could voters make sense out of the things that happen each day, each month, or each year? The answer to all three questions is no. Reporters are needed because voters do not have the time to govern themselves and because they dare not trust their representatives to govern in private. If the world were not complex and if power were not corrupting, journalism could be declared a luxury. Until those conditions obtain, voters must adjust to its fallibility.

Besides, the media are not as bad as some claim. I could detect no overarching favoritism here. Instead, the press adhered to news norms with considerable dedication. Admittedly, one rough examination such as this one cannot exonerate the press completely, but a great many texts were studied and a great many language patterns searched. If systematic bias existed, it would have shown itself somewhere, but it did not. Still, the news is a complicated text. It provides facts but also offers interpretations, and that conjunction (or disjunction) upsets many. The news explains what is wrong with the world, and that upsets still more, especially when the press delights in doing so. The news, especially televised news, puts us in personal touch with our leaders, and that seems like a good thing except when it seems like a bad thing. Because the news is so complex and because it is so vital to democratic life, it will probably always make voters quarrelsome. Democracies have long been animated by such quarrels.

NOTES

1. Portions of this paper draw on work published in Hart (2000).

2. The DICTION program can be accessed at <http://www.scolari.com>.

3. Optimism: Means = 50.613 (politicians), 48.970 (press); $F(1, 11436) = 933.696$, $p < .000$.

4. Commonality: Means = 49.994 (1948–1960), 49.658 (1964–1976), 49.258 (1980–1996); $F(2, 8525) = 68.201$, $p < .000$.

5. For the press, the drop-off is small but intriguing: Commonality: Means = 49.892 (to September 15), 49.793 (September 16–30), 49.581 (October 1–15), 49.330 (October 16–end); $F(3, 8448) = 22.534$, $p < .121$. The picture was different for the politicians in my sample: Commonality: Means = 49.775 (to September 15), 49.804 (September 16–30), 49.607 (October 1–15), 49.567 (October 16–end); $F(2, 227) = 1.939$, $p < .121$.

6. Activity: Means = 50.179 (politicians), 52.933 (press); $F(1, 11436) = 1380.341$, $p < .000$.

7. Activity: Means = 53.066 (print), 52.133 (broadcast); $F(1, 8526) = 100.905$, $p < .000$.

8. Realism: Means = 47.831 (print), 49.588 (broadcast); $F(1, 8526) = 537.034$, $p < .000$.

9. Insistence: Means = 41.090 (politicians), 74.145 (press); $F(1, 11436) = 953.812$, $p < .000$.

10. Insistence is a measure of code restriction and semantic "contentedness." The assumption is that repetition of key terms indicates a preference for a limited, ordered world. In calculating the measure, all words occurring three or more times that function as nouns or noun-derived adjectives are identified (either cybernetically or with the user's assistance), and the following calculation is performed: (Number of Eligible Words × Sum of Their Occurrences) ÷ 10. For small input files, high frequency terms used *two* or more times are used in the calculation.

11. Realism: Means = 51.999 (politicians), 48.082 (press); $F(1, 11436) = 4717.273$, $p < .000$.

12. Realism: Means = 48.3610 (1948–1960), 47.8077 (1964–1976), 48.076 (1980–1996); $F(2, 7306) = 97.60$, $p < .000$.

13. After all language scores were standardized, the Detachment Index was assembled in the following manner: (Activity + Numeric Terms + Leader References + Party References) – (Leveling Terms + Tenacity + Self-References) + 40.

14. Detachment (by party focus): Means = 42.568 (Democrat), 42.893 (Republican); $F(1, 5149) = 23.373$, $p < .000$. Detachment (for third parties): Means = 42.530 (all coverage; $n = 6,824$), 43.287 (third-party coverage, 1980), 43.832 (third-party coverage, 1992), 43.787 (third-party coverage, 1996).

15. Detachment (print coverage only): Means = 42.375 (1948–1960), 42.800 (1964–1976), 43.311 (1980–1996); $F(2, 7306) = 95.139$, $p < .000$. Detachment (for polling spread): Means = 42.896 (0–9 points), 42.214 (10–19 points), 42.526 (20–36 points); $F(2, 8406) = 56.562$, $p < .000$. Detachment (for "sense of care"): Means = 43.180 (–50%–0%), 43.038 (1%–20%), 42.365 (21% and up); $F(2, 6760) = 76.833$, $p < .000$. Detachment (for unemployment): Means = 42.355 (4.5% and down), 43.074 (4.6%–7.0%), 43.110 (7.1% and up); $F(2, 8525) = 70.687$, $p < .000$. Detachment (for "economic fear"): Means = 42.531 (0%–24%), 43.263 (25%–45%), 43.010 (46% and up); $F(2, 7306) = 60.947$, $p < .000$. Detachment (for front-runner stories): Means = 42.173 (Democrat), 42.635 (Republican);

F (1, 6941) = 48.908, p < .000. The sense-of-care and economic fear measures were dummy variables extrapolated from Stanley and Niemi (1998, 133).

16. Detachment (by medium): Means = 42.867 (print), 40.508 (broadcast); F (1, 8526) = 952.527, p < .000.

7

Media Effects: Paradigms for the Analysis of Local Television News

Shanto Iyengar

In the modern era, it is common knowledge that people learn about the larger world beyond their immediate experience primarily through television news presentations. Scholars from every discipline have weighed in at length on the meaning and significance of the shift from print media to television as the news medium of choice.

Although television is still the dominant source, in recent years the public's consumption of news programming has shifted noticeably. While formerly audiences tuned in to the networks' national newscasts with regularity, today more people rely on local news programs than on network news. Opinion surveys recorded this shift as early as 1993, when the Roper Organization's annual survey of television viewing noted that a plurality of Americans cited local news on television as their major source of information.

More compelling evidence than media-use surveys is the relative share of the viewing audience commanded by network and local news programs. Based on Nielsen audience ratings from the country's two largest media markets (Los Angeles and New York), it is clear that the number of Americans who tune in to local news programs on a daily basis far exceeds those who watch national newscasts. Averaging across both markets, the cumulative audience for evening local news easily surpasses the cumulative audience for national news (see Gilliam and Iyengar forthcoming).

The huge audiences for local news reflect fundamental changes in television programming. In most areas today, local news programs air during the morning, afternoon, evening, prime time, and late night. Between 1991 and 1996, the amount (expressed in hours) of weekly local news programming available in Los Angeles increased from 80 to 97. For New York, the weekly total rose from 85 to 91. During the same period, the total amount of network news programming remained stagnant at less than twelve hours per week. In terms of the volume and availability of news programming, local news dominates the broadcast day.

When the local news turns to serious subjects, the focus is invariably on crime or other threats to public safety. This comparative advantage in programming actually means that local news fares well when it competes head-to-head with national news. One study examined twenty-two media markets; for eighteen of them, the local programs attracted more viewers by an average margin of four gross ratings points (see Hess 1991).[1] Of course, when the comparison is made between the total number of viewers who watch local news on any given day and the number who tune in to network news, the results are even more one-sided. The daily audience for local news in Los Angeles and New York exceeds the audience for network news by a margin of three to one. Even when we ignore the huge differences between national and local news in the length and availability of programming and focus on the average audience for a thirty-minute local newscast, local news enjoys the statistical edge. That is, on any given day, the average number of people watching a thirty-minute local newscast is greater than the average audience for the three national newscasts. In short, no matter how one measures broadcast audiences, local news is the undisputed leader (for a more detailed analysis of these data, see Gilliam and Iyengar forthcoming).

The dominance of local news has important consequences for the viewing audience and American society at large. Local news is defined by a distinctive perspective on public issues and events, that is, by its emphasis on (and frequent exaggeration of) drama, conflict, and violence. Every effort is made to appeal to the public's appetite for "blood and guts." All local broadcasters are well aware that if local news is to be economically successful, it must emphasize violent crime. Simultaneously, the demand for personalized news means, more often than not, that a suspected perpetrator occupies center stage in news stories about crime. This script means that viewers' attention is directed at salient and visible attributes of criminal suspects, such as their race and ethnicity. In the course of watching the news, the audience inevitably notices that criminal suspects are nonwhite males.

The prominence of violent crime in local news and the tendency of crime reports to feature nonwhite perpetrators cry out for research into two broad classes of media effects. The first—media agenda setting—refers to shifts in the public's political priorities induced by the amount of news coverage accorded particular issues. In the case of local news, the obvious prediction is that the unrelenting attention to violent crime has boosted the centrality of crime in viewers' political consciousness. In addition to changes in the salience of crime, the agenda-setting paradigm predicts further that viewers across the nation have become more dependent on their crime-related beliefs and opinions when formulating more general political attitudes.[2]

Local news coverage of crime may also be examined as a particular case of framing—"subtle alterations in the definition or presentation of judgment or choice problems and the changes in decision outcomes resulting from these alterations" (Iyengar 1991, 11). It is well known that broadcast news outlets rely on an "episodic" frame for public affairs in which political issues are depicted in terms of concrete instances.

Thus, in the case of crime, the focus of the typical local news report is directed at a particular act of violence by a specific (usually nonwhite) perpetrator. Prior research suggests that episodic framing of issues of public order (crime and terrorism in particular) encourages viewers to advocate a more punitive approach to criminal justice (see Iyengar 1991). The evidence also indicates that episodic framing of crime, when accompanied by racial imagery, evokes racial stereotypes and race-based reasoning about policy issues (Iyengar 1991; Mendelberg 1997). Based on this evidence, it can be anticipated that exposure to local news will strengthen public support for punitive approaches to crime and encourage the expression of racist attitudes.

In summary, local news has emerged as the ordinary citizen's major source of information. The content of local news programming is marked by two themes: Crime is violent, and those who engage in crime tend to be nonwhite males. As described in the following, these themes are likely to make their presence felt in the minds of viewers.

AGENDA SETTING AND PRIMING EFFECTS

More than any other issue, Americans consider crime to be the "most important problem facing this country today." The Gallup Poll has asked this question twelve times since January 1994; in eleven of the surveys, crime has dominated all other problems. What role has the media played in fanning public fear of crime? The fact that the rate of crime—and violent crime in particular—has dropped dramatically over the past decade would seem to suggest that the public's beliefs about crime are based not on some personal experience as a crime victim but rather on what they see in the news media, namely, that violent crime is a frequent daily occurrence. In the Los Angeles area, a report on violent crime airs every three minutes during local newscasts. Murder accounts for less than 1 percent of all crime in Los Angeles but makes up 20 percent of all local news reports on crime (see Gilliam and Iyengar forthcoming). In the sheer frequency of crime news, Los Angeles is no outlier; violent crime accounted for two-thirds of all local news in a recent study of news programming in fifty-six U.S. cities (Klite, Bardwell, and Salzman 1997).

In keeping with the notion of media agenda setting, the research evidence suggests that exposure to news coverage of crime contributes to the perception that crime is a serious problem. Iyengar and Kinder included illegal drugs as a "target" in one of their experiments on network news coverage. Examining various indicators, they found that viewers exposed to news coverage accorded significantly greater importance to drug abuse (Iyengar and Kinder 1987, chap. 3). In a series of similar experiments, this time manipulating the amount of local news coverage, Gilliam and Iyengar found that exposure to a single crime-related story heightened viewers' fear of being victimized (Gilliam and Iyengar forthcoming). Comparable results have been obtained in studies of newspaper coverage. For example, Erbring, Goldenberg, and

Miller (1980) found that crime was the only issue for which the amount of news nationwide correlated with the level of audience concern. This body of experimental and correlational evidence thus helps explain the paradox of continued high levels of public concern for crime in the face of declining rates of criminal activity. Crime may be declining overall; information about specific acts of crime is all too visible.

In addition to estimating the net impact of news coverage on issue salience, agenda-setting researchers have attempted to identify the factors that moderate the effects of the news. Do people differ in their susceptibility to coverage of particular issues? Iyengar and Kinder (1987) hypothesized that agenda setting would be enhanced when the target issue was personally consequential for the audience. They yoked their manipulation of news coverage to specific personal characteristics of their participants so that the issue under investigation would be especially compelling to one group of viewers. For example, news reports about the financial difficulties facing the social security system were shown to elderly and young participants. In general, their results revealed a significant interaction between personal relevance and news coverage—the impact of the news was greatest for viewers personally affected by the issue. The identical pattern was uncovered in the Erbring et al. study of newspapers. Readers most likely to be "at risk"—women and the elderly—were especially receptive to news stories dealing with crime.

The evidence on the individual-level moderators of agenda setting suggests that the impact of local news will be conditioned by viewers' personal experience with crime. In addition to factors known to be correlated with exposure to crime (e.g., gender, race, and age), we might expect the news to exert greater influence among viewers who live in relatively high-crime areas. In addition to such experiential factors, several other potential moderators are worth considering. These include patterns of media use (people who rely exclusively on local news versus those who watch a variety of news shows), evaluations of the credibility of local news, level of political involvement and expertise, and so on.

In summary, spiraling coverage of crime by local news has contributed significantly to the current furor over crime. Most Americans do not experience crime directly. They do, however, receive huge doses of crime news. With increasing numbers of Americans tuning in to local news, crime occupies a privileged position on the public agenda.

The fact that crime is a salient issue has important ramifications for public opinion. The so-called priming effect refers to changes in the weight that individuals assign to their specific opinions on issues when they make political evaluations and choices as a result of the amount of news coverage accorded issues. The basic finding—which has been replicated extensively—is that the more prominent an issue in the news stream, the greater the impact of that issue on political attitudes (for reviews, see Iyengar and Kinder 1987, chap. 7; Krosnick and Brannon 1995; Miller and Krosnick 1997).

In the context of election campaigns, the core implication of priming is that issues in the news become the principal talking points for voters. In 1980, for example, the media's sudden preoccupation with the Iranian hostages in the closing days of the campaign caused voters to consider the candidates' credentials on the issue of terrorism when choosing between Carter and Reagan. Naturally, this logic proved disadvantageous to President Carter. More recently, the fact that news of the economy drowned out news of the Gulf War at the time of the 1992 election cost President Bush dearly. Had the media played up military or security issues, of course, the tables would have been turned, given Bush's reputational advantage over Clinton on matters of national defense (see Iyengar and Simon 1993; Krosnick and Brannon 1993).

The perennial newsworthiness of crime has forced all candidates for elective office—no matter what their political leanings—to address the issue. Given the state of public opinion (with large majorities favoring a "tough" approach to crime), it is no coincidence that increasing numbers of public officials advocate the death penalty and stringent law enforcement. While the "law and order" posture was previously associated with Republican and conservative candidates, today the position is consensual; to be on the other side of this issue is generally considered politically fatal. Thus, the impact of the news media on the audience's political agenda has resulted in a substantial shift in the policy positions of political elites.

FRAMING EFFECTS

Not only is violent crime central to local newscasts, but the episodic, or personalized, style of reporting means that the news is typically about specific crimes and perpetrators. In local newscasts in Los Angeles, the ratio of episodic to thematic crime stories exceeds four to one (for details, see Gilliam and Iyengar forthcoming). Nearly 60 percent of the crime reports provide some information about a suspect.

Research into the framing effects of news coverage suggests that the episodic frame draws viewers' attention to the actions of particular individuals rather than societal conditions (see Iyengar 1996). Poverty is understood as a consequence of insufficient effort and motivation, and crime and terrorism are understood as a consequence of lawlessness and disregard for human life. Confronted with news coverage describing particular instances of complex issues, people reason accordingly: Poverty and crime are caused not by deep-seated economic conditions but by dysfunctional behavior. The appropriate remedy for crime is not improved job training programs and economic opportunity but, rather, harsh and unconditional punishment. By shaping viewers' attributions of causal and treatment responsibility for crime, the episodic frame indirectly influences crime-related attitudes. People who subscribe to individualistic accounts of crime, for example, are more likely to favor greater spending on law enforcement and to express greater support for the police (see Iyengar 1991, 1996). By influencing attributions of responsibility, episodic framing of crime also shapes attitudes toward the criminal justice process.

What is especially striking about the episodic news frame for crime is the frequency with which it conveys explicit racial cues. The focus on a particular perpetrator and the visual emphasis of television mean that, as depicted in the news, the principal antecedent of criminal behavior is race (see Entman 1992; Gilliam and Iyengar forthcoming).

By associating crime and race, local news necessarily interjects racial stereotypes into the public's understanding of crime. Viewers are compelled to evaluate their racial beliefs in light of what seem to be empirical realities. Iyengar's framing experiments suggested that news of crime in black neighborhoods made viewers more likely to offer either individualistic (e.g., character flaws) or punitive (e.g., insufficient retribution) attributions of responsibility for crime (Iyengar 1991). Because attributions of causal and treatment responsibility for crime and poverty proved to be significant attitude cues, the racial component of crime news also contributed to opinionation more generally.

The most unequivocal evidence concerning the racial element of the crime news script has been provided by Gilliam and Iyengar (see Gilliam and Iyengar 1997, 1998). Their experiments demonstrate that the presence of a black rather than white perpetrator in local news reports is meaningful to viewers. Specifically, the skin color of the alleged perpetrator matters to viewers' opinions concerning both race and crime. Using computer-based editing techniques, the researchers present the *same* individual as either a white or an African American male. The results show that when the suspect in the news was African American, significantly more viewers endorsed punitive criminal justice policies (the death penalty, "three strikes," or increased funding for prisons). In addition, the racial manipulation strengthened viewers' racial stereotypes (ratings of blacks as lazy and unintelligent) and lowered evaluations of black leaders such as Jesse Jackson (Gilliam and Iyengar 1998). However, Gilliam and Iyengar found that the racial element of crime news was overshadowed by any exposure to crime news as an antecedent of racial attitudes. That is, viewers' tendency to stereotype African Americans and their negative evaluations of black leaders became more pronounced in response to the crime/no crime than to the white perpetrator/black perpetrator manipulation (see Gilliam and Iyengar 1998). This result suggests that viewers have internalized the racial element of crime news, so much so that any reference to crime is sufficient to trigger negative racial attitudes.

Not only does exposure to crime news influence viewers' attitudes, but we can expect that it will also serve to increase the relevance of racial stereotypes as a basis for judging the performance of elected officials or for choosing between candidates for elective office. In effect, local news programming "racializes" public discourse by making policy choices increasingly intertwined with questions of race. A recent study by Mendelberg (1997) is revealing. Mendelberg found significant priming effects of exposure to the 1988 "Willie Horton" advertisement used by the Bush campaign. Among participants exposed to the Horton ad, racial prejudice was a stronger predictor of support for particular social welfare and civil rights policies than among control participants who did not view the ad (Mendelberg 1997). Race-based news coverage of crime primed racial stereotypes. Of course (as the use of the Horton ad by the Bush campaign itself reveals), the audience's exquisite sensitivity to matters of race is grist for vote-seeking public officials. We can only anticipate that racial appeals —either explicit or coded—will become even more frequent during political campaigns. In short, the prominence of local news makes race an even more central component of American public life.

CONCLUSION

The political implications of agenda setting and framing effects with respect to crime are all too clear. Elected officials must, of course, take heed of their constituents' political concerns. In response to the media-induced public outcry over crime, elected officials—Republican and Democrat, liberal and conservative, running for executive and legislative office—have endorsed "law and order" as an immediate policy goal. Heightened attention to the issue of crime necessarily means reduced attention to other pressing problems. In California, for example, the annual budget for the Department of Corrections has increased at a significantly faster rate than the annual budget for the Department of Education.

The frequent association of crime with race in the news also means that exposure to the news will trigger racial identity and the resulting "in-group" bias (e.g., Tajfel and Turner 1986). It is well documented that people categorize themselves into groups instinctively and that group identity exerts powerful attitudinal consequences, including the expression of discriminatory affect for in-group and out-group members. The current journalistic paradigm thus does not bode well for the state of race relations; white viewers of the news will only become more likely to stigmatize black Americans, while black viewers will increasingly malign the motives of a "hostile" media.

The psychological implications of agenda setting and framing effects are no less significant. The fact that a mere three-second insertion of a photograph into a fifteen-minute news segment significantly alters viewers' racial attitudes and their views about the appropriate means of controlling crime suggests that there is much more to race relations and political attitudes than acculturation and one's formative experiences. No doubt racial prejudice is deeply rooted in American culture, and there is considerable evidence suggesting that racial and other group-related sentiments are acquired early in life. Moreover, core values such as individualism and the work ethic encourage citizens to hold individuals rather than societal factors responsible for issues such as poverty or crime. The research summarized here, however, suggests that despite the "drag" provided by such lifelong socialization processes, the daily flow of news can provide significant added value. People seem to resort to a more dynamic process of reasoning about racial groups in which the frequency of particular actions by individual group members is taken as revealing about the group as a whole. In this sense, people are Bayesian, "updating" their stereotypes to correspond to the latest round of "evidence." Thus, models of racial attitudes that grant dominant status to stable personal influences (most notably, party identification and political ideology) must be revised to allow for circumstantial influence.

NOTES

1. One gross rating point represents approximately 920,000 viewers.
2. This effect is commonly referred to as "priming."

Part 4

Media Representation of Social Movements

8

Movement Strategy and Dramaturgic Framing in Democratic States: The Case of the American Civil Rights Movement

Doug McAdam

In this chapter, I examine the "dramaturgic framing" of movement actions within democratic states. My argument is straightforward. First, the legitimating ideology of democratic governance creates "framing opportunities" unique to nominally democratic states. That is, the need for state actors to maintain what might be termed "democratic appearances" affords insurgents a powerful dramaturgic weapon in their struggle to advance group interests. By choosing action sites and forms of protest that invite nondemocratic responses by state actors, movements in democratic polities have the ability to transform the greater coercive power of the state from an asset into a liability. Resting as it does on the consent of the governed, legitimate state authority can be delegitimated should it appear that it is attempting to maintain consent through coercive means.

Second, this symbolic weapon is not as generally available to movements in nondemocratic polities. Since state authority in such systems does not depend as much on popular support, state officials are less obliged to preserve the appearance of democracy in their dealings with insurgents. Instead, they have more latitude to repress movements, thus denying to dissidents the same level of strategic framing opportunities available in nominally democratic contexts.[1]

Third, this difference may lead us to equate "extremism" with movements in nondemocratic polities. It may well be true that the suppression of peaceful dissent in such polities tends over time to encourage certain highly dramatic, consequential forms of extremism. What is much less certain is that democratic states invariably mute extremist tendencies. On the contrary, building on the perspective developed here, I would argue that the institutional logic of democratic polities encourages movements to engage in forms of "moderate extremism" designed to undermine the legitimacy of state opponents by inviting nondemocratic responses that grant to insurgents new moral and political capital with which to press their claims. The

117

presence of the kind of relatively independent mass media that one finds in democratic polities also inclines movements in this direction. This is so for at least two reasons. First, disruptive actions attract media attention. Second, it is the presence and relative freedom of the media that make it possible for the movement to achieve its broader strategic aims. That is, only by publicizing the nondemocratic responses of state opponents to a wider set of reference publics can the movement hope to generate the leverage needed to offset the superior power and resources of its opponents. The "free press," then, serves as the critical consumer and purveyor of the movement's strategic dramaturgy.

Finally, there is an "ideational bias" in the literature on framing processes (Snow and Benford 1988, 1992; Snow et al. 1986). In a later section, I develop this critique a good bit more. For now it is enough to say that the literature on framing has focused almost exclusively on the formal ideological pronouncements of insurgents while neglecting the important action component of a movement's "signifying work." The relevance of this distinction should be clear for the perspective sketched previously. The strategic possibilities that distinguish democratic from nondemocratic contexts are primarily action oriented rather than pronouncement oriented. This is not to deny the very real constraints on free expression in nondemocratic states, but, within the limits of these constraints, insurgents can seek to disseminate their message to a subterranean constituency. What they absolutely cannot do, however, is engage in the forms of public strategic dramaturgy alluded to previously. In short, the unique framing opportunities available to movements in democratic polities are, for the most part, action opportunities. Thus, if we are to understand the distinctive strategic dynamics characteristic of movements in democratic contexts, we have to broaden our definition of framing processes to include the important signifying function of movement tactics and strategies. Before elaborating on this general critique, let me first review the work that has been done to date on framing processes.

FRAMING AND FRAME ALIGNMENT PROCESSES

Among the most provocative and potentially useful of the works on the cultural dimensions of social movements have been the writings of David Snow and various of his colleagues (Snow and Benford 1988, 1992; Snow et al. 1986) on the role of "framing" or "frame alignment processes" in the emergence and development of collective action. Movements, note Snow and Benford (1988, 198), are "actively engaged in the production of meaning for participants, antagonists, and observers. . . . They frame, or assign meaning to and interpret, relevant events and conditions in ways that are intended to mobilize potential adherents and constituents, to garner bystander support, and to demobilize antagonists." By framing, then, Snow and Benford have in mind the conscious, strategic efforts of movement groups to fashion meaningful accounts of themselves and the issues at hand in order to motivate and legitimate their efforts.

The concept of framing is an important one and a necessary corrective to those broader structural theories that often depict social movements as the inevitable byproducts of expanding political opportunities (political process), emerging system-level contradictions or dislocations (some versions of new social movement theory), or newly available resources (resource mobilization). The very notion of framing reminds us that mobilization and ongoing collective action is an accomplishment, even in the face of favorable environmental conditions. The point is that any of the facilitating circumstances noted previously can only create a certain structural potential for collective action. Whether that potential is realized depends on the actions of insurgents, and those actions are, in turn, shaped by and reflect the understandings of the actors involved. "Mediating between opportunity and action are people and the . . . meanings they attach to their situations" (McAdam 1982, 48).

The framing concept has also focused analytic attention on what ironically has been a neglected topic in the study of social movements, that is, the everyday activities of movement participants. Reflecting the influence of the broad structural theories noted previously, most recent empirical work has tended to focus on the role of system-level factors in either facilitating or constraining movement activity. Consequently, we know comparatively little about the lived experience of activism and the everyday strategic concerns of movement groups. The concept of framing calls these topics to mind and invites us to theorize and ultimately study the ways in which insurgents seek—largely through various forms of "signifying work" (Snow and Benford 1988, 198)—to manage the uncertain and typically volatile environments in which they find themselves.

Framing Processes and Movement–Environment Relations

Political movements face at least six strategic hurdles that typically must be surmounted if they are to become a force for social change. Specifically, movement groups must be able to

1. attract new recruits;
2. sustain the morale and commitment of current adherents;
3. generate media coverage, preferably, but not necessarily, of a favorable sort;
4. mobilize the support of various "bystander publics";
5. constrain the social control options of its opponents; and
6. ultimately shape public policy and state action.

The first two goals in this list can be thought of as "internal" to the movement. That is, they center on the effort to maintain the movement's internal strength through the recruitment and retention of activists. Obviously, this is a critically important challenge confronting the movement. However, it is one that has been studied quite extensively by those seeking to understand the dynamics of "differential recruitment" (Gould 1991, 1993; Marwell, Oliver, and Prahl 1988; McAdam 1986; McAdam and Paulsen 1993; Rosenthal et al. 1985; Snow, Zurcher, and Ekland-Olson 1980). In contrast, the last four of these goals have been the subject of very little empirical research by movement scholars. In what follows, then, I want to make them the principal focus of attention. Together they constitute the broader "environmental challenge" confronting the movement.

For all the importance attached to the question of movement emergence, it could well be argued that movements face a tougher set of challenges following initial mobilization. The emergence of collective action requires only that a relatively small number of activists seek to exploit what they see as the increased receptivity or vulnerability of whatever system they seek to change. Following initial mobilization, however, the movement and the specific social movement organizations (SMOs) that are its carriers face a very different, and arguably tougher, challenge. They now confront an established political environment composed of a number of critically important constituent publics with very different interests vis-à-vis the movement. Just how successfully the movement and its carrier SMOs negotiate the conflicting demands imposed by these established constituents will largely determine the ultimate fate of the struggle; and, in seeking to manage the demands of this highly fluid and often hostile environment, the principal weapon available to the movement is its strategic use of framing processes. That is, in trying to attract and shape media coverage, win the support of bystander publics, constrain movement opponents, and influence state authorities, insurgents depend first and foremost on various forms of signifying work. In this chapter, I seek to show how the American civil rights movement was able, through the strategic framing efforts of Martin Luther King Jr. and his Southern Christian Leadership Conference (SCLC), largely to accomplish these four goals. However, before turning to the empirical case, I want first to address what I see as the strong "ideational bias" in the prevailing conception of framing.

The Ideational Bias in the Literature on Framing

The prevailing conception of collective action frames and framing processes betrays an almost exclusive concern with ideas and their formal expression by movement actors. Thus, empirical research on the topic tends to focus on the speeches, writings, statements, or other formal ideological pronouncements by movement actors. These conscious ideational expressions are an important component of the overall framing effort of a given social movement. However, they are not the whole of that effort. Indeed, I am tempted to argue that especially during the initial stages of mobilization, the old adage is true: Actions do speak louder than words. That is, the actions taken by insurgents and the tactical choices they make represent a critically important contribution to the overall signifying work of the movement.

Encoded in a group's actions and tactics are a good many messages, but none more significant than the degree of threat embodied in the movement. As many theorists remind us, movements derive much of their effectiveness as agents of social change from their ability to disrupt public order (Lipsky 1970; McAdam 1982; Piven and Cloward 1979; Tarrow 1994). Given the critical importance of this capacity, we should likewise attach great significance to the specific types of movement framing efforts that signify this capacity. In my view, no component of a movement's overall framing work is more important in this regard than the tactical choices it makes and the actual activities in which it engages.

The practical significance of these observations stems from the conviction that the degree of perceived threat conveyed by a movement's actions and tactics is a powerful determinant of other groups' responses to the movement. There are other influences as well, the most important of which perhaps is the movement's stated goals. Taken together, the tactics and goals of the movement largely shape the reactions of various publics to the conflict. Figure 8.1 attempts to capture this dynamic by noting the typical environmental response that a movement can expect, *within a democratic context,* given a particular mix of goals and tactics. The emphasis in the previous sentence cannot be too strongly underscored. Given the very different legitimating philosophy that underlies nondemocratic systems, the interaction between movements and other sets of actors is expected to conform to very different dynamics than those evident within ostensibly democratic systems.

To simplify the discussion, I have treated both variables—goals and tactics—as dichotomous. Goals are defined as favoring either "revolution" or "reform," depending on whether they require a major redistribution of wealth and/or power. As regards tactics, movement groups are differentiated on the basis of their primary reliance on either "noninstitutionalized" or "institutionalized" forms of action. When combined, these two variables largely determine the extent to which a given group is perceived as threatening by established political actors. In turn, this "perceived

Figure 8.1　Expected environmental responses to movements characterized by the following combinations of goals and tactics

		Tactics	
		Noninstitutionalized	Institutionalized
Goals	Revolution	Repression	Indifference/ surveillance and harassment
	Reform	Heightened public attention/polarized conflict	Indifference/minimal opposition and/or support

threat" can be expected to powerfully shape the broader environmental response to the group in question.

Crossing the two dichotomous variables yields a two-by-two table (see figure 8.1). Each cell of the table lists the general environmental response that a group can expect given a particular mix of tactics and goals. I will touch briefly on each cell of the table, beginning with the upper-left-hand corner. As a broad category, the most threatening movement groups are those that espouse revolutionary goals and rely on noninstitutionalized tactics. Such groups signify threat through both their pronouncements and their actions. Nowhere is this more true than in regard to those groups willing and able to make use of violence in pursuit of their aims. Groups that do make use of violence should, however, be prepared for the undifferentiated opposition and extreme repression that their actions invariably invite. Examples of such groups include the Baader-Meinhof gang and the Irish Republican Army.

The upper-right-hand cell would include those groups who pursue revolutionary ends primarily through institutionalized means. At first blush, this might appear to be an empty cell, but, in fact, one can think of any number of groups whose rhetoric and substantive aims are far more radical than their tactics. The Communist Party in various western European countries affords a good case in point. Even in the United States, with its history of Communist paranoia, the Communist Party thrived for a period of time (during the 1930s and 1940s) as a fairly conventional organization devoted to a radical restructuring of the American political and economic system. During the late 1960s and early 1970s, the radical black-power group, the Black Panthers, essayed a similar blend of rhetorical radicalism and institutionalized tactics. The ultimate fate of the latter two groups suggests the poverty of this particular blend of goals and tactics. As William Gamson points out, this strategy makes little tactical sense given the social control costs that the open advocacy of revolutionary change is likely to entail. Groups that pursue this strategy "seem to pay the cost of violence without gaining the benefits of employing it. They are both threatening and weak, and their repression becomes a low-cost strategy for those whom they attempt to displace" (Gamson 1990, 87).

I would modify Gamson's analysis only slightly. While certain groups in this category have indeed been repressed, many more have been greeted by a combination of indifference and low-level surveillance and harassment. In a democratic country, the espousal of revolutionary aims does not, in and of itself, legitimate violent repression on the part of authorities. It is the means by which these aims are pursued that dictate the social control response. Should the group remain within "proper channels," they are likely to remain powerless, thus affording the authorities the luxury of indifference combined on occasion with low-level efforts at surveillance and harassment. In those rare instances when tactically conventional revolutionary groups gain notoriety and a following, authorities are apt to either exaggerate the threat posed by the group—as in the Communist "witch hunts" that took place in the United States during the early 1950s—or seek to lure the group into violent confrontations with the police, as was done in the case of the Black Panthers (Marx 1974, 1979). Either way, the intent is the same: to depict the group's tactics as illegitimate in order to justify overt repression. My emphasis in the preceding sentence serves to underscore the point I made previously concerning the "ideational bias" evident in earlier discussions of framing. Interactive frame contests involving movement groups, the state, the media, and various bystander publics are very likely to turn on the signifying function of action. This is especially true in nominally democratic states where freedom of speech—including the advocacy of revolutionary aims—is protected. What is not protected is the right of movement groups to use any means necessary to achieve their aims. This disparity between freedom of speech and the limits on action makes action and the battles over its interpretation the fulcrum on which many frame battles turn.

The least threatening and probably most common type of movement group would fall into the lower-right-hand cell of figure 8.1. These are SMOs that work through "proper channels" to achieve reform goals. These are the professional advocacy organizations described by John McCarthy and Mayer Zald (1973) in their initial formulation of the resource mobilization perspective. While McCarthy and Zald may have erred in equating this specialized type of movement group with social movements in general, they were clearly prescient in describing formal movement organizations as "the trend of social movements in America." Recent work on the founding of movement groups in the United States over the past forty years confirms the increasing preponderance of the kind of professional advocacy organizations described by McCarthy and Zald (Berry 1989; Minkoff 1993).

Typically, such groups can expect a highly differentiated set of responses from other parties based on the latter's perception of convergence/divergence between their own interests and that of the SMO. By virtue of their narrow, reform focus, most professional SMOs stand to engender the opposition of only those few "polity members" who perceive their interests as directly threatened by the group. By the same token, such groups are likely to receive facilitative support only from those elites who see their interests as clearly aligned with those of the SMO. The vast majority of member groups can be expected to remain unaware or indifferent to the SMO. Thus, when professional reform groups eschew the leverage that often comes from disruptive action, their hopes hinge on their ability to mobilize more allies than opponents. Should they succeed in this, they are likely to prove an effective agent of slow, piecemeal change. Failing to do so, they are apt to die a slow, unpublicized death.

When compared to the reform SMO, our final type of social movement group, located in the lower-left-hand cell in figure 8.1, represents a considerably rarer but arguably more effective blend of goals and tactics. I am referring to those movement groups that pursue reform goals through noninstitutionalized means. The genius of this blend derives from the cognitive ambiguities encoded in the approach. In their willingness and demonstrated ability to disrupt public order and, by extension, the realization of their opponents' interests, radical reform groups often come to be seen as powerful and threatening. Their adherence to moderate reform goals, however, bespeaks a respect for the broader system that invites support from various publics while simultaneously restraining the social control proclivities of opponents. This optimal mix of outcomes, however, is not easily achieved and must ultimately depend on a highly developed and flexible capacity for framing. In effect, radical reform groups must master the art of simultaneously playing to a variety of publics, threatening opponents, and pressuring the state while appearing nonthreatening and sympathetic to the media and other publics. It is a difficult balancing act to pull off, but when achieved it is the source of tremendous political leverage. It is the social movement equivalent of Teddy Roosevelt's admonition that one "walk softly but carry a big stick."

Martin Luther King Jr.'s organization, the SCLC, affords a perfect example of a movement group that was able, for a time, to achieve the aforementioned balancing act. The balance of this chapter is given over to an analysis of the ways in which King and the SCLC were able, by their tactical choices and framing efforts, to surmount the four "environmental challenges" noted at the outset of this chapter and, in so doing, to achieve a significant restructuring of race relations in the United States.

TACTICS, FRAMING, AND MOVEMENT–ENVIRONMENT INTERACTION IN THE AMERICAN CIVIL RIGHTS MOVEMENT

To fully appreciate the daunting challenge that confronted the civil rights movement, one has to understand the depths of black powerlessness on the eve of the struggle. In 1950, fully two-thirds of all blacks continued to live in the southern United States. Yet, through a combination of legal subterfuge and extralegal intimidation, blacks were effectively barred from political participation in the region. Less than 20 percent of all voting-age blacks were even registered to vote in 1950 (Bullock 1971, 227). In the states of the so-called Deep South, the figure was many times lower. In Mississippi, for example, barely 2 percent were registered in 1950. Fear kept more from trying to register. Small wonder that as late as 1955, two blacks were killed in Mississippi for refusing to remove their names from the voting roles (Bennett 1966, 201).

Nor on the eve of the movement were there any signs of a crack in the "solid South" or any diminution in the will of the region's political and economic elite to maintain "the southern way of life." On the contrary, the 1954 Supreme Court decision declaring educational segregation unconstitutional set in motion a regionwide "resistance movement" aimed at preserving white supremacy at all costs. At the heart of the movement were the local white citizen councils and state legislatures throughout the region. The councils mobilized to preserve segregation locally, while the state legislatures passed statute after statute in defense of the racial status quo. Among the measures passed were bills in various states outlawing the National Association for the Advancement of Colored People (NAACP), the only civil rights organization that had been previously active in the region.

Thus, on the eve of the movement, southern blacks remained barred from institutional politics and deprived of any real leverage within the region. If change were to come, it would have to be imposed from without. This, of course, meant intervention by the federal government. However, with a moderate Republican, Dwight Eisenhower, in the White House and southern Democrats exercising disproportionate power in Congress, the movement faced a kind of strategic stalemate at the national level as well. To break the stalemate, the movement would have to find a way of pressuring a reluctant federal government to intervene more forcefully in the South. This, in turn, meant attracting favorable media attention as a way of mobilizing popular support for the movement.

Attracting Media Coverage

If one were to conduct an ethnographic study of virtually any social movement organization, be it local or national, one would be very likely to uncover a pervasive concern with media coverage among one's subjects. The fact is, most movements spend considerable time and energy in seeking to attract and shape media coverage of their activities. With the exception of Charlotte Ryan (1991) and Ralph Turner (1969) and his students (Altheide and Gilmore 1972), movement scholars have granted the topic very little attention. The question is, which of these views more accurately reflects the realities of social movement life? Is the media really as irrelevant in the life of most movements as the lack of scholarly attention would suggest? Or does the activist's view capture a critical dynamic too long neglected by movement scholars?

I subscribe to the latter view. Activists are neither deluded into thinking that the media are important nor driven by their egos to court media attention. The simple fact is that most movements lack the conventional political resources possessed by their opponents and thus must seek to offset this power disparity by appeals to other parties. The media come to be seen—logically, in my view—as the key vehicle for such influence attempts. The civil rights movement represents a prime example of this dynamic in action, and no group in the movement mastered this dynamic and exploited its possibilities better than the SCLC and its leader, Martin Luther King Jr.

The media's fascination with King was evident from the very beginning of the Montgomery, Alabama, bus boycott. Launched in December 1955, the boycott inaugurated the modern civil rights movement and catapulted King into public prominence. From then until his death in April 1968, King never strayed far from the front page and the nightly news. What accounts for King's media staying power, and why were he and the SCLC, alone among movement groups, so successful in attracting favorable media attention? In seeking to answer these questions, I will emphasize the role of three factors.

1. *Disruptive actions are newsworthy.* First, the SCLC and King mastered the art of staging newsworthy disruptions of public order. The first requirement of media coverage is that the event be judged newsworthy. Their experiences in Montgomery convinced King and his lieutenants of the close connection between public disruption and media coverage. All of King's subsequent campaigns were efforts to stage the same kind of highly publicized disruptions of public order that had occurred in Montgomery. Sometimes King failed, as in Albany, Georgia, in 1961–1962, when Police Chief Laurie Pritchett responded to King's tactics with mass arrests but without the violence and disruptions of public order so critical to sustained media attention. At other times in other places—most notably in Birmingham, Alabama, in 1963 and Selma, Alabama, in 1965—local authorities took the bait and responded with the kind of savagery that all but guarantees media attention.

Still, his mastery of the politics of disruption explains only how King and the SCLC were able to attract the media but not the overwhelmingly sympathetic tone of that coverage. Given the openly provocative nature of the King/SCLC strategy, the generally favorable coverage accorded King's actions demands explanation. The key to the puzzle would seem to rest with King's consummate ability to frame his actions in highly resonant and sympathetic ways. The final two factors focus on King's framing efforts, first in conventional ideational terms and then in terms of the signifying function of his tactics.

2. *Ideational framing.* As noted previously, all work on framing betrays an exclusive concern with ideas and their formal expression by movement actors. These conscious ideational pronouncements-speeches, writings, and so on are an important component of a movement's overall framing effort; and, in accounting for King's success in attracting sympathetic media coverage, much of the credit must go to the substantive content of his thought. Quite simply, no black leader had ever sounded like King before. In his unique blending of familiar Christian themes, conventional democratic theory, and the philosophy of nonviolence, King brought an unusually compelling yet accessible frame to the struggle. First and foremost, there was a deep "resonance" (Snow et al. 1986) to King's thought. Specifically, in employing Christian themes and conventional democratic theory, King succeeded in grounding the movement in two of the ideational bedrocks of American culture. Second, the theme of Christian forgiveness that runs throughout King's thought was deeply reassuring to a white America burdened (as it still is) by guilt and a near phobic fear of black anger and violence. King's emphasis on Christian charity and nonviolence promised a redemptive and peaceful healing to America's long-standing racial divide. Third, King's invocation of Gandhian philosophy added an exotic intellectual patina to his thought that many in the northern media (and northern intellectuals in general) found appealing. Finally, while singling out this or that theme in King's thought, it should be noted that the very variety of themes granted those in the media (and the general public) multiple points of ideological contact with the movement. Thus,

secular liberals might be unmoved by King's reading of Christian theology but resonate with his application of democratic theory and so on.

3. *The signifying function of SCLC actions.* King and his SCLC lieutenants' genius as "master framers," however, extended beyond the ideational content of their formal pronouncements. In their planning and orchestration of major campaigns, the SCLC brain trust displayed what can only be described as a genius for strategic dramaturgy. That is, in the staging of demonstrations, King and his lieutenants were also engaged in signifying work—mindful of the messages and potent symbols encoded in the actions they took and hoped to induce their opponents to take.

Arguably the best example of SCLC's penchant for staging compelling and resonant dramas is their 1963 campaign in Birmingham. Like virtually all major cities in the Deep South, Birmingham in 1963 remained a wholly segregated city, with blacks and whites confined to their own restaurants, schools, churches, and even public restrooms. In April of that year, the SCLC launched a citywide campaign of civil disobedience aimed at desegregating Birmingham's public facilities; but why, among all southern cities, was Birmingham targeted? The answer bespeaks the SCLC's strategic and dramaturgic genius. As a major chronicler of the events in Birmingham notes, "King's Birmingham innovation was pre-eminently strategic. Its essence was . . . the selection of a target city which had as its Commissioner of Public Safety 'Bull' Connor, a notorious racist and hothead who could be depended on not to respond nonviolently" (Hubbard 1968, 5).

The view that King's choice of Birmingham was a conscious, strategic one is supported by the fact that Connor was a lame-duck official, having been defeated by a moderate in a runoff election in early April 1963. Had the SCLC waited to launch its campaign until after the moderate took office, there likely would have been considerably less violence and less press coverage as well. "The supposition has to be that . . . SCLC, in a shrewd . . . stratagem, knew a good enemy when they saw him . . . one who could be counted on in stupidity and natural viciousness to play into their hands, for full exploitation in the press as archfiend and villain" (Watters 1971, 266).

King and his lieutenants had learned their lessons well. After several days of uncharacteristic restraint, Connor trained fire hoses and unleashed attack dogs on peaceful demonstrators. The resulting scenes of demonstrators being slammed into storefronts by the force of the hoses and attacked by snarling police dogs were picked up and broadcast nationwide on the nightly news. Photographs of the same events appeared in newspapers and magazines throughout the nation and the world. The former Soviet Union used the pictures as anti-American propaganda at home and abroad. Thus, the media's coverage of the events in Birmingham succeeded in generating enormous sympathy for the demonstrators and putting increased pressure on a reluctant federal government to intervene on behalf of the movement.

In short, by successfully courting violence while restraining violence in his followers, King and the SCLC were able to frame the events in Birmingham as highly dramatic confrontations between a "good" movement and an "evil" system. Moreover, the movement's dominant religious ideology granted this interpretation all the more credibility and resonance. These were no longer demonstrators; rather, they were peaceful, Christian petitioners being martyred by an evil, oppressive system. The stark, highly dramatic nature of this ritualized confrontation between good and evil proved irresistible to the media and, in turn, to the American public.

Mobilizing Public Support

While favorable media coverage was the immediate goal of King and his lieutenants, it was never conceived of as an end in itself. Instead, the SCLC courted the media for the role that it might play in mobilizing greater public awareness of and support for the movement. That support, in turn, was seen as the key to breaking the strategic stalemate in which the SCLC and the broader movement found itself. With no chance of defeating the white supremacists in a direct confrontation, the SCLC knew that its prospects for initiating change would turn on its ability to prod a reluctant federal government into more supportive action on behalf of civil rights. Ironically, the election of John F. Kennedy as president in 1960 only intensified the government's long-standing aversion to "meddling" in southern race relations. The specific explanation for Kennedy's reluctance to intervene had to do with his narrow margin of victory in 1960 and the "strange bedfellows" that comprised his electoral coalition. Not only had Kennedy garnered the so-called black vote and the votes of northern liberals and labor, but he was also beholden to the "solid South." In rejecting the Republican Party as the party of Abraham Lincoln, white southerners had voted consistently Democratic since the late nineteenth century. Thus, Kennedy, no less than his party predecessors, counted racist southerners and civil rights advocates among his constituents. The electoral challenge for Kennedy, then, was to preserve his fragile coalition by not unduly antagonizing either white southerners or civil rights forces. More immediately, Kennedy knew that the success of his legislative agenda would depend, to a large extent, on the support of conservative southern congressmen whose long tenure granted them disproportionate power within both the House and the Senate. For both electoral and legislative reasons, then, Kennedy came to office determined to effect a stance of qualified neutrality on civil rights matters.

In this context, the SCLC saw its task as destroying the political calculus on which Kennedy's stance of neutrality rested. It had to make the political, and especially the electoral, benefits of supporting civil rights appear to outweigh the costs of alienating southern white voters and their elected officials. This meant mobilizing the support of the general public, thereby broadening the electoral basis of civil rights advocacy. In concert with the other major civil rights groups, the SCLC was able to do just that. Between 1962 and 1965, the salience of the civil rights issue reached such proportions that it consistently came to be identified in public opinion surveys as the "most important" problem confronting the country. In six of the eleven national polls conducted by Gallup (1972) between January 1961 and January 1966, it was designated as the country's most pressing problem by survey respondents. In three other polls, it ranked second. Only twice did it rank as low as fourth. Moreover, the imprint of the SCLC's dramaturgic genius is clearly reflected in these data. The two highest percentages attached to the issue correspond to the SCLC's highly publicized campaigns in Birmingham (April to May 1963) and Selma (March 1965). Quite simply, the SCLC's ability to lure supremacists into well-publicized outbursts of racist violence kept the issue squarely before the public and ensured the growing support necessary to pressure Kennedy and Congress into more decisive action.

Constraining the Social Control Options of Segregationists

To this point, I have said very little about the effect of the SCLC's tactics on southern segregationists, but, in a very real sense, the success of the SCLC's politics of disruption depended not on the media or the general public but on the movement's opponents in the South. Had segregationists not responded to the SCLC's actions with the kind of violent disruptions of public order seen in Birmingham, the SCLC would have been denied the media coverage so critical to its overall strategy. Indeed, the SCLC's most celebrated failure turned on its inability to provoke precisely this response from segregationists. I am referring to the citywide campaign that the SCLC launched in Albany, Georgia, in November 1961. In all respects, the campaign was comparable to the organization's later efforts in Birmingham and Selma. However, while the campaigns themselves were similar, the opponents' response to them was anything but. What was absent in Albany were the celebrated atrocities and breakdown in public order characteristic of Birmingham and Selma. This difference owed to Albany Police Chief Laurie Pritchett's clear understanding of the SCLC's strategy and his firm resolve to deny them the villain that they so badly needed. While systematically denying demonstrators their rights, Pritchett nonetheless did so through mass arrests rather than the kind of reactive violence that proved so productive of sympathetic media coverage in Birmingham and Selma. The data in figure 8.1 support this conclusion. At the very height of the Albany campaign in March 1962, public concern with the issue of civil rights was at its virtual nadir.

There is, of course, a wonderful irony in all this that was not lost on the SCLC or its supremacist opponents. On the one hand, by framing action in the way that they had, King and the SCLC had taken the supremacists' ultimate strategic weapon—violence and the threat of violence—and transformed it into a liability. In so doing, they effectively broke the terror on which the system ultimately depended. In effect, any response on the part of the segregationists furthered the aims of the movement. Restraint, as in Albany, may have denied the movement its immediate need for media coverage, but it also lessened black vulnerability and fear of racist violence. On the other hand, celebrated instances of violence generated media coverage, public outrage, and increasing pressure for federal intervention on behalf of black civil rights. In his own way, President Kennedy acknowledged the dynamic under discussion here when he offered the following "tribute" to Bull Connor. In a remark to King, Kennedy said, "[O]ur judgement of Bull Connor should not be too harsh. After all, in his own way, he has done a good deal for civil rights legislation this year" (cited in King 1963, 144).

Shaping Public Policy and State Action

Little remains to be said in this final section. The ultimate goal of King and the SCLC was to prod the government into action and to reshape federal civil rights policy in the process. That they were able to do so is clear from the various histories of the movement (Branch 1988; Garrow 1978, 1986; McAdam 1982; Rosenberg 1991). What is also clear is that the extent and pace of their achievements were inextricably linked to their success in orchestrating the politics of disruption described here. In particular, the movement's two most significant legislative victories—the Civil Rights Act of 1964 and the Voting Rights Act of 1965—owed, in large measure, to the Birmingham and Selma campaigns, respectively.

Birmingham, as we have seen, featured the brutality of Bull Connor and, in the waning days of the campaign, a Sunday morning bombing of a black church that claimed the lives of three little girls. As broadcast nightly into the living rooms of America, these atrocities mobilized public opinion like never before and, in turn, put enormous pressure on President Kennedy to act forcefully on behalf of civil rights. The ultimate result was administration sponsorship of the Civil Rights Act, which, even in a much weaker form, had earlier been described as politically too risky by Kennedy himself. Finally, there was Selma. One last time, King and the SCLC orchestrated the by-now familiar politics of disruption to perfection. Initiated in January 1965, the campaign reached its peak in March with a series of widely publicized atrocities by segregationists:

> On March 9, state troopers attacked and brutally beat some 525 persons who were attempting to begin a protest march to Montgomery. Later that same day, the Reverend James Reeb, a march participant, was beaten to death by a group of whites. Finally, on March 25, following the triumphal completion of the twice interrupted Selma-to-Montgomery march, a white volunteer, Mrs. Viola Liuzzo, was shot and killed while transporting marchers back to Selma from the state capital. (McAdam 1982, 179)

In response to this consistent breakdown in public order and the public outrage that it aroused throughout the nation, the federal government was forced to once again intervene in support of black interests. On March 17, President Lyndon Johnson submitted to Congress a tough voting rights bill containing several provisions that movement leaders had earlier been told were politically too unpopular to be incorporated into legislative proposals. The bill passed by overwhelming margins in both the Senate and the House and was signed into law on August 6 of the same year.

However, Selma was to represent the high-water mark for King, the SCLC, and the movement as a whole. Never again was King able to successfully stage the politics of disruption at which he had become so skilled. The reason for this is simple: As the movement moved out of the American South and sought to confront the much more complicated forms of racism endemic to the North, King was deprived of the willing antagonists he had faced in the South. As King had learned, southern segregationists could be counted on, when sufficiently provoked, to respond with the violence so critical to media attention and the increased public and government support that sympathetic coverage inevitably produced. No such convenient foil was available to the movement outside the South. In fact, more often than not, after 1965 civil rights forces came to resemble a movement in search of an enemy. Kenneth Clark captures the amorphous quality of the opposition the movement came increasingly to confront in the late 1960s:

> What do you do in a situation in which you have the laws on your side, where whites smile and say to you that they are your friends, but where your white "friends" move to the suburbs leaving you confronted with segregation and inferior education in schools, ghetto housing, and a quiet and tacit discrimination in jobs? How can you demonstrate a philosophy of love in response to this? What is the appropriate form of protest? (Clark 1970, 288)

Even when the movement was able, as in the 1966 open housing marches in Cicero, Illinois, to provoke southern-style violence in the North, local authorities were unwilling to intervene because they feared the political consequences of doing so. They knew that while the general public was prepared to accept an end to Jim Crow segregation in the South, it was assuredly not ready to acquiesce in the dismantling of de facto segregation in the North. Thus, the absence of supportive public opinion in the North denied the movement the critical source of pressure that had helped compel federal action in the South. The ability to command public and, by extension, state attention and support had been lost. In no public opinion poll since 1965 has the American public ever accorded black civil rights the status of the number one problem confronting the country, nor since then has Congress passed, with the exception of the Civil Rights Act of 1968, any significant civil rights legislation.

CONCLUSION

The veritable explosion in theory and research on social movements that has taken place in Europe and the United States over the past twenty years has profoundly altered our understanding of movement dynamics and resulted in an impressive body of knowledge regarding the phenomenon. Still, many gaping holes remain in our knowledge. In this chapter, I have sought to address three of those holes.

First, although the recent emphasis in the literature on the importance of "framing processes" represents an important corrective to the somewhat mechanistic opportunity- or resource-based models proposed earlier, there remain problems with the framing concept. For one, it has thus far resisted much in the way of systematic empirical application. With a few notable exceptions (e.g.,. Gerhards and Rucht 1992), the literature on framing processes has been long on ringing, programmatic statements and short on the kinds of detailed empirical applications that would allow for a real assessment of the worth of the concept. A second problem concerns what I see as the pronounced "ideational bias" inherent in our current usage of the concept. Framing has been equated with the formal ideological expressions of a movement. However, as I have tried to show here, it is impossible to fully understand the "signifying work" of a movement group without paying close attention to its tactics and the actions in which it engages. In my view, the unique genius of Martin Luther King Jr. lay in his ability to frame action in such a way as to invoke a set of predictable responses from not one but four references publics. The key lies in King's ability to lure segregationists into acts of extreme racist violence while still maintaining his followers' commitment to nonviolence. When combined with the religious themes that King invoked, the juxtaposition of peaceful black demonstrators and virulent white attackers created powerful and resonant images that triggered critically important reactions in three additional publics. The media were drawn to the drama inherent in the attacks. Through the media's sympathetic coverage, an increasingly outraged American public was moved to call for more action on behalf of the movement. Finally, as a result of the increasing public pressure, a previously reluctant federal government was prodded time and again into more decisive action. It was on the basis of this dynamic that the movement—with King as its driving wedge—was able to achieve the significant victories that it did. However, it was the compelling dramaturgy of King's tactics rather than his formal pronouncements that keyed the dynamic.

This recounting of the important parties—segregationists, the media, the general public, and the federal government—to the civil rights struggle underscores a second major point of this chapter. If we are ever to develop a full understanding of collective action and social conflict, we must transcend the limits of the prevailing movement-centric view of social movements. Most movement scholarship focuses exclusively on a given movement or even a specific movement organization. Even those visionary scholars who have recently asserted the importance of the state to a full understanding of movement dynamics have tended to stop there (e.g., Amenta and Zylon 1991; Duyvendak 1992; Koopmans 1992; Quadagno 1992). However, I would argue that virtually all instances of state–movement interaction are mediated by other publics. This was clearly the case in the American civil rights movement. Only by focusing equal attention on the actions of the movement, southern segregationists, and the media, plus the consequent shifts in public opinion, could the analyst ever hope to make sense of federal action and inaction in regards to the movement. In general, as movement scholars, we need to broaden our analyses to include the full range of publics relevant to whatever movement we seek to understand.

Finally, in closing, let me return to the theme with which I began this chapter. Although virtually all contemporary movement research draws its cases from democratic polities, movement scholars have been generally silent on the significance of this "selection bias" for an understanding of collective action dynamics. I have sought to explore what I take to be one of the distinctive features of collective action in nominally democratic states. I am referring to the richer possibilities for strategic dramaturgy in democratic than in nondemocratic polities and the role of a "free press" and various reference publics in shaping the outcome of the strategic interaction of state and movement actors. However, this is only one example of how polity type affects the emergence and development of collective action. In general, movement scholars need to take more seriously polity type as a variable and to explore the different characteristics, strategic logics, and ultimate outcomes of collective action in nondemocratic as well as democratic contexts. Only by doing so will we be in a position to know just how much of the movement scholarship of the past two decades has theoretical resonance outside the particular political contexts in which it was first produced.

NOTES

This chapter appeared originally in *Research in Democracy and Society*, vol. 3 (Greenwich, Conn.: JAI Press, 1996) 155–176.

1. The wide range of state responses to the democracy movements of 1989 (think only of the events in Prague and Beijing) remind us that nondemocratic regimes vary considerably in the extent to which they are vulnerable to the kind of dramaturgic tactics under discussion here. Indeed, rather than simply asserting democratic vulnerability and nondemocratic impunity from such tactics, it would be interesting to learn more about the conditions under which such tactics are effective in each of these two general regime contexts.

9

Body Rhetoric: Conflicted Reporting of Bodies in Pain

Gerard A. Hauser

In *The Human Condition,* Hannah Arendt (1958, 50–51) makes an argument for differentiating a world of personal experiences that are privately encountered and, therefore, real to no one but the individual who has them and those that are commonly encountered and, therefore, worldly realities for all those who share them. To make this distinction concrete, she points to the utterly undeniable but equally unsharable personal experience of pain. Arendt reminds us that great bodily pain is both the most intense of human feelings and "at the same time the most private and least communicable of all." Yet, even though intense pain can deprive us of our ability to feel reality, once relieved it can be instantly forgotten. "Pain, in other words, truly a borderline experience between life as 'being among men' (*inter homines esse*) and death, is so subjective and removed from the world of things and men that it cannot assume an appearance at all" (51).

Arendt's formulation of pain's utter privacy seems unassailable as long as we restrict pain to the actual physical suffering of a body in distress, but what of the power of a body in pain to form deep and powerful identification among an audience that feels empathy for the sufferer's anguish? In addition to the utterly private and unshared physical experience of the body's own pain, there also are rhetorical and political dimensions to pain that, regrettably, Arendt did not address. Without refuting her point, we would err to deny the suffering body's impressive rhetorical potential. As the twentieth century has taught us, bodies in pain are a tragic constant of the public realm. It also has taught us that despite exerting impressive rhetorical force that exhorts humanity to relieve their suffering, sometimes their pleas go unheard and their suffering goes ignored. Whatever else politics might include, democracy ties it inexorably to our capacity to invent and respond to responsible rhetoric, including the rhetorical power of bodies in pain.

Regarding the body as a rhetorical site is not new. Homer's *The Iliad* (1990) immerses the reader in heroic actions that often convey the *areté* of its characters and strong emotions that accompany their deeds through corporeal reference. In Book 5, for example, Homer structures his narrative of a world in chaos through the anatomical destruction wrought by spear, arrow, and club during full-scale combat before Troy's gate. His graphic depiction of Acheans and Trojans meeting their demise made each individual body's destruction synecdochic for the devastation that war was visiting on Attica and Troy. His battlefield scene fastens the physical piercing and breaking of flesh and bone to the devastation each death visited on that warrior's family and its world.

More academically, since antiquity the rhetorical canon of delivery has included gesture and posture among its sources of influence. Rhetoric's oral tradition continues to theorize discourse in a manner that, at least implicitly, acknowledges its worldly appearance as an embodied performance. At the opposite pole from public performance and closer to our own time, Sigmund Freud's theory of psychopathology established the pleasure principle as the basic motivation for individual conduct, thereby wedding the body inescapably to the formation of subjectivity and an explanatory mechanism for human action.

Explicit attempts to theorize the body as a discursive formation are, however, relatively recent, with a flood of work since the mid-1960s. Most prominent among the contributions to our understanding of bodies as contested sites are the writings of feminist intellectuals and of Michel Foucault. As Randi Paterson and Gail Corning (1997, 6) observe, feminist scholarship has made a massive contribution to our understanding of the body as a discursive construction that extends beyond the provinces of medicine and psychology, and they provide an annotated bibliography of more than thirty recent scholarly works in which this extension is elaborated. The Foucaldean exploration of the other as insane (Foucault 1973), as subjected to the medical gaze (Foucault 1975), as disciplined through panoptic surveillance (Foucault 1979), and as a sexuality defined through confession to a higher authority (Foucault 1980) is a monument to the body as a discursive formation. Through its discursive construction, the body becomes an object of desire whose appropriation authorizes knowledge and power.

Feminist and poststructuralist research is not alone in centering a discussion of meaning and influence, which is to say a discussion of knowledge and power, on the body. Richard Sennett's *Flesh and Stone: The Body and the City in Western Civilization* (1994) chronicles how symbolic representations of architecture and urban design historically have reflected cultural understandings and attitudes toward the body. Likewise, Gilles Lipovetsky's *The Empire of Fashion: Dressing Modern Democracy* (1994) details a similar relationship between cultural understanding of the body and the way it is displayed as an object of social attraction and influence. Elaine Scarry's *The Body in Pain: The Making and Unmaking of the World* (1985) offers a meditation on our search for language capable of giving voice to the body's vulnerability. Russian poet Irina Ratushinskaya's *Grey Is the Color of Hope* (1989) takes the reader into the surrealistic labor camp at Barashevo, in which its women prisoners of conscience used their bodies as contestive sites to challenge the authorities' denial of their personal and political identity and rights. Among dissident explorations, perhaps the most noted, Jacobo Timerman's *Prisoner without a Name, Cell without a Number* (1981) details the horrors of psychological and physical torture at the hands of Argentinean army officers whose own identities seem perversely tied to the anguish that they can impose on their political captives.

Sennett's *Flesh and Stone* especially illuminates the deep incongruity between the body's private sufficiency and public insufficiency. Historically, he argues, the incongruity between personal lessons of self-sufficiency and public ones of insufficiency has been transferred to the tension between domination and civilization in urban spaces. This tension is manifested in public spaces, principally cities, whose structures mirror a cultural/historical understanding of bodily experience. Urban design reflects Western civilization's attempt to shape a civic realm that can protect us from our own weaknesses and those of others but also can accommodate our desire to turn toward those others and be open to experiencing them as the Other. Sennett's account of urban experience presents a *conflicted publicness* residing in communal encounters of a discourse about privacy: the experience of the body, including the most intimate aspects of its private contact with other bodies.

The urban discourse Sennett examines is, itself, part of a larger historical and cultural dialogue on the body. The voices engaged in this conversation speak in many arenas: the pulpit and confessional, medical practice, psychotherapy, legislatures and courts, urban and architectural design, fashion design, the arts, and, of course, the streets. These discursive arenas transform the personal and private experiences of the body into an object of public expression. Our pain or ecstasy may be our own and known only secondhand to those with whom we share its secrets, as Arendt argues, but our bodies also are in the world. Beyond the gates of our privacy, we become aware of our flaws, our weaknesses are exposed and even exploited, and we experience rebuke for our personal insufficiency. As these discourses acquire official status, whether by virtue of trust (as in the efficacy of medicine), faith (as in the redemptive power of religion), or ballot, they speak a discourse of power in which the individual's self-sufficiency is made the object of protection and regulation. Our bodies are made subject to a larger authority that tries to discipline them.

On the other hand, as effective as regimes of discipline may be, the body, especially the body in pain, also is capable of resisting discipline. A number of the works noted previously offer compelling testimony to the body's capacity to evoke responses to their peril and cause from a witnessing public, to bring pressure to bear on a disciplining authority, and sometimes even to overturn the plans of their oppressors. This is to say that the body is a source as well as a site of signification and, therefore, of rhetoric.

To maintain that the body is a rhetorical site requires qualification. Certainly the body may attract attention by its form and treatment, and we may impose an interpretation on it, as when, witnessing a body in extreme pain, we search for a cause and respond empathetically to its anguish. However, the body itself is an ambiguous form of signification, and the meaning that we attribute to one in pain is not necessarily the assertion being advanced. This ambiguity is evident in the seeming disparities in public responses to public controversies in which bodies are used as a form of evidence to advance larger political claims.

Insofar as a body may make a public statement, it requires a context and words to explain its actions. Absent context and words, the body's declarations remain largely inchoate. Moreover, we seldom directly encounter the anguished body advancing a public appeal to redress a public problem. The web of discourse that forms around its suffering mediates its claim. Claim making, in short, requires *framing* for a body to appeal to the conscience of its public and move it to exert pressure on official bodies authorized to act.

Framing is a function of publicity that hails and focuses our attention. The press is an important voice in this publicizing process. Press coverage influences how readers perceive ownership of public problems, the nature of issues, and how to interpret public words and deeds. The body's status as a public statement is tied to this framing process of publicity, to whether and how it is reported.

In this chapter, I wish to interrogate an aspect of the way in which publicity alters the body's rhetorical functions. My concern is with why certain modes of body rhetoric succeed at capturing attention and moving an attending public to compassion and even action while others seem to be largely ineffectual. Although a complete answer is beyond my current purpose, attention to specific cases may suggest some dimensions that a complete answer would include. I wish to explore this concern through two contrasting cases of reporting bodily anguish: those of the bodies of prisoners of conscience and those of women who have been sexually abused in contexts involving pornography.

Political prisoners often use their bodies as their rhetorical means of last resort but often also as their most (perhaps only) effective rhetorical weapon to confront and best the state. The empathy generated by their body rhetoric contrasts with the general difficulty women have had inserting pornography-related violence of sexual abuse against their bodies into a serious public dialogue about their pain as a public problem. I will argue that one of the features separating their cases is their different status as exemplification of the ills they purport to represent. Simply put, in the cases of both prisoners of conscience and victims of sexual abuse, the body becomes a particular case, a source of evidence and argument, an exemplification or what Aristotle (1991) would have called argument by *paradigma,* or example.[1] However, their status as an exemplification is contingent on how their pain is framed in the public imagination. In the case of the political prisoner, the body seems to achieve the argumentative status of a paradigm, whereas sexual violence gets treated as anecdotal evidence. The contrasting press coverage of Bobby Sands's hunger strike and of the Meese Commission report on pornography offers cases that can aid in elaborating this difference and suggest how press coverage contributes to it.

THE BODY AS PARADIGM

The political prisoner's rhetoric is inherently entwined with the dissident's body. The political prisoner typically chooses incarceration over the Faustian bargain of his name for his freedom. Dissidents in former communist states who called for a velvet revolution in the form of a viable civil society were acutely aware of this bodily tension between self-sufficiency and regulation. Many of them, such as Kuron (1968) and Michnik (1985) in Poland, Havel (1989) in Czechoslovakia, and Bonner (1986), Shcharansky (1988), and Ratushinskaya (1989) in the Soviet Union spoke as political prisoners whose bodies were regulated, sometimes extremely so, in order to protect the larger body politic.

Although removal and control of the dissident's physical body is administered as a form of therapy for the body politic, it underscores the body's rhetorical potency. Rebuking the dissident's self-sufficiency in this extrasymbolic fashion creates a tension with the state's own self-sufficiency. Removing the opposition by forcibly controlling its body serves as an admission that dissident ideas cannot be refuted, thereby bestowing a hyperrhetorical presence on the political prisoner's body. This is another way of saying that the prisoner of conscience, having lost control of her body and its attendant freedoms of movement, assembly, and expression, has her body transformed into her last but most potent resource for subverting her oppressors. The most graphic form of this bodily argumentation is the hunger strike.

Self-starvation is inexplicable without words. The anorexic body can capture our attention by the sheer spectacle of its wasting away, but we require words to tell us whether we are watching a religious fast, an involuntary famine, a manifestation of cultural psychosis, or a hunger strike. The hunger strike particularly is tied to words. The hunger strike is an attempt at subverting a superior power by becoming helpless before it. Without words, the point of the protest remains mysterious.

The authorities, mindful of how fundamental words are to the protest's meaning, attempt to control the hunger striker's voice by banning his words from the light of publicity (Ellmann 1993). Even if muted, however, the hunger striker's body manages to speak. By appealing to the state's power to act, the hunger striker offers a perverse form of legitimation. He recognizes the authority's power by placing his life in its hands. The death fast opposes within the hierarchy and, by not denying it, unmasks it. It seeks to overpower the oppressor through a display of powerlessness. Insofar as this act of helplessness succeeds in eliciting pressure from external groups, it actually subverts the superior power.

The spectacle of the striker's starvation poses a moral dilemma to the authorities: either yield to save my life or, by refusing to fold, stand publicly condemned for your moral intransigence. The moral economy of wordless starvation before a seemingly unbending authority calls its witnesses to an exercise of conscience in hopes of saving another human's life. It calls them into a public sphere where predefined premises frame a discourse on the society's civility. In itself, wordless and wasting, the fasting body cannot force the authority to cave in, but its public display of anorexic helplessness before a superior power presents itself as *paradigmatic* for the society's moral economy. Through a pageant that plainly indicates the authority might end the death march should it choose, the strike focuses attention on seemingly misguided values that, absent *phronêsis,* would allow a person to perish rather than negotiate the complaint. The spectacle of the striker's disintegrating body thus becomes a form of rhetoric by indirection (Natanson 1978).

The striker's body becomes a corporeal manifestation of her grievance. It drives a wedge (Johnstone 1990) between our identification of the state's actions as an expression of national values and the state's exercise of its authority. This wedge functions rhetorically as an opening that invites critical reflection on the taken-for-granted fusion of power with the persona of the state's leader. Witnessing the body's self-consumption simultaneously fixes our gaze on the authority's display of intransigence in the face of appeals for civil accommodation. As the physical body diminishes, its rhetorical incarnation grows, touching the conscience of ever enlarging circles of society. Sometimes, as in the cases of Gandhi in India, Sakharov and Shcharansky in the former Soviet Union, and Bobby Sands in Northern Ireland, its rhetorical presence crosses national borders and even spans oceans to elicit a common urging that the authority be responsive to the larger demands of civility. The body's rhetorical identity becomes a literal manifestation of the rhetorical topos of magnification: words magnify the wasting body's moral weight, enlarge its mass through publicity, and transform its powerless physical form into a powerful moral invocation that advances the striker's demands while questioning the legitimacy of rulers unwilling to compromise. Through the pressure that its helplessness elicits from external groups, it becomes a subversive threat to its oppressor's superior power. Finally, as the body vanishes into death, its corporeal frailty conquers its physical master by acquiring transcendent rhetorical life as a martyr. In death, it robustly survives, drawing life from words that memorialize past grievances and give meaning and force to a cause of opposition.

The suffering body's march from personal pain to public symbol requires voices to spread news of its anguish. They must publicize its gradual demise by linking the body's ordeal to a cause and its opposition. The inevitable selectivity of the press in reporting the striker's decline and how the custodians of its fate responded encourages readers to perceive self-inflicted suffering either as emblematic of a decayed body politic or of political blackmail. Insofar as perception functions as reality, framing counts massively, reinforcing existing prejudices and swaying the uncommitted.

These claims are illustrated in the rhetorical power exerted by Irish Republican Army (IRA) inmates in Northern Ireland's Maze Prison at Long Kesh during the late 1970s and early 1980s. Then, the more than 400 IRA prisoners in H-Block engaged in continuous protest through rhetorical displays of their bodies for over four years to have their "special status" as de facto political prisoners restored. Their grievance culminating in the 1981 fast-to-death by Bobby Sands and nine other IRA inmates before the strike was terminated.

Following the surge of guerrilla activity that accompanied the insurgence in Belfast in 1969, the British had established a policy of detention without trial for those arrested for terrorist acts. Prisoners who were members of the Provisional IRA and other groups with Irish Republican sentiments were awarded "special status," which allowed them to be treated as political prisoners. They were segregated from the criminal population, allowed to wear their own clothes, not required to engage in the industrial work of the prison, allowed to congregate among themselves, and permitted to conduct their own educational programs. England reversed its policy of detention without trial in 1976, when it criminalized terrorist acts and established a policy of treating those convicted of such acts as ordinary criminals.

The Criminalization Act provided individuals arrested for terrorist activities with summary trials in which the accused was tried by a judge without benefit of a jury of peers. It further abolished the currency of political motivation from the moral economy of its penal system. These convicts no longer were to be segregated from the criminal population, would be required to wear prison attire, would be assigned to the normal work details with the other prisoners, and would be denied freedom of congregation and freedom to conduct their own educational programs. Men convicted of Republican terrorist acts after March 1, 1976, were to be incarcerated in the recently constructed addition to Maze Prison at Long Kesh, called H-Block, rather than in the older part of the prison, whose configuration permitted greater freedom of movement.

In retaliation against being treated as convicted felons, the prisoners used their bodies for a sustained solidarity strike. First, they engaged in the "blanket" protest, wherein they went naked except for their prison blankets rather than wear standard prison garb. In March 1978, the "blanket" protest escalated to the "no-wash" protest when the authorities refused the Republican prisoners' request for a second towel to conceal their nakedness from their guards while in the washroom. Refusal to visit the washrooms meant that the prisoners had no way to empty their own chamber pots. Their warders refused to empty them and administered beatings instead. The prisoners retaliated by emptying their contents through the spy holes and out the windows of their cells. The officials responded by sealing the spy holes and windows. The prisoners refused to call off their defiance of the authorities and instead escalated the confrontation to a "dirty" protest, in which they disposed of excreta by smearing it on the walls and ceilings of their cells.

The debasement of their bodies became the text for the important voice of Tomas Cardinal Ó Fiaich, who, after visiting the squalor of Long Kesh, wrote a public letter in which he issued a stinging indictment of British policies that had led to these vile internment conditions. He asserted that the men's refusal to wear a prison uniform did not entitle the prison administration to deny them rights to physical exercise, freedom of association, and outside contact. In his view, these were "basic human needs for physical and mental health, not privileges to be granted or withheld as rewards or punishments." He concluded with passionate insistence on a political identity that framed their imprisonment and their voluntary acts of debasement as meaningful claims against the legitimacy of the state:

> The authorities refuse to admit that these prisoners are in a different category from the ordinary, yet everything about their trials and family background indicates that they are different. Special courts without juries sentenced them. The vast majority was convicted on allegedly voluntary confessions which are now placed under grave suspicion by the recent report of Amnesty International. Many are very youthful and come from families which had never been in trouble with the law, though they lived in areas which suffered discrimination in housing and jobs. How can one explain the jump in the prison population of Northern Ireland from 500 to 3,000 unless a new type of prisoner has emerged? (cited in Beresford 1987, 139–140)

In the late fall of 1980, Republican prisoners went on a hunger strike to force concessions on issues such as their right to wear their own clothing, not perform standard prison work, participate in programs of self-education, and communicate regularly with their relatives. In effect, they were striking for de facto reinstatement of their political status. Just before Christmas, as its leader neared death, the strike was aborted in belief that an agreement had been reached. However, the British government claimed that it had not offered to meet the prisoners' demands, and the prisoners, after a month of futile attempts to clarify the confusion, concluded that the government was not going to make the concessions that they thought had been agreed on. Bobby Sands, the Provo prisoners' leader, announced that he would commence a hunger strike to death on March 1, to be followed two weeks later by Frank Hughes and then a few weeks later by more inmates and so on with new inmates taking the place of those who died until their demands were met.[2]

Sands died sixty-six days later on May 5, 1981, having just turned twenty-seven and been elected a member of Parliament. His hunger strike received international press coverage and focused world opinion and anger on Prime Minister Margaret Thatcher and the British government. His death was reported on the front page of newspapers in every major American city and most cities around the world. The newspapers condemning Thatcher included *Le Monde, Izvestia, Hindustan Times, Hong Kong Standard, Noticias* (the semiofficial newspaper of Mozambique), and *Sowetan* (South Africa's mainly black newspaper). Anti-British demonstrations occurred in Antwerp, Athens, Brisbane, Chicago, Ghent, Milan, Oslo, and Paris, among others. The New Jersey State Legislature passed a resolution honoring Sands's "courage and commitment." Teheran announced that the Iranian government would send a representative to the funeral. The Indian parliament split as the opposition stood for a minute of silence in Sands's memory while members of Indira Ghandi's ruling party refused to join in. World leaders, such as Lech Walesa, paid Sands tribute as a "great man who sacrificed his life for his struggle." British targets were bombed in Lisbon, Milan, and Toulouse (Beresford 1987, 98–99; O'Malley 1990, 4).

While governmental bodies elsewhere were questioning the wisdom of Britain's refusal to negotiate an end to Sands's hunger strike, the House of Commons assigned blame for the international furor more to news coverage than misbegotten policy. During the Commons' questions to the prime minister on May 5, 1981 (reported in "Political Status a Licence to Kill," *Times* [London], May 6, 1981, p. 6), a Unionist member of Parliament (MP) from North Down, James Kilfedder, asked Mrs. Thatcher, "Will she do something to win the propaganda battle because foreign television crews are putting out a wrong version of what is happening." In the same article, the "wrong account" was expressed emphatically by Mr. Patrick Duffy, Labour MP from Sheffield, who broke ranks to ask the prime minister, "Is she aware of the widespread impression overseas notably on the part of the *New York Times,* until recently a staunch ally, that the death of Mr. Sands—who the Speaker has already described as a fellow MP—will be due to the Prime Minister's intransigence?" One did not have to travel beyond England and Ireland, however, to capture a sense of the rhetorical power on press coverage wielded by Sands's wasting body. There is good evidence that the framing of Sands's strike in the *Irish Times* provided a basis for its readers to interpret Sands's dying body in ways that supported the prisoners' demands and, incidentally, their interpretation of Anglo-Irish politics. Even the contrasting point of view represented by the *Times* (London) could not muffle the political point that Sands's strike was making.

The initial stages of the strike received relatively light coverage from both the *Irish Times* and the *Times* (London). Still, from its inception, both reported starkly contrasting versions of events that were predictably Republican or Unionist in their emphasis. The *Irish Times* marked the onset of the strike with articles on the activities of supporters and the response by the British government. It reported the comparatively small number of supporters mustered by an IRA rally in Belfast—4,000 versus 10,000 in the fall—to mark the strike's beginning. It speculated that the suspension of the 1980 strike had dampened public enthusiasm for supporting a tactic that was unlikely to succeed. The British government was portrayed as steadfast in ignoring the strike. When Humphrey Atkins, secretary of state for Northern Ireland, repeated to Commons the government's determination never to concede special status, the *Irish Times*'s Martin Cowley reported that he was greeted with applause. No mention was made of the hue and cry that his account raised in Parliament, which was the focus of the reporting by the *Times* (London). Instead, Cowley noted in the *Irish Times* (March 3, 1981, p. 1) that several MPs "made it clear that they did not want frequent statements" and that Atkins "reciprocated with the strong hint" that he had no intention of making them. This Republican perspective framed Sands's body as in callously indifferent hands.

By contrast, on March 4, 1981, an article titled "Government Unmoved by IRA Prisoners" (*Times* [London], p. 8) reported the actual exchanges in Parliament, during which MPs on both sides upbraided Atkins to stop making such statements as "we shall not give way on the issue of political status" and "the Maze prison is one of the most modern in the United Kingdom and . . . compares favorably with any prison anywhere in the world" since they publicized only the IRA's cause. Atkins's reproachment for talking about these matters is indicative of British awareness that

Sands's body was rhetorically potent. From a loyalist perspective, in which Sands's body personified criminal terrorism and was undeserving of public discussion, the policy of not emphasizing the strike itself could be sustained only by ignoring Sands. To talk about him went beyond enumerating the government's reasons for rejecting his claims to political status or reiterating that he was a convicted felon. It meant that one also had to address the fact that the government had his body on its hands, with the insurmountable pathos that his dying frame would soon evoke for some form of accommodation.

The dynamic for press coverage changed dramatically when the sudden death on March 5 of Frank Maguire, MP from Fermanaugh/South Tyrone, required a special election. Two weeks later, with the press still ignoring his strike, the IRA's Executive Committee declared that Sands would stand for the vacant seat. The other Republican candidates withdrew, and the Reverend Ian Paisley's Democratic Unionist Party elected not to field a candidate rather than face embarrassing defeat in a Republican stronghold. The election came down to a two-man contest between Sands and Harry West, official Unionist candidate. When Sands won on April 9, his strike assumed international dimensions. The election effectively fused Sands's dying body with a Republican construction of Northern Ireland's body politic. Coverage by the *Irish Times* lent credence to this interpretation.

Two days after the election, an *Irish Times* article by Thomas Ó Cathoar (April 11, p. 5) normalized the election results by recounting past instances in which a jailed political dissident had been elected to Parliament, both from Fermanaugh/South Tyrone and from other counties in Ireland. Five days later, on April 16, another article analyzing the election, titled "Sands" (p. 8), made the same point and further argued that close scrutiny of election results in the counties where jailed Republicans had been elected in the past showed that voters also had a record of defeating Republicans. According to the article, this indicated that the Sands vote did not reflect a blind Catholic-Nationalist sentiment. Instead, it was "a vote for the specific policy Sands put forward, political status for the prisoners in the H Blocks and Armaugh." The article concluded with a note indicating that much of its material came from a file in the Northern Ireland Public Record Office that had been closed to the public and asked, "Is this because of the rather embarrassing story it reveals?"

The frame of prison reform, not support of terrorism, was buttressed in news reporting of related incidents in which Sands's supporters were confronted by the Royal Ulster Constabulary (RUC). For example, a 3,000-person demonstration by the Trade Union Sub-Committee of the Anti-H-Block Campaign found its April 15 march to the center of Belfast blocked by a large contingent of the RUC and British soldiers:

> When they were stopped in College Square North, on the edge of the city centre, they sat down in the street for half an hour in the bright sunshine to listen to a number of speakers, all of whom emphasised that there should be no confrontation with the security forces.

Stewards then made sure the marchers dispersed peacefully back along Falls Road, the only route left open to them after rows of RUC Land Rovers and armoured cars had sealed off all other routes to the city centre. The only trouble was a little desultory stoning and the burning of a van by a group of youths outside Divis Flats. ("3,000 Stopped," *Irish Times,* April 16, 1981, p. 8)

The depiction of peaceful marchers with responsible leaders sitting in the sun while surrounded by the menacing force of the RUC and British army whose Land Rovers and armored cars sealed off their access to the city center offered a metonomic representation of the Republican version of Sands's strike and the relationship of his frail body to the British authorities with whom they claimed his fate rested. Without compromise by the British, the spectacle of Sands's self-consumption became a corporeal manifestation of his grievance.

Coverage in the *Times* (London) laid its emphasis more on the forgone conclusion that Sands would be elected, given the Catholic majority of Fermanaugh/South Tyrone, and that this would be a propaganda victory for the IRA. After the election, it focused on deliberations within the government and among MPs over whether to unseat Sands and how to interpret the election. Following Sands's victory, the *Times* (London) articles commonly began with "Mr. Robert Sands, Provisional IRA gunman." Having inscribed him as a felon and terrorist and therefore unfit to serve, the implications of Sands's body seated in the House of Commons were seen as grave. The vote for him was depicted both as a blow to moderate Roman Catholic opinion in the Social Democrat and Labour Party (SDLP) and as Catholics laughing at the gravesite of a slain loyalist. Was it a vote for the IRA? against union? for a gunman? for the H-Block issue? Although the focus of the *Times* (London) was decidedly on dampening the propaganda value of his election, these accounts were confronted with the indisputable fact that the voters in Fermanaugh/South Tyrone, who had been reported as going to their polling place out of fear and intimidation, could have spoiled their ballots but chose not to. The voters had made Sands representative of their political aspiration in a way that gave it and him official status. The British government might construe his election in ways that diminished its IRA mandate, but Westminster could no longer ignore him. It had to discuss Sands and the claims for which he stood.

The credibility of Sands's insistence on the need for reform in the H-Block was supported as postelection press coverage steadily became a deathwatch. His deteriorating body increasingly appeared paradigmatic of Anglo-Irish relations in the North. Following the election, the international press carried the continuing story of his steady physical decline, including appeals by his supporters who spoke of Long Kesh as a "concentration camp" and excoriated the colonial practices of England as at the root of Sands's protest and "the troubles" of the North (*Washington Post,* April 21, 1981, C3).

On April 21, the *Irish Times* began counting the number of days that Sands had been fasting and reporting medical accounts of his deteriorating condition. Although it quoted some local voices dissenting from the publicity being given to Sands's hunger strike in comparison to that accorded victims of IRA terrorism, the reporting by the *Irish Times* more typically fused his dying body with the issue of political status. Its coverage framed Sands's strike in terms of the prison reform issue. In that context, British refusal to accommodate Sands appeared heartlessly stubborn. Over the following two weeks, it also reported a steady stream of visits by world leaders, representatives of the International Commission for Human Rights, a papal nuncio, local clergy, and public figures such as Ramsey Clark and Father Joseph Barrigan, who issued statements denouncing terrorism while urging Great Britain to find a reasonable accommodation to the long-standing dispute in the H-Block. Despite Thatcher's point that Sands could save his own life by calling off the strike, the frames of the election as a mandate for prison reform and international concern directed to the Northern Ireland Office (NIO) and Thatcher for humanitarian response legitimated Sands's claim that his cause was just and reasonable, as England's was not.

As death neared, Sands's body, frail and wasted, grew in its capacity to provoke heated exchange as a source of competing political interpretation between the British and Republican Irish moral economies. Starting on April 16, one week after he was elected and immediately after Westminster determined not to unseat him through May 8, when Sands was buried, the *Times* (London) ran fifteen articles reporting violence or fear of violence precipitated by Sands's fast to death. For the *Times* (London) reader, Sands's dying body was not framed as the exemplar of an Irish body politic but of a terrorist group that brought only strife, bloodshed, and grief to Ulster. For example, the *Times* (London) of May 2 reported that Secretary of State Atkins accused the IRA of planning to provoke sectarian warfare in the event of Sands's death, including evacuation of a section of Belfast so that they could burn the houses and then blame it on Protestant parliamentarians. This was met with ridicule by those in the neighborhood in question, who, Catholics all and involved with the IRA, marveled at being suspected of plotting to burn their own houses. As a further example, in a *Times* (London) letter to the editor (May 20, p. 15), General Sir John Hackett rhetorically obliterated the geopolitical identity of Ireland as he wondered, "When was Ireland in any real sense ever united, even before the cruel liquidation of native Catholic Irish in Ulster, its most recalcitrant kingdom, and their replacement by Protestant lowland Scots? . . . 'Ireland' has long been little more than a geographical expression, a name on what happens to be an island."

For his supporters, the symbiosis of Bobby Sands's body with the body politic expressed their struggle for Irish self-determination. For the British, Robert Sands was a convicted felon whose body had no meaning beyond his individual person. For Republicans, Bobby Sands was struggling for the Irish right to self-organization. For the British, he relinquished that right when he engaged in criminal acts. To spare him amounted to legitimizing this claim and relinquishing the state's authority over his body as a convicted criminal. The rhetoric of Sands's hunger strike advanced a politics of absolutes: absolute helplessness, absolute power to spare another's life, absolute adherence to the law, nonnegotiable principles of political right, nonnegotiable principles of human rights, and nonnegotiable principles of control. It left no middle ground for compromise positions.

Without compromise, the spectacle of Sands's self-consumption became a corporeal manifestation of his grievance. Regardless of what the British might say in response, Sands's body fixed the world's gaze on Britain's unyielding stance in the face of a clamor for civil accommodations. The swell of sentiment for the government to end the crisis reflected Britain's inability to silence Sands's emaciated and dying body or to deflect its claim that its fate lay in British hands. Thus, as his body diminished, its rhetorical incarnation grew, touching the conscience of ever enlarging circles of society and crossing national boundaries until its plea for civility became colossal. Sands's body had become a literal manifestation of the rhetorical topos of magnification; as words increased his wasting body's moral weight and enlarged its mass to span continents, its frail physical form metamorphosed into a mighty moral invocation that advanced his demands while questioning the legitimacy of masters unwilling to compromise.

Finally, as Sands's body sank into death, *Irish Times* coverage (May 8, pp. 1, 8) constructed a narrative of his corporeal frailty conquering his physical master's domination by acquiring transcendent rhetorical life. In death, his body was claimed by the IRA and given a military funeral. Thousands of mourners were reported to line the three-mile route from the church to the graveyard while thousands more paraded behind the cortege. His coffin was draped with the tricolors and a barrette and glove symbolic of a slain soldier. A lone piper playing a dirge led the funeral procession. At one point, the procession stopped while IRA soldiers, dressed in military garb, fired three rifle volleys in salute. At the graveside, Owen Curron, Sands's election agent, eulogized him as "a hero in the struggle that will drive the British out of our country for once and for all" (*Irish Times,* May 8, pp. 1, 8). He quoted Sands's words from the *Republican News:* "They may hold our bodies but while our minds are free, victory is assured." Sands's death was "a cruel murder" that marked "a watershed in Irish history." His hunger fast was eulogized for having achieved lasting meaning for all Ireland. Curron praised Sands as "a symbol of Irish resistance . . . a symbol of hope for the poor, the oppressed and homeless and for those divided by partition. . . . We have never surrendered and we never shall. . . . We haven't got tanks and guns, but, please God, it won't always be so. We must take what they will not give" (*Irish Times,* May 8, pp. 1, 8). In death, Sands's body survived with rhetorical robustness that drew life from words that memorialized past grievances and that gave meaning and force to a cause of opposition. He was now the paradigm for the Republican cause. He had become a martyr; he had become immortal.

WOMEN'S STORIES AS ANECDOTAL EVIDENCE

In contrast with the rhetorical potency of the hunger striker's body, women's appeals concerning episodes of sexual violence provoked by their attacker's consumption of pornography have difficulty escaping their local, even personal context. One source of evidence for this claim is the disparity in the press discussion accorded fictive works dealing with this issue. For example, Rosa Eberly (1993) has compared press discussion of Andrea Dworkin's *Mercy* and Bret Easton Ellis's *American Psycho*. Her detailed examination of the argumentative strategies of Dworkin and her critics in the literary public sphere underscores the disparity in treatment of voice on sexual abuse of women. Ellis's protagonist engages in serial acts of violence so extreme that Simon & Schuster reneged on its contract at the last minute, forfeiting its advance of several hundred thousand dollars rather than bring it to print, only to have Vintage acquire the book two days later. Nor did Ellis's content, "interpreted as an implicit argument for men to rape, kill and dismember women" (Eberly 1993, 276), deter the arbiters of literary merit from engaging in serious debate in the literary public sphere, with more than seventy reviews and feature stories, including no less a Brahman than Norman Mailer, who declared that it indeed was worthy of serious literary consideration (Eberly 2000). Dworkin's *Mercy* is no less consumed by graphic details of sexual violence. However, her point of view, militantly feminist, which by novel's end has its protagonist, Andrea, calling for random killing of men and embarking on a life of guerrilla warfare, had difficulty gaining the attention of the literary public sphere, with a scant eleven reviews.

Dworkin's difficulty in getting her voice heard is of a piece with the striking difficulty of the women's voices that had appeared before the Meese Commission. The Commission's *Final Report,* published in 1986, is in two volumes of nearly 2,000 pages (United States Attorney General's Commission, Pornography 1986). Individual statements by the commissioners, occupying nearly 200 pages, are followed by a 218-page statement written by Frederick Schauer, a commission member and professor of law at the University of Michigan, and endorsed by the other members. The Schauer statement offers the commission's analysis and argument. A section that specifies ninety-two recommendations to curb the spread of pornography follows this. The remaining 1,500 pages consist of selected testimony and evidence, excerpts from pornography, summaries of pornographic books and movies, a rather extensive bibliography of pornographic literature and videos, and photos of the commission in action. These materials, composed by the commission staff and more strident in tone and less thoughtful in analysis, led commission member Judith Becker to advise readers to stop on completing Schauer's report. Were readers to focus on the first quarter of the two-volume document, or its initial 458 pages, they might conclude that it was attempting to present balanced and responsible analysis and recommendations (Vance 1986, 78).

The version of the report portrayed in the American press, however, was anything but balanced and responsible. Although sparsely covered by television, the report became a source of national debate at the newsstand. Its notoriety was attributable principally to American Civil Liberties Union attorney Barry Lynn, who, as a self-appointed commission watchdog, followed the panel to each location, securing court orders for the release of information and providing the working press with a steady stream of information and quotable interviews. From its inception through the *Final Report*'s reception and debate in the press, Lynn successfully galvanized a portrayal of the Attorney General's Commission as an object of suspicion to the liberal community, as anathema to the publishing industry, and as a palpable threat to the civil liberties of the average American.

The press version of the report transformed it from a framing statement for pornography as a public problem that required local dialogue, community attention, and citizen action into an attack on the First Amendment. Elsewhere, I have detailed the way in which press accounts reframed the discussion from harms to women and children into the scientific validity of the commission's findings (Hauser 1999). In summary, mitigating factors of commissioner bias, a skewed evidentiary base, and a lack of demonstrated causality between consumption of pornography and subsequent behavior were summoned to support the press claim that the report was an attempt to legitimate censorship. Significantly absent in this account were the actual voices of women who claimed to be victims of physical abuse in a context where their attacker was enacting a sexual fantasy found in a pornographic portrayal.

For adherents to the scientized epistemology of modernism, the objectivist/relativist binary dictated that the evidence of women who had been sexually assaulted in a context involving consumption of pornography was deeply flawed. For example, the binary suggested that the general indictment of magazines such as *Hustler* as a cause of sexual violence was an oversimplification at best. Were it true, the several million monthly readers of these publications would have constituted a massive public menace, not to mention the corrosive effects on the commissioners who were steeped in far worse for a full year.

Press accounts and commentaries skipped over witness testimony by abused women to focus on the commission and its agenda. Press coverage emphasized the activities of the commission itself and its recommendations, not the testimony of commission witnesses. As the commission and its actions became the focal point of the story, it framed commentaries depicting the commission as engaged in an ideological witch-hunt. Doubtless these opponents found little rhetorical advantage in challenging victim accounts of overwhelmingly vicious attacks. However, equally, since the press essentially refocused the discussion from the public and personal harms inspired by pornography to the threat posed by a "witch-hunting" committee, the attending public had little chance to connect with the pathos of these accounts because they were seldom publicized.

I have consulted accounts in the *New York Times, Washington Post, Los Angeles Times,* major newsweeklies, and other magazines that reported and commented on the commission's work. The more than 250 news stories and commentaries that I examined contained not a single verbatim report of a woman's testimony. The few mentions of witnesses that did appear characterized them in a way that reflected more on the commission as a source of controversy than on those who testified to tell their stories. For example, Carole Vance asserted, "The commission's 300-plus hours of public hearings and business meetings featured zany, if unintended, comedy: vice cops, born again Christians and prosecutors thundering indictments of pornography and its progeny" (Vance 1986, 65). Testimony that was reported typically was by contrite men whose accounts of sexual depravity involved admissions of alcohol and drug abuse at the time of their acts or stories so extreme in their perversity that the reader was invited to suspect that the person had a psychological disorder. In these cases, the stories were treated as anecdotes that failed to establish a causal relationship between the consumption of pornography and sexual violence. Tragic as any individual case may have been, it came to the reader through the filtering process of press and commentator or special interest voice intent on debunking the commission's work as inquisitional.

The women who testified lost control of their story; readers of press accounts were not engaged *by* the plight of their bodies but by redacted versions that were *about* their plight. Unlike Sands, who used his body to make a point that fused his pain with the problem of IRA prisoner treatment in H-Block and that was publicized as such, these sexually abused bodies had neither elected to be harmed nor benefited from the principle of publicity to present their pain directly through news accounts and discussion. Rather than a discourse *of* the body, it was *about* the body, presented to readers at a distance several steps removed from their physical pain. It was a discourse about words and images whose consequences were subject to myriad interpretations.

The bodies depicted in sexually explicit materials, ranging from erotica to obscene depictions of abuse and degradation of the subjugated partner, initiated a complex discourse difficult to confine to any single overriding issue. Was the question of pornography really about freedom to engage in erotic expression, about violence, or about public health? These alternatives framed pornography and sexual violence as a public problem requiring technical discourse among expert elites: lawyers and jurists, ethicists, psychiatrists, publishers, researchers, and official entities. These expert and special interest groups, not the victims, were owners of the public problem, meaning they defined the critical issues and controlled the discussion (Gusfield 1981). They, not the victims themselves, controlled the victims' narrative. In turn, the victims' inability to control their narrative or its treatment as merely a personal story diminished its evidentiary status. Within the frames of the commission itself and free speech, press accounts interpreted their plight as a form of bodily insufficiency subordinate to scientific criteria of causality for justifying state action. Their bodies' synecdochic representation of the issue was lost as others appropriated their stories as merely one more datum to consider. This public insufficiency prevented their bodies' assertions of pain from becoming paradigmatic in a way that might compel social action (Hauser 1999). Quite the contrary, the issue of sexual acts inspired by pornography could be inserted into benign contexts, such as Sallie Tisdale's defense of erotica, *Talk Dirty to Me: An Intimate Philosophy of Sex* (1994), which challenged the negative interpretation of pornography's consequences.

Tisdale's and the commission's contrasting interpretations of women's bodies in the context of pornography reflect an instability of signification that opens accounts of these bodies to multiple readings. Their range of meaning denies them the force of Sands's public suffering and the press' identification of the hunger striker's body with his political cause. This difference is more than that between a body that is symbolic of a political cause and a body that is the victim of a crime. For example, a public furor arose in 1990 and 1991 over the brutal rape and assault of a young Wall Street executive while she was jogging in New York's Central Park. New Yorkers identified her body with the city's prototypical success story. Her body spawned a discourse of class and race that polarized the city along lines, as Joan Didion (1991) argues, closely related to how the story was reported by the New York press.

Equally, the testimony of Bosnian women before Helsinki Watch to their systematic rape by their Serbian captors received wide publicity and endorsement as evidence of war crimes that validated UN intervention (Tindemans 1996). In the case of Bosnia, the Western press framed these rapes as part of Serbia's virulent anti-Muslim discourse that portrayed them as Christ slayers who had to be purged from the land. The juxtaposition of these violated bodies with Serbian rhetoric preaching a policy of ethnic cleansing escalated international furor and eventuated in charges of war crimes brought against the Bosnian Serb military leaders. It also strengthened the resolve of NATO to use military force when Serbia seemed determined to repeat history in Kosovo.

In both these cases, molested bodies were framed by larger identities that transcended the specific violence and were represented by it. Unlike the stories of particular women whose pain is confined to their personal trauma, theirs was a public pain, presented to and experienced by the larger community they had come to represent. Their bodies spoke a rhetorical language that grounded the historicity of a city and a people they had come to exemplify as no anecdotal representation possibly could. Certainly, other factors also contributed to the differences in public sentiment evoked by the Meese Commission witnesses and the Muslim women or the Central Park jogger. However, chief among them surely must be how their pain was reported.

CONCLUSION

Bodily anguish makes claims on our compassion. Publicized, it becomes a rhetorical statement urging sympathetic response to end its suffering and safeguard its well-being. As with all rhetoric, its capacity to move is neither vaguely generic nor general but tied to its status as a particular case. In its particularity, its pain is its own. Yet, as its pain makes its worldly appearance as inflicted by an oppressive other, its relief becomes the possibility of concerted response. Relationships can be altered, and how the attending public understands its particularity bears directly on the body's evocative power to instigate change.

Aristotle's *On Rhetoric* (1991) discusses *paradigma* as the use of particular cases to influence the audience's judgment. In most cases, he observes, the particular case serves as familiar evidence drawn from the audience's experience to exemplify the point being made. Its illustrative character makes it a form of support. However, on occasion, when there is no ready premise to bring the audience to a sound judgment, particulars can serve as the primary argument. In such cases, he held, particulars assume paradigmatic strength. In more recent times, Chaïm Perelman and Lucie Olbrechts-Tyteca (1969, 350–371) point out that in these cases where the particular goes beyond the argumentative function of illustration to actually make the rhetor's case, they serve as models articulating the shape of the world and how we might be in it. Particulars can so exemplify a point or mode of conduct that it serves as a model.

The hunger strike can satisfy this paradigmatic function through its potential to be a lightning rod for the energy of public discussion. By calling society and the world to witness its grueling anorexic ordeal, the starving body can alter the public currency for assessing its master's worth. Public starvation posits civility as a fundamental coin of the political realm, as the fundamental ethical basis on which a society organizes itself. The prisoner of conscience, finding his voice silenced, can speak with his body. As his acts of resistance are punished, the authorities risk the danger of an outside world, incensed by the eloquence of a body in pain, finding that body's suffering representative of a misguided political structure. As dangerous as a political prisoner is alive, he is more dangerous martyred and dead.

Conversely, sexual violence is not typically enacted in public. Women's stories of pain inflicted outside the glare of publicity are accounts of personal experience. They are not part of a common experience whose reality each observer must acknowledge. Without a frame that gives them some paradigmatic value, they are susceptible to being received as merely anecdotal. The stories of battered and raped women who have been subjected to horrendous forms of degradation and humiliation are urgent pleas by bodies in pain for a civil society's compassionate intervention. However, her transportability to multiple contexts makes each woman's story just a story. Ultimately, the inability to control their narrative or its treatment as a personal story and, therefore, its evidentiary status prevents this rhetoric of the body from becoming paradigmatic in a way that compels social action.

Our public experience of the body in pain is part of a larger historical and cultural dialogue on the body. In this dialogue, the bodies of the hunger striker and the sexually assaulted differ in their capacity to control their own bodies, to end or continue their pain, to author their own public narrative of what they experience or to have it co-opted, to make their pain symptomatic of a larger issue or to have it reduced to their personal story, or to engage us with and by their pain or with a story about it. These differences in authorial capacity are further inflected by press coverage that frames their anguish. Despite the inherently rhetorical situated and particular discourse that these bodies in pain speak, they are unable to speak their own meaning unassisted. Their claims acquire traction on public imagination as they are cast in a public language that articulates their specific vulnerability and need for our response. If their claims are foremost to the immediacy of their circumstances, ultimately they seek to make their bodies paradigmatic through their fusion with a larger cause. By fusing their pain with the power that has caused it and by making us witness to it, they pose the ominous burden of self-indictment should we remain inactive when we have the power to act. How we hear and respond to them is influenced by how the press frames them as particular cases.

NOTES

1. Aristotle's *On Rhetoric: A Theory of Civil Discourse* (1991) counsels that *paradigma* is one of two modes of rhetorical arguments; it is a rhetorical induction that argues from part to part. Usually, the term *paradigma* is translated as "example," and Aristotle holds that in most cases the example should be employed as a form of illustration properly used after an enthymeme, or rhetorical syllogism, has been constructed. However, in some cases, when enthymemes are not available, the argument proper is made through the rich example, or the paradigm case. For a discussion of this doctrine in Aristotle, see Hauser (1968, 1985).

2. The IRA prisoners made five demands, which would have given them the same treatment as political prisoners and were the manifest cornerstone of the hunger strike. Padraig O'Malley (1990, 3) summarizes them as follows: "the right to wear their own clothes; to refrain from prison work; to associate freely with one another; to organize recreational facilities and to have one letter, visit, and parcel a week; and to have lost remission time restored."

10

Media Portrayal of "Second Wave" Feminist Groups

Anne Costain and Heather Fraizer

Adding the voices of new and challenging groups to ongoing democratic discourse is what keeps the public sphere inclusive and allows it to represent changing trends in the broader public. This process is particularly important in the case of social movements, for they form to foster social change by educating people and challenging social and political institutions. For this to happen democratically, they must initiate a dialogue with citizens and politicians. When movements enter the political arena, typically, their best-organized groups and the leaders of those groups soon become more visible and better known to the public than the movement's more loosely structured network of activists and sympathizers. This occurs, in part, because the mass media cover news by interviewing spokespersons for organizations. For example, when an abortion clinic is bombed, a substantial portion of the media coverage focuses on the meaning of the bombing as interpreted by leaders of pro-choice and pro-life groups. The size and complexity of American society virtually dictate that movements work through the mass media to gain this kind of influence. Thus, entrepreneurial leaders of social movements court the press as a means to publicize their causes.

Women have remained a powerful interest that is frequently consulted by the U.S. media despite the fact that the protest phase of the women's movement declined throughout the 1980s and 1990s. The "second wave" women's movement in the United States arose in the mid-1960s as one among many protest movements that defined that era socially and politically.[1] The mid-1970s saw the movement reach a peak of press coverage before beginning to lose ground with the defeat of the proposed Equal Rights Amendment (ERA) to the U.S. Constitution in 1982 (Costain 1992, 79–99). Yet, while the highly mobilized "protest" phase of the women's movement lost momentum, far from disappearing from public view, the movement transformed itself into an effective actor in the arenas of interest group and electoral politics (see Costain 1983, 1992; Gelb and Palley 1987; Schlozman 1990; Spalter-Roth and Schreiber 1995). This period, when protest movements give way to the more routine representation of their interests, is frequently a time when the press will ignore or downplay the importance of both the movement and its issues. Since few movements have been as successful in making the transition from a social movement to a mainstream lobbying and voting bloc as the women's movement, this research looks at the press's role in allowing this adaptation.[2]

The media play a huge role in shaping the content of American political discussion (Gamson 1992; McCombs and Shaw 1972; Page and Shapiro 1989). Much has been written about biases in the media and their effect on citizens' political positions (Ansolabehere, Behr, and Iyengar 1993; Iyengar 1987; Iyengar, Peters, and Kinder 1982). Several studies have demonstrated that media coverage does not necessarily tell citizens what to think, but it does tell them what to think about (Iyengar et al. 1982; Rochon 1998; Zaller 1996). Newspapers and television play central roles in making citizens aware of which national movements and controversies are most influential in American politics (Tarrow 1994). The influence of movements seems to depend a great deal on the ability of its leaders and organizations to communicate an appealing vision of the movement's issues and goals to the public through the media.

Thomas Rochon's (1998) theory of culture shift develops the links between movements and the media. He asserts that although changes in values or norms are generated and grow first within a critical community of scholars or scientists, once new language and concepts are well developed, a social movement becomes the principal agent for its social diffusion.[3] Movements spread the new values or norms by mobilizing individuals, educating the public, and pressuring the political and social systems to accept change (Rochon 1998). The position of the media is pivotal for movement success since most people learn of events outside their direct experience from the mass media. As a result, "would-be agents of cultural change must be centrally concerned with their relationship to the mass media" (Rochon 1998, 177). Successful social movements recognize the critical agenda-setting and agenda-building functions of the media (Rochon 1998, 178).

Accepting the importance of this connection between social movements, groups within them, their leaders, and the media, we ask what kind of coverage second-wave feminist groups received in the press and how the message coming from them was spread. Since the women's movement has had significant influence on U.S. political culture and public policy, its treatment by the press may be viewed as both a model for other movements to follow and an example of media facilitation of social change (Rochon 1998, 165–199; see also Gelb 1995; Gelb and Palley 1987). A number of specific questions guide our analysis. How has the elite press characterized groups growing out of the women's movement that emerged in the mid-1960s, often referred to as "second wave" feminist groups? Is this coverage, on balance, negative and denigrative, neutral, or supportive? Does it change over time? What movement policy issues are conveyed through the media? Do some movement groups receive more favorable coverage than others? Can this persist over many years? To what extent is reporting determined by external occurrences? Does involvement with particular U.S. political institutions yield more access and press coverage than with others? Finally, what is the image of the movement that remains after its more passionate and volatile early period has passed?

REPRESENTING FEMINIST GROUPS

Our data consist of the 1,852 articles, published between 1980 and 1996 in the *New York Times,* that make specific reference to one or more of the nine second-wave feminist groups chosen to represent the most recent national women's movement.[4] We used Lexis-Nexis as the searching mechanism to find these articles. The complete text was then downloaded from Lexis-Nexis. During this period, the number of articles in the *Times* mentioning these second-wave women's groups ranged from a low of 55 in 1996 to a high of 168 in 1984. We then entered the full texts into Q.S.R Nudist, a content analysis program that permits searches for patterns of language within texts.

To divide the data set into favorable and unfavorable references to specific groups and their issues, we searched for articles containing the following words and phrases: "reform," "rebuild," "fight discrimination," "progressive," "better," "improve," "improvement," "productive," "success," "successful," "effective," "well organized," and "constructive." We likewise searched for critical words, including the following: "radical," "extreme," "disruptive," "confrontational," "destructive," "counterproductive," "setback," "fail," "disorganized," "controversial," "staid," and "stodgy." Although in many cases these descriptors did not characterize the groups themselves, their proximity to group references can be assumed to create either a positive or a negative association with the organization. For example, if an article discusses an issue favored by one of our groups promoting "reform of rape laws" or an effort "to fight discrimination based on gender in employment," the context is far different from an article that discusses "a failed attempt to win legislative passage of the Equal Rights Amendment" or a "controversial proposal to draft women." As a check, to make sure that we were not pulling up the same articles under both positive and negative categories, we examined cross listings and counted how many articles were coded under both. Only 3 articles of the 922 total that contain at least one positive or negative descriptor (or less than one-half of 1 percent) fell under both positive and negative categories. This indicates that although most coverage (930 articles) is neither positive nor negative, the inclusion of either type of language normally precludes use of the other. With this coding, we describe changes in both the number of articles and their portrayal over time.

We were also interested in variations in the issues covered during this seventeen-year period. We used the following words to identify issue areas. "Abortion and antiabortion" proved to be simple descriptors that flagged abortion issues. "School, teacher, and education" were used to identify education issues. Topics concerning work and economics were isolated with the words "employ," "job," "work," and "economic." Finally, we uncovered civil rights stories using "civil rights," "equal rights," "discrimination," and "Equal Rights Amendment." We examined yearly coverage for each issue area. This allowed us to track fluctuations by issue over time. We then determined the extent to which each issue was presented by the press in a positive or negative light and how this varied across time.

We similarly considered how coverage of particular second-wave women's groups changed over time. Because such a high proportion of the articles mentioned the National Organization for Women (NOW), we wound up comparing coverage of NOW with treatment of all eight of the other groups. Alternatives would have created more volatility in the analysis because of the small numbers of articles in most years mentioning any single group other than NOW. These data, along with other studies that have been done, provide empirical evidence of NOW's high profile in the news coverage featuring women's movement groups. This meant that much of the public's impression of the women's movement during this period was based on NOW.

Because positive and negative descriptors are only one method through which the news can convey a positive or a negative image to the public, we also contrasted the incorporation of a family frame of reference that was heavily promoted by the countermovement that arose to challenge the goals of the women's movement, with articles treating women as a more autonomous social group. Family descriptors were identified using the words "mother," "father," "family," "families," and "children."

Finally, we considered the political involvement of women's movement groups with national political institutions. Were these organizations gaining access to national debates and policy decision making primarily through one institution or through many? To find which articles referred to Congress, we used "Congress" and "congressional" in word searches. For the presidency, we used "president" and "presidential." Particularly the use of "president" created problems not encountered in the Congress search. "President" falsely identified articles discussing the presidents of many interest groups, labor unions, boroughs in New York City, and foreign leaders. Also, "president" picked up a large number of references to U.S. vice presidents and vice presidential candidates. To correct for these false finds, we read through the language surrounding "president" and removed articles making no reference to current or former American presidents. Because the use of the word "court" alone created even more problems than "president," we conducted our search for involvement of the judiciary using just "Supreme Court." In examining these articles on second-wave groups and political institutions, we were especially interested in which issues and events brought the movement into closest contact with the institutions of government.

BIAS IN THE NEWS

Figure 10.1 shows how many articles the *New York Times* published each year mentioning these second-wave feminist groups, along with the balance between positive and negative coverage. The number of articles referencing these groups has declined slightly over time—from an average of 107 articles per year in the 1980s to 100 in the 1990s. Despite this decrease in overall coverage, the extent to which positive mentions outnumber negative ones remains quite steady throughout the period. Thus, although there are fewer articles in the *Times* for the public to read, the overall positive impression conveyed to the public has remained fairly constant. This view is reinforced by examining the proportional balance of positive and negative articles (figure 10.2). The shaded area shows the size of the gap between favorable and unfavorable coverage, with consistently 15 to 25 percent more positive than negative stories throughout the period.

VARIATION AMONG ISSUES

After this initial yearly division of the articles, we then split them into four issue content areas: abortion, economics/jobs, education, and civil rights (figure 10.3). The numbers sum to more than the total since many of the articles address multiple issues and consequently are counted more than once. While reporting on economic and education issues remained relatively constant throughout the decades, the number of features covering civil rights and abortion varied widely. In the 1980s,

Figure 10.1   Balance between positive and negative coverage in the *New York Times*, 1980–1996

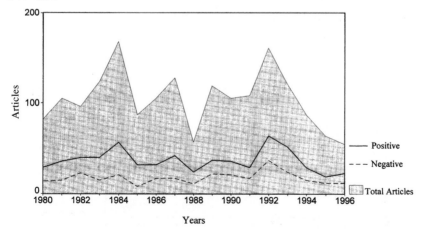

Figure 10.2   Proportion of positive and negative coverage in the *New York Times,*
1980–1996

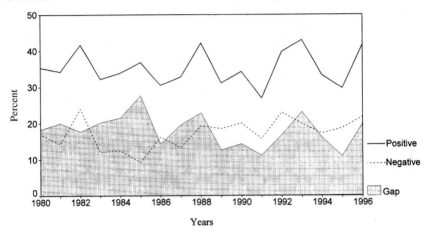

many of the articles dealt with the civil rights of women. This civil rights focus continued even after the final defeat of the ERA in 1982. In fact, 1984 had the largest number of civil rights articles in the period (sixty-nine). However, by the 1990s rights was the least reported-on category in this data set. Abortion replaced civil rights as the issue most likely to be written about. The number of abortion articles peaked at eighty-five in 1992.

Because abortion has always generated so much public controversy, we expected that the media would employ more negative language covering it than they did on the other topics examined. In fact, although there was a closer balance between

Figure 10.3   *New York Times* coverage by issue, 1980–1996

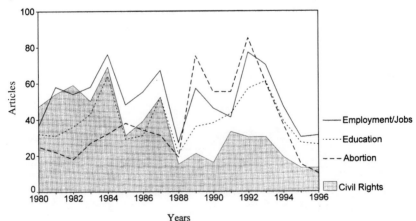

Figure 10.4   Positive and negative coverage of abortion, 1980–1996

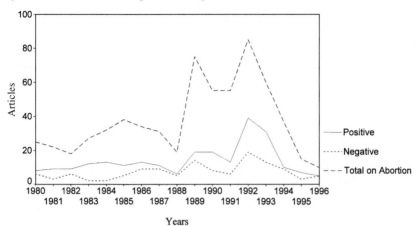

positive and negative articles on abortion than on other issues examined, as figure 10.4 shows, there was no year during this seventeen-year span when negative articles dealing with abortion outnumbered positive ones. This was particularly surprising since "controversial" was one of the negative descriptors used. On its face, one would imagine that many articles on abortion would refer to controversy. Yet civil rights has nearly as close a balance between positive and negative references as abortion. (Abortion had 235 positive articles and 124 negative ones. The comparable figures for civil rights were 237 positive and 108 negative.) One might also expect that the failure of the ERA to win ratification in 1982 would explain much of the negative civil rights coverage. Yet figure 10.5 shows that the close balance between negative

Figure 10.5   Positive and negative coverage of civil rights, 1980–1996

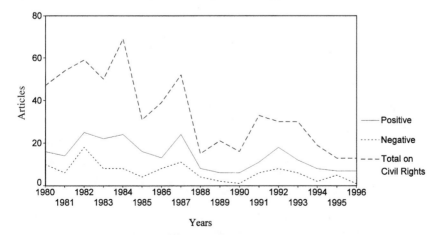

Figure 10.6   Positive and negative coverage of employment, 1980–1996

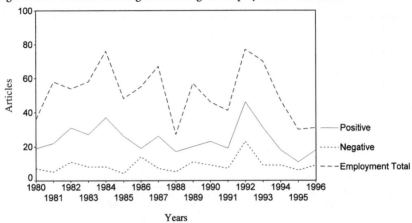

and positive mentions on civil rights issues continued throughout the 1990s. These findings reinforce those from an earlier study showing that throughout the period of the modern women's movement, legal equality for women was more controversial than many public policies aimed at women's special needs, including education, child care, and employment issues (Costain 1992, 123).

Figure 10.6, showing the *Times*'s coverage of jobs and economic issues, departs from this relatively close mix of positive and negative treatment that characterized abortion and civil rights issues. Discussion of women's employment and working conditions had consistently more positive coverage throughout this period. The pattern for education issues is strikingly similar, with the vast majority of the coverage positive, especially during the 1990s (figure 10.7). In summary, the less volatile

Figure 10.7   Positive and negative coverage of education, 1980–1996

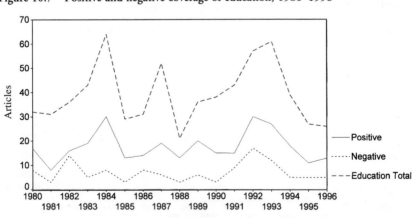

and thus more enduring women's issues throughout these decades are also those presented in the most consistently positive light.

DEPICTION OF INDIVIDUAL GROUPS

NOW was the first national group to organize as part of the second wave of feminism. The decisive event creating NOW occurred at the Third Annual Conference of the Commissions on the Status of Women, held in Washington, D.C., in 1966. This conference brought together representatives of all the state commissions on women's status with those active in the National Commission on Women's Status. Catherine East had invited feminist Betty Friedan to attend. Friedan's book *The Feminine Mystique* had sparked a national discussion of women's discontent popularly referred to by the terminology used in the book as the "problem that has no name" (Friedan 1963). When Wisconsin state delegate Kathryn Clarenbach was told that she could not offer resolutions supporting reappointment of Richard Graham as a commissioner for the Equal Employment Opportunity Commission (EEOC) or asking for stronger enforcement of the ban on sex discrimination in employment in the 1964 Civil Rights Act, those became catalytic events. Clarenbach and Friedan, along with thirteen other women, met in Friedan's hotel room and organized the National Organization for Women. By the end of the Conference on the Commissions on the Status of Women, there was a new group, called NOW, with Betty Friedan as its first president and twenty-eight members from across the United States.

NOW remains the largest and most influential of the second-wave feminist groups. Although we included a number of organizations that focus on women's issues—ranging from radical groups such as SCUM (Society to Cut Up Men) to single-issue groups such as the National Abortion and Reproductive Rights Action League (NARAL) to groups with a reputation for moderation such as the Women's Equity Action League (WEAL)—the group that consistently attracted the most press coverage during this period was NOW. Figure 10.8 shows the proportion of all the second-wave articles that mention NOW. The intensity of this focus on NOW can be explained, at least in part, by the organization's size and broad goals. Throughout the period, it has remained the largest and nationally most active women's group. It has continued to pursue its initial objective, namely, to engage in "action to bring women into full participation in the mainstream of society now, exercising all the privileges and responsibilities thereof in truly equal partnership with men" (Slavin 1995, 403–404). By contrast, most of the other national groups have more narrow foci. For example, the National Women's Political Caucus was started and continues to apply pressure to increase the numbers of women in elective and appointive political offices. NARAL, as its name implies, works almost exclusively on abortion issues. Federally Employed Women promotes the interests of women employed by the federal government. Because NOW is engaged in a broader range of issues than

Figure 10.8   Coverage mentioning NOW and all coverage, 1980–1996

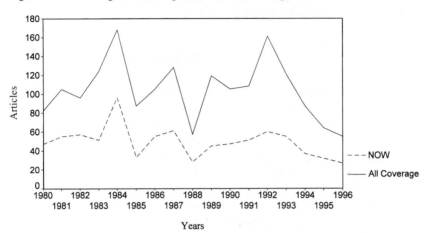

these other groups, it makes sense that the media would more frequently turn to its leaders to comment on a variety of news events.

Examining the balance between positive and negative articles featuring NOW gives another perspective on this coverage. As figures 10.9 and 10.10 show, throughout the period, NOW alone is referred to as frequently as all the other second-wave women's groups combined. In each year of our study, there are more positive than negative articles about both NOW and the cluster of other organizations. Yet NOW's coverage, on balance, is slightly less positive than that of the other groups taken together. As significantly, NOW's advantage in news coverage throughout the 1980s declined in the 1990s as other groups began to command more press attention. It

Figure 10.9   Positive and negative articles mentioning NOW, 1980–1996

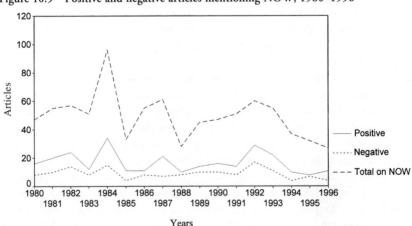

Figure 10.10   Positive and negative articles mentioning groups other than NOW,
1980–1996

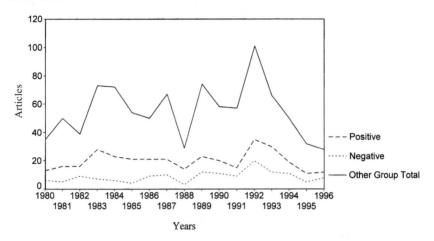

appears that NOW as the first, largest, and most active second-wave feminist organization formed the cutting edge on issues in the 1980s. As the women's movement
became more institutionalized in the 1990s, NOW's influence began to be overshadowed by other more specialized and perhaps less tactically confrontational women's
groups.

EVENTS THAT DRIVE COVERAGE

As issues and specific organizations shaped the coverage of the women's movement
by the mass media, events also drove the news. Figure 10.11 provides a time line of
the dominant news stories from this data set. In the 1980s, the leading features were
the defeat of the ERA, debate over the abortion issue, the increasing number of
women in elective office (including the Democratic party's nomination of Geraldine
Ferraro to run as vice presidential candidate with Walter Mondale in 1984), and the
emergence of a gender gap in voting. In many respects, the 1989 Supreme Court
decision *Webster v. Reproductive Health Services* (109 S.Ct. 3040), which greatly increased states' options to discourage and restrict legal access to abortion, was the
watershed event dividing the 1980s from the 1990s.

   In the 1990s, controversy over abortion escalated in the wake of the *Webster* decision, which reopened the question of whether there was a constitutionally guaranteed right for women to decide to have an abortion. In addition, the charges of
sexual harassment aired by Anita Hill at the confirmation hearings for Supreme Court
nominee Clarence Thomas focused attention on sex discrimination within the work-
place. The elections of 1992 were dubbed the "Year of the Woman," as an unprec-

Figure 10.11 Events time table

1980	1981	1982	1983
Older women mobilize and are more active (older women's league [OWL])	Legal controversy surrounding extension of ERA	Legal dispute over ERA extension	President Reagan chooses woman to head Department of Health and Human Services
Controversy over government funding of abortion	Discussion of sex discrimination in education and Title IX	Lose ERA	Gender gap becomes wider
Women have record number of seats in Congress	Politics surrounding state regulation of abortion	Focus on women winning political office	Women's pay equity, "comparable worth" theory asserted
Reagan elected—boosts liberal surge women's mobilization	Congress debates ways of bypassing *Roe v. Wade*	Abortion mobilization on both sides	Introduction of congressional legislation addressing sex distinctions in insurance
Illinois rejects ERA	Girls' increasing participation in athletics	Abortion bombings?	First time women are political directors of both Republican and Democratic National Committees
President Reagan wants ERA removed from Republican platform	President Reagan nominates first woman to Supreme Court: Sandra Day O'Connor	Women in political offices: senate, judges, networks	Reagan tries to win over female voters
Selective Service Act declared unconstitutional because it excludes women	Antiabortion movement in disarray after success with Reagan	Gender gap becomes apparent	

Figure 10.11 *continued*

1984	1985	1986	1987
Number of women higher in professions	Abortion clinic bombings, clinics anxious and on alert	President Reagan supports antiabortion rally	Continued controversy around discriminatory insurance laws
Gender gap clear	Black women mobilize and speak out	NOW turns twenty years old	Pat Schroeder potential Democratic presidential candidate
Geraldine Ferraro as Walter Mondale's running mate	U.S. Commission on Civil Rights rejects comparable-worth pay theory	Abortion protests and antiabortion mobilization	Supreme Court rules in favor of job protection for pregnant women
Abortion protests	Economic Equity Act of 1985 introduced	Reagan nominates William Rehnquist as chief justice of the Supreme Court	Confirmation hearings for Supreme Court nominee Robert Bork
Women's pay rising but still behind that of men		Pornography becomes an issue	
Mondale loses to Reagan		Increased numbers of women in political office	
Republicans attempt to mobilize women		Debate over pregnancy leave	
Women support Mondale		OWL active	
NOW sues over sex-based insurance rates		Gains for women predicted in state races	
Women becoming more important in Republican Party			

Figure 10.11 *continued*

1988	1989	1990	1991
Women support Michael Dukakis campaign	*Webster* abortion case decided by Supreme Court; generates heavy protesting by pro-choice groups	FDA approves contraceptive implanted under skin	Anita Hill, Clarence Thomas confirmation hearings
President Bush's election seen as good for antiabortion campaign	Contentious politics surrounding *Webster* decision	Better climate for women in 1990s predicted	President Bush vetoes bill that would allow federally funded clinics to discuss abortion with patients
Study suggests different hormone levels in women affect ability to perform tasks	Gender bias in classroom recognized	OWL mobilizes	Antiabortion protests
Women's groups charge bias in merit scholarship testing	Study finds SAT discriminates against girls	Right-to-life movement and abortion politics	Women's groups ask Supreme Court to hear Pennsylvania abortion case and reassert *Roe* decision
NOW submits proposal/petition for ERA	States adopt stricter restrictions on abortion	"Decade of the Woman"	
Operation Rescue protests at abortion clinics		Justice David Souter's confirmation hearings	
Insurance sex discrimination		Dianne Feinstein runs for governor of California	
		Catholic church fights abortion	

Figure 10.11 *continued*

1992	1993	1994	1995
"Year of the Woman"	Emily's List successfully supports	Women in political campaigns	Women-only investment clubs on
Bill Clinton elected president	female candidates	Bob Packwood accused of sexual	the rise
Increase in women in statewide	Debate over federally funded	harassment, making comeback	Seventy-five-year anniversary of
offices and Congress	abortion continues	*Bobbitt* case	women's suffrage
Women raising money for politics	Controversy over women in		Women press for hearings on Bob
Supreme Court decides to take	Clinton's cabinet		Packwood
Pennsylvania abortion case	Senator Bob Packwood accused of		Antiabortion killings
Female candidates campaign	sexual harassment		Nicole Brown Simpson allegedly
Religious Right active in Bush	Janet Reno nominated for		murdered by ex-husband O.J.
campaign	attorney general		Simpson; event brings national
Amendment 2 in Colorado leads	Success with Clinton leads to		attention to problem of domestic
to boycott	division within pro-choice movement		violence
Abortion politics	Nationalized health care debate		
Pornography politics	Confirmation hearings for		
Sexual harassment cases are up	Supreme Court nominee Ruth Bader		
(Equal Employment Opportunity	Ginsberg		
Commission)	Freedom of Choice Act to abolish		
	state restructions on abortion dies		

Figure 10.11 *continued*

1996

NOW thrives among inmates
President Clinton vetoes bill
banning late-term abortions
NOW organizes march for liberal
causes
  Domestic violence
  Abortion pill
  Senate passes welfare bill
  Clinton signs welfare bill
  1996 election—women make only
  modest gains despite many
  candidates

edented number of female candidates were elected to public office. In this year, women voters provided Bill Clinton with his victory margin, defeating incumbent president George Bush. Charges of sexual harassment were brought against Oregon Senator Bob Packwood, ending his tenure in Congress. Finally, the murder of Nicole Brown Simpson, former wife of O.J. Simpson, focused national attention on the problem of domestic violence.

ISSUE CONTEXT

A battleground in the "culture wars" opened up over the issue of whether women should be treated as individuals or considered fundamentally as part of the family unit. Second-wave women's groups were adamant that women should be viewed autonomously. They encouraged women to claim rights for themselves, whether they wanted to apply for financial credit in their own name, enter a U.S. military academy, have a surgical abortion, or go to medical school. By contrast, the countermovement argued that a liberal individualistic perspective of this sort would destroy conventional families and family life. Those opposing feminism, in general, advocated preserving and honoring a special role for women as daughters and mothers. These competing frames of family and individualism provide another look at the representation of second-wave women's groups by the media at the dawn of the twenty-first century.

As figure 10.12 shows, there is evidence in this period of a rise in the number of articles discussing women's issues in conjunction with the family. This is particularly evident from the *Webster* decision in 1989 through the electoral campaign of 1992. The issues most frequently looked at in this context were abortion, education,

Figure 10.12   Issues presented in a family context, 1980–1996

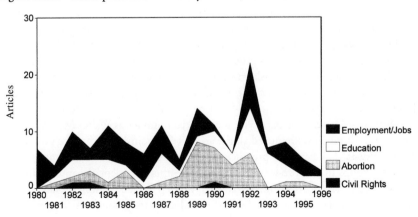

Years

Figure 10.13   Percentage of issues using a family context, 1980–1996

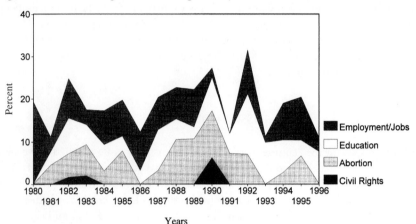

Years

and employment. Civil rights as an issue area was never infused with this family perspective. This is not surprising since the dominant legal basis of rights in the United States has always been the individual. Figure 10.13 shows the magnitude of this shifting emphasis toward the family. At its peak, slightly over 30 percent of the articles include this context, with the norm for these decades varying between 20 and 25 percent. Even following the defeat of the ERA, the family perspective achieves only limited inroads. Thus, despite the challenge of conservative opponents, the majority of issues of special concern to second-wave feminists are not redefined as family issues.

INTERACTION WITH THE GOVERNMENT

As figure 10.14 shows, the most consistent coverage of women's groups and their issues in the *New York Times* comes from their work with Congress. Although there is a brief upward peak in congressional coverage around the time of the defeat of the ERA, second-wave women's groups are generally engaged in a continuing effort to influence congressional legislation through the media. By contrast, presidential politics shows far greater fluctuation. The exceptionally large number of articles dealing with the presidency in 1984 can be directly traced to Geraldine Ferraro's nomination as Democratic party vice presidential nominee as Walter Mondale's running mate. Although we removed all the articles discussing only the vice presidency, it was evident that Ferraro's presence on the ticket actively engaged many more women's groups in the 1984 campaign than in other presidential contests. In fact, with the exceptions of 1984 and 1992, when women elected Clinton president along with an unprecedented number of women candidates to national office, most presidential election years have unusually low reported activity by second-wave women's

Figure 10.14   Institutional involvement with second-wave women's groups, 1980–1996

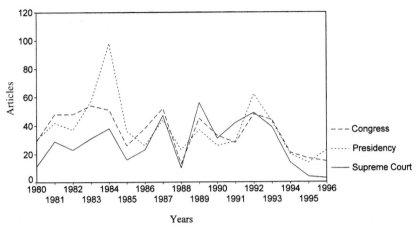

groups. The changeable role of women's groups with respect to the courts mirrors that of the presidency. The peak of coverage occurred in 1989, when the *Webster* case was handed down by the Supreme Court. The other identifiable blip in coverage occurred in 1987, when women's groups mobilized to defeat President Ronald Reagan's conservative nominee to the Supreme Court, Robert Bork. Bork's weak record of support for civil rights, together with his opposition to a constitutionally guaranteed right to privacy, led women's groups to ally with other interests in resisting his confirmation. Second-wave women's groups, in this period of relative inactivity by the broad social movement, were consistently engaged with Congress, the presidency, and the courts. Although much of this involvement was spurred by consequential events, such as the defeat of the ERA, the nomination of the first woman to be part of the presidential ticket of a major political party, and the *Webster* decision, there can be little doubt that women's movement groups were influential in affecting many of the important news stories of these decades.

CONCLUSION

In this overview of coverage of second-wave feminist groups by the *New York Times,* several tendencies emerge with clarity. First, although articles mentioning these groups become less frequent in the 1990s, that coverage remained overwhelmingly positive. Second, a disproportionate number of the stories referred to NOW as contrasted with other second-wave feminist groups. Third, economic and educational issues, on balance, generated more favorable articles than did articles on abortion or civil rights. Although civil rights was clearly a dominant media focus in the 1980s, by the 1990s abortion had replaced civil rights as the most frequently written about and controversial issue involving women's groups. Fourth, 1984, 1989, and 1992 were the years with the largest number of stories involving second-wave women's groups. Coverage in these years was driven by: the nomination of Geraldine Ferraro as vice presidential candidate, the handing down of the *Webster* decision on abortion, and the electoral "Year of the Woman." Although at first blush these seem to be external events driving coverage, as one explores the origins of these stories, it becomes evident that the women's movement and second-wave groups within it played significant political roles in getting Representative Ferraro added to the Mondale ticket and turning public anger against the charges of sexual harassment against Supreme Court nominee Clarence Thomas into electoral victories for women candidates in 1992. Similarly, opponents of the women's movement can largely claim credit for spurring the conservative *Webster* decision.

To conclude, by 1996 coverage of second-wave women's groups remains remarkably positive, even with the quieting of the protest movement supporting them. NOW and its leaders continue as the dominant spokespeople for the feminist movement. Although a significant minority of articles incorporate a family frame to discuss women's concerns, that perspective never seriously challenges the dominant individualistic focus of news about women. Press coverage of educational, economic, abortion, and civil rights issues is, on balance, favorable when containing the perspective of women's organizations. Finally, second-wave women's groups are portrayed as actively and constructively engaged with all three branches of government. This picture both confirms the growing institutionalizing of the women's movement and likely facilitates it.

NOTES

1. First-wave feminist groups are those that formed as part of the women's suffrage movement, including the League of Women Voters, the American Association of University Women, and the National Woman's Party.

2. There are many sources that detail legislative, legal, and electoral gains made by the women's movement. See, for example, Costain (1992, 1998), Gelb and Palley (1987), Mansbridge (1986), and Schlozman (1990).

3. This view, that social movement emergence is tied in an important way to changes in language and thinking, draws significantly on the work of Alberto Melucci (1996).

4. We selected the following second-wave feminist groups for this search: National Organization for Women, National Women's Political Caucus, Women's Equity Action League, Federally Employed Women, Congressional Caucus on Women's Issues, Society to Cut Up Men, Redstockings, Older Women's League, and National Abortion and Reproductive Rights Action League. These groups were chosen because they include the largest national women's organizations as well as spanning a wide range of feminist interests, issues, and styles. The literature on women's organizations identifies each as politically active (Carden 1974; Costain 1978, 1979, 1981, 1983, 1992; Gelb 1995; Gelb and Palley 1977, 1982, 1987; Katzenstein 1987, 1990, 1995; Schlozman 1990; Spalter-Roth and Schreiber 1995).

Part 5

Culture and Rhetoric

11

The Banality of Evil, the Evil of Banality

Mark Kingwell

HUMAN RIGHTS AT FIFTY: FACING A CRISIS

The thoughts presented in this chapter were prompted initially by the signal anniversary of 1998, which marked the half century since the United Nations adopted the Universal Declaration of Human Rights (United Nations General Assembly 1949). That document, substantially drafted by a Canadian law professor, John Humphrey of McGill University, offers thirty articles of faith for the shattered global landscape after World War II, beginning with the assertion that "all human beings are born free and equal in dignity and rights, endowed with reason and conscience, and should act towards one another in a spirit of brotherhood" and ending with the warning that "nothing in this Declaration may be interpreted as implying any right to act in destruction of the rights and freedoms set forth" within it.

The Declaration is a stirring document because it uses the plain language of faith and hope without embarrassment. It is couched in tough-sounding declarative sentences, almost every article beginning with the phrase "Everyone has a right to" or the phrase "No one shall be subjected to." What everyone has a right to includes life, security, freedom, property, work, equal pay for equal work, leisure, due process, free assembly, suffrage, medical care, intellectual property rights, and education. What no one shall be subjected to is, among other evils, slavery, torture, arbitrary imprisonment, slander, seizure of property, and exile. The "will of the people" will be the basis of all legitimate government, according to the Declaration, and that will "shall be expressed in periodic and genuine elections."

Perhaps anticipating the sorts of objections that would soon be leveled against this so-called rights discourse by nonliberal critics, the Declaration also articulates the responsibilities and duties of humans living in society. In Article 29—significantly, near the end of the document, almost as a counterpoint or recursive metarule—we

177

are told, "Everyone has duties to the community in which alone the free and full development of his personality is possible." Moreover, in the exercise of rights, everyone will be subject to the limitations of law—but only "for the purpose of securing due recognition and respect for the rights and freedoms of others and of meeting the just requirements of morality, public order and the general welfare of democratic society." The resulting notion of citizenship is stronger than is often defended by liberals, moving toward a more civic republican view of political activity as part of the set of goods enjoyed by any person in his or her role as citizen; more than this, it extends the range of our understanding of human rights from the prophylactic or protection-based conception—human rights as a shield—toward a host of positive duties and activities.

It is easy to pick over a high-minded statement such as this in search of gaffes or missteps; it is also easy to make the obvious point that, despite the language of *everyone having a right to* and *no one shall be subjected to*, people around the world are subjected to and fail to have a right to all kinds of things on a daily basis.[1] That is not as damning an objection as it is usually thought to be since documents such as the Declaration are—and are intended to be—statements of ideals. In the best case, they act as *regulative* ideals, guiding principles for an imperfect world, and not simply as utopian fantasies. That is, they act to edge actual states of affairs ever closer to the ideal state without any too robust belief that such a state will ever be fully achieved. That a rosy picture does not reflect the nature of the world as it now stands is not, contrary to cynical opinion, a rap against the picture.

However, my problem with the Declaration is not of that kind. It is, rather, that the sentiments of the Declaration are systematically unstable, and unstable in a way that makes it hard for us to think clearly about our political context, that is, a world in which a form of universalism has indeed been achieved in human affairs, but without many of the guarantees that animated the authors and early adopters of this document and with so little stability that we are not indulging in millenarian doomsaying or aimless fear when we say that it is in crisis. Yet, I believe that this crisis is also an opportunity.

THE TRIUMPH OF MODERNITY: THE FAILURE OF REASON

The story of how that world came to be has many possible starting points, and here I choose one that will seem controversial only until we realize its connections to the deep tensions of our own political experience. I start with Immanuel Kant, the Enlightenment thinker responsible for much of our reigning view of the moral and political self and, in turn, for the spirit that animates the Declaration. There are some echoes of Rousseau in the Declaration (e.g., people are born free, the will of the people), but in its emphasis on human dignity, the centrality of reason, and the very idea of universalism itself, the document is clearly driven by Kantian ideals of cosmopolitan order. Indeed, the Kantian legacy cannot be overestimated in the idea of universal human rights because it is Kant's version of liberalism, building on the pioneering efforts of the seventeenth-century English philosophers, that takes the ideas of freedom and equality to a higher plane of abstract reality, moving past the fear-driven propertarianism of Hobbes or the minimalist religious toleration of Locke to embrace the idea of each and every individual as valuable simply in virtue of being alive.

I will leave aside for the moment any consideration of the dignity and rights of nonhuman life and note simply that Kant's triumph is modernity's triumph. Against the old orders of privilege based on social hierarchy, bloodline, and salvational status, he offers the modern world a vision in which every human, regardless of station or wealth, must be treated as an end in him- or herself and not merely as a means to an end. Extending the range of that "regardless" clause to take in nationality, race, gender, ethnic origin, sexual preference, and physical ability has been the work of the past two centuries—work that is by no means complete. Whatever we may think of Kant personally—and he was not much to like, if biographical tales are to be trusted—he bequeaths to us a twinned vocabulary of individualism and universalism that runs through the modern world like the buzz of conversation at a good party. An individual is worthy of respect simply by virtue of being alive, and that worthiness extends without borders to encompass every individual, ignoring all particularities.

There are difficulties here, however, and many of them. I will mention only two kinds and really focus only on the second. The first kind of problem arises as a result of the fact that, for Kant and his followers, individuals were actually worthy of respect not in virtue of being just any kind of human being but because they were moral agents, and they were moral agents in virtue of being rational. That is, it was a central part of the worthiness of individuals that they could, by the light of reason, perceive the structure of the moral law and of their duty to it and so act as to make the maxim of their action a universal law. That, indeed, is one prominent formulation of Kant's categorical imperative: a test of dutifulness that says that an action is justifiable if and only if it can be universalized for everyone.

The trouble is that the attribute "rational," and its unexamined characterization, does all the work in this conception of human action, so much so that a negative judgment on a person's actions could lead, without difficulty, to the judgment that they were not fully rational. Or, by the same token, groups of individuals could be ruled out of moral and political play ex ante by declaring them incapable of reason—"minor," in Kant's usage, much the same way that police in 1950s melodramas might speak of minors—a procedure that will be familiar to women, blacks, the handicapped, and many others. Even if the attribute "rational" is taken to be uncontroversial, there are many heterogeneous elements that tend to creep into Kantian moral decision making, as John Stuart Mill famously noted a half century after Kant. Calculations of universal extension are notoriously subject to situational limits and various other forms of special pleading, often reducing the allegedly pure dutifulness of the categorical imperative to the decidedly hypothetical instrumentality of calculating consequences for and against a certain action: Lying is wrong, finally, not because it entails a self-contradiction (as Kant insisted) but because it undermines the web of social relations.

That, however, is not my present concern. It is, rather, the specifically political issues arising from the twinned discourses of individualism and universalism, in particular the tension that exists between them—a tension noticed and thematized most recently by the Canadian political theorist Charles Taylor (1992). That tension comes to the fore in recent political events, but it also nestles in the heart of the Declaration in the unstable relationship between Article 29 and the rest of the document. It is the tension between the avowed focus on the individual, which emphasizes the uniqueness and worthiness of the individual's projects in this life, and the overarching demand for universalism, which attempts to transcend the particularities of the individual's life in favor of some global property or properties of humanness that demand protection and promotion.

We can articulate this tension, which will not come as news to political observers today, in several ways. It is not just that universalism is being challenged in various appalling conflicts that turn on resurgent ethnic nationalisms or tribal blood feuds. We might place those facts, in their very extremity, beyond the political pale. However, even if we choose to do that, we cannot do the same when it comes to the social struggles within Western liberal democracies such as our own, the struggles in what has come to be called the politics of identity. The attempt to secure group rights, cultural recognition, or simply a rich acceptance of my reality as an individual have been written and acted as oppositions to the prevailing liberal norm of those democracies, a norm that is perceived to secure individual rights only by robbing individuals of their lived particularity. In other words, when individualism is universalized, it has the self-contradictory effect of rendering individuals null, mere ciphers in a formal array of rights.

This is a familiar story, if also an alarming one, to anyone who has read the newspapers during the past decade or so. From the civil rights movements of the 1950s and 1960s, which sought to extend the range of universal recognition in the manner I described earlier—that is, they sought to work out the implied promise of universalism by securing rights for previously excluded individuals—the 1970s, 1980s, and 1990s moved into a period in which that kind of victory was rewritten as a defeat. From the point of view of new generations of feminists, race theorists, and gay activists, it was not enough to have individual rights because individual rights were ultimately conceived and made into policy by straight white men who wished, consciously or otherwise, to reduce everyone to a straight white man.

Individual rights, once the prize, now become the tool of a new, more subtle form of oppression: They were a particular masquerading as a universal. There is no Kantian standard of universal rationality functioning beneath all our particularities, and political stability cannot be secured by stripping those particularities away. Suborning one's particularity to that false universal means only losing one's self, not preserving it. The political imperative is not to secure individual rights under a larger political structure of generalized and therefore empty respect but to demand real respect for *my* particularity in the uniquely valuable project of living my life—or, if not my particularity per se, then that of the exclusive group to which I belong, whatever it may be, especially if that group has been, as a group, historically excluded from power and privilege.

I will not retail the intricacies of these conflicts here, as they are widely known. Nor will I declare myself on the various conflicts that ensued, except to say that I still believe that a language of individualism can be politically useful if its limits are constantly acknowledged and any tendency to eliminate otherness or difference is ruthlessly resisted. What must equally be resisted, however, is the tendency to celebrate particularity at the expense of any larger political goals, the sort of self-regard that closes off all rational challenges by pointing out that the challenger is not a member of the particular group in question. In short, I believe that the tension between these two extremes of elimination and separatism can be made productive. (Of course, I'm a straight white man, so you'll have to judge for yourself.) My main concern at the moment is the very existence of this conflict between particularity and the prospect of a larger political justice. Now, that is the first time I have used that word in these remarks, but I hope you will grant that it is what we have been talking about all along. Human rights are about justice, and the Declaration was an attempt to help secure them—or at least give us some guidelines in working to do that. It was, I have suggested, a flawed attempt, but only because the very political culture from which it sprang is riven by this deep conflict. It is a powerful and indispensable touchstone in an era where there is much confusion, and even outright cynicism, about human rights. The question remains: What can we do about justice when the interests of the individual seem everywhere at odds with the interests of a larger body politic, *even* one based on the idea of the individual's interest?

In order to suggest an answer to that question, I am first going to complicate it with another one: What becomes of universalism in a world where the particularity of the individual must always be respected, possibly to the exclusion of other goals? Without exaggeration, we can suggest some proximate tendencies. The prevailing idea of the sovereign individual is, like all prevailing ideas, liable to pathology. If people's identities must be respected absolutely, then presumably so must the preferences and desires that proceed from those identities. If an identity cannot be challenged by reference to some larger shared goals, then neither can the preferences and desires that proceed from it. Thus, in a twisted way, we arrive at the toxic forms of narcissism, complaint, and self-justification that pass for individualism today: not just the rock-'em, sock-'em talk shows, in which people act out their depressing conflicts under Jerry Springer's cynically moralizing eye, but also the high-toned literary memoirs and confessions that are the functional equivalents for people with more money and education.

You may say that I am moving a little too fast here, conflating legitimate claims to identity with these lowest-common-denominator excesses. However, as the Declaration itself teaches us, it is always important to consider the worst case to illuminate the whole field of cases. Not everyone need fear imminent prospects of torture, but everyone should be able to articulate a right not to suffer it. I am highlighting these excesses mainly in order to illustrate a point, that individualism is not the uncomplicated good that it may seem to be. While it has brought us much good, it has also led to many perversities that have the ultimate effect of cutting against justice rather than fostering it.

This becomes even clearer when we take a look at how the discourse of universalism has fared in practice. Again this will be a story of worst cases and excesses and therefore only part of the story, but I think that it can be validly argued that functional universalism today has little to do with the propagation of justice and almost everything to do with the growing reach and influence of the cash nexus. This story is so depressingly familiar that I will not spend much time making my claim about it. Capitalism has now decisively entered what the Marxist economist Ernest Mandel called its third, or late, stage—each stage determined quite precisely by the dominant technology of capital's spread. The first stage, coinciding with the machine production of steam engines since about 1848, was market capitalism. This was eventually encompassed and surpassed by monopoly or imperialist capitalism based on the production of electric and combustion motors since the last decade of the nineteenth century. In turn, that form was sublated by the postindustrial, or multinational, capitalism of the 1940s and beyond, based on electronic and nuclear technology.

The stages of capitalism also determine new sets of spatial relations, such that the world of multinational capital is speedily transformed into a weirdly annihilated space in which every point touches every other simultaneously, a rhizome of fiberoptic relations. In a world dominated by multinational capital, not only is everything reducible to exchange value, in the traditional manner, but the exchanges themselves become distorted and metastasized because of a speed and virtuality of exchange that ultimately defies the old logic of supply and demand, not to mention the now archaic, if not risible, idea that markets exist to facilitate the movement of useful products to the people who need them. That view now has the quaintness of a fairy tale— something represented vividly by the near failure, in the fall of 1998, of a private, transnational derivatives fund whose sudden plunge into trading free fall, while its operators were on vacation, threatened the stability of the entire global economy. If not for the panicked intervention of "various governments and agencies"—a phrase that has for us the same menacing vagueness that the words "certain matters of import to discuss" might have for a character in a Kafka novel—that fund's failure would have pitched us all into chaos.

GLOBALIZED MARKET CULTURE: THE EVIL OF BANALITY

The first reality of universalism today, therefore, is our universal subjection to these economic forces that appear to function beyond our conscious control. I say "appear" because the belief that they are literally beyond control is one of the most disabling ideas we can surrender to.[2] However, if you believe the newspapers, it is far from clear that even those who directly benefit from those forces have a much better idea of how they function than you or I do. The world of late capitalism is more dependent on its material technological base than the earlier stages were because computer technology functions so often in an opaque, black-box manner.[3] Sophisticated communications and media technologies also have a tendency to deliver what Fredric Jameson calls a "technological bonus," such that the act of consumption includes not only the first-order product—the film, the shoes, the song, the computer—but also the second-order product of the technology that produced it, in itself (Jameson 1991, 276, 384–386). When consumers ingest a successful Hollywood blockbuster, for example, how much of that success comes from the greedy consumption of the money on the screen in the form of technological showing off? Moreover, there is a peculiar—and highly pleasurable—reductio of this second-order bonus, when, as J. G. Ballard noted of dystopian science fiction films such as *Blade Runner* or *The Terminator,* we observe technology advanced enough to depict the violent decline of advanced technology.

I do not mean to be facetious here, but perhaps the most appropriate tag we could use for the situation is the name that Homer Simpson, in an episode of the animated television series, *The Simpsons,* gave the Internet provider company that he decided to set up in competition with Microsoft's Bill Gates—without benefit of a computer, knowledge of computers, capital, or even a second phone line. Homer called his company Compu-Global-Hyper-Mega-Net, and that's as good a description as any of where we now live. (The company, by the way, did not hold out against Gates for long. The Microsoft honcho and some thuggish nerds quickly descend on Homer's house to break all his pencils, smash up his desk, and tear out the phone.)

These facts have numerous political and cultural consequences that we must note. The first is that the de facto universalism of the transnational market has more devastating effects on the idea of the individual's particularity than any liberal attempt to articulate formal rights ever could. It is a function of late capitalism not only that technology and capital go global but also that culture—or at least a simulacrum of it—goes global, too. We now have, all protests and cries of incredulity aside, a genuine global culture. In fact, taking a page from the book of Homer, we could give it a name: Mono-Global-Culture-Corp. It is not perhaps the culture that you or I would consider worth attending to, although I do not presume to speak for anyone on this account. I have myself listened to the music of the Spice Girls without suffering debilitating effects and watched their surprisingly witty movie *Spice World* with keen enjoyment. I have personally purchased Nike running shoes because, among other things, I wanted to wear the swoosh that Michael Jordan also wore. I have never watched *Baywatch* with much pleasure, mainly because of a scarring childhood experience with the earlier David Hasselhoff vehicle, *Knight Rider,* but I accept that it has its uses as a morality play about the temptations of cosmetic surgery and extremely skimpy bathing suits. I do not drink Coke or Pepsi except at the movies—

but then, why not there? Where else does flavored carbonated water cost more than four dollars a cup?

Mono-Global-Culture-Corp is ripe for parody, as always. However, I think that it is important not to indulge that tendency, at least for a moment, so that we can note something more significant than the risibility of the product: the net effects of Mono-Global-Culture-Corp on the project of securing individual identity. We hear so much from postmodernist intellectuals about the death of the individual under conditions of late capitalism that it often does not sink in that there is a reality to the claim, precisely because of the unparalleled success of a pathological version of that modern aspiration, the universalization of regard for individuals. The net effect is a self-contradiction, but that fact is but rarely noted in the rush to extend the reach of market, technology, and culture to every corner of the world. It is not crazy to call this three-pronged initiative a global virus, for, like a virus, it free rides on the otherwise healthy functions of its hosts, namely, the desires for personal comfort and security that animate individuals, and gradually rewrites those functions to such an extent that the original host is, in a sense, no longer present. In effect, Mono-Global-Culture-Corp, with its enabling technological and market conditions, colonizes individuals around the world one by one until they are assimilated into the smoothly functioning logic of production. Anyone who believes desires cannot be colonized in this way has not been paying attention to his or her own shopping patterns and self-reassuring connoisseurship about advertising techniques, that third-order consumerism in which we consume our own sophistication along with the ads and the products.

What becomes of political power under these circumstances? It probably goes without saying that the political power of individuals, those elements of the will of the people that made for legitimacy according to the Declaration, is attenuated, if not eliminated, under extreme conditions of this kind. Power reduces in many cases to little more than spending power, the vaunted "voting with our feet" that free marketeers seem to think so much of. The populism of the market's availability, its wide dissemination of what was formerly thought to be the preserve of an elite few, is nothing but a false form of democratization. When the contours and offerings of the market are beyond question, when choice is just a game of eenie-meenie between infinitesimally different brands, power of that truncated sort is little more than a bad joke. The individual disappears even further, reduced to an unconnected series of expressed preferences in market surveys and political opinion polls, whose once essential differences are no longer discernible even to those who administer them.

Worse than this, however, is the attenuation of legitimate national power and the resulting distortion of its exercise. We see every day more and more obvious manifestations of the bland, bureaucratized, responsibility-deflecting management style of political leaders who have become all too aware of their insignificance on the larger world stage. Bureaucracy, not patriotism, is the last refuge of the scoundrel—especially if the scoundrel cannot avoid constant reminders of his own ultimate powerlessness. I evoked Hannah Arendt in the title of this chapter, and I will not shrink from making the connection clear. Arendt's vivid depiction of the banality of evil in her *New Yorker* report, "Eichmann in Jerusalem," gave us an important new way to understand the nature of power, especially when mobilized around technological and economic imperatives of rationalization. In the hands of the functionary, the dutiful servant of larger forces, evil can itself be rationalized as a perverse instance of Kant's categorical imperative: follow the will of the leader without question. Such was Adolf Eichmann's notorious defense of his own role in facilitating the extermination of Polish Jews.

Evil becomes banal, in other words, when it becomes mechanical, routinized, heedless, and thick. Eichmann is no monster out of the Satanic mold; on the contrary, he is a featureless family man with few distinguishing interests and no obsessions. He is simply doing a job. Of course, his ordinariness is precisely what makes him noteworthy, the blunt instrument of a great evil. I will not belabor the point, for this is a familiar story. The connection to the bureaucratized and implacable power of our world is perhaps less familiar. Drawing comparisons to the Holocaust is always a risky business, and I do not mean to suggest that every attempt to shrug off an instance of police brutality or a policy of complicity with a visiting dictator is equivalent to mass murder. However, I do mean to suggest that there is a connection, on the continuum of banality, between the exemplar, Eichmann, and many of our more proximate political functionaries whose indifference to questions of legitimacy and accountability is their most obvious defining feature. Thus does the banality of evil become, under less extreme and even more routine political conditions, the evil of banality—which may nevertheless erupt at any moment into something worse. Indifference can swiftly breed callousness, arrogance, and eventually contempt.

That is one aspect of the inversion of Arendt's famous phrase.[4] There is, of course, another. The evil of banality is cultural as well as political, and indeed the two forms are related. What is evil about mass culture is not simply its massive reach and apparently unopposable force but its relentless downward drag on the rich possibilities of media and performance. At the same time, the creation of such lowest-common-denominator product is naturalized by producers and consumers alike by asserting, without argument, that this is simply "what people want." Depending on where you situate yourself, that claim is either outright cynicism, on the order of there being a sucker born every minute, or a well-heeled elitism that presents itself as democratic geniality: "*I* don't like *Baywatch,* certainly, but you can't argue with the people, and what they want is *Baywatch.*" This position abdicates responsibility for critical judgment at the same time that it abandons these "people," whoever they are, to a cultural hell allegedly of their own making.

We all act to obscure our complicity in the banalization of the cultural world and in the social and economic arrangements reinforced by that world. We might even note a new form of reification here: not the translation of social forces into things, as leftist critics used to speak of reification, but rather the "effacement of the traces of production" itself.[5] What does that mean? Well, consider the unremarkable facts that you can get Nike shoes made in Indonesia in your local Foot Locker store, that the person who made them was paid about sixteen cents an hour to do it, and that you pay your hundred dollars and feel pretty much okay about doing it. Indeed, these facts are so unremarkable that they do not feel like news. What is deeply worrying here is not just the unconscious acceptance of a brutalizing economic determinism but also the concomitant fact that we lose any connection whatsoever between the objects purchased and the facts of their production.

Globalization of the labor market does not just allow this disconnection; it demands it. We must remember always to forget the conditions of the creation of consumer and cultural goods because otherwise we might become disgusted with our own needs and desires and what is necessary to satisfy them. It is in the interest of global markets to keep us from thinking too deeply or too long about the conditions of production lest, in alarmed self-disapproval, we begin to withdraw our consumer dollars. The forces of transnational capital very much want us to remain blithe, happy, and freely spending; all the elaborate and fine-tuned machinery of influence and desire formation they marshal—advertising, marketing, focus groups, and demographic targeting—is in the service of precisely this, and no nation on earth is powerful enough to regulate that kind of influence.

Cultural products no longer come to us signed, as when they were the result of personal artisanship and commitment; they come only branded, with the heavily underscored logos and trademarks of the corporate project. In that multiple branding, the relentless mechanical reproduction of equivalent objects whose very goal is to be the same in Tokyo as in Topeka, in Belgrade as in Burlington, the objects begin to lose their reality as things created by humans. Style and contour, once identified with artistic genius and individual talent, remain, but they are henceforth emptied of all meaning, retaining only a hollowed-out status of the commercial sheen, the glossy patina, that catches the eye—and coaxes the dollar.[6] More than this, reality itself begins to lose its reality: it disappears, or threatens to, in a pervasive system of mass reproducibility where there are multiple tokens but no types, many simulacra but no true representations, for there is nothing real left to represent.[7] Cultural products are therefore consumed precisely in a manner that studiously ignores the (usually exploitative) conditions of their mass production and that, further, ignores the implications of that consumption for our sense of ourselves.[8]

Banal means trite, as in aesthetically or morally inferior; but it also means, more precisely, commonplace, taken for granted. The banality of evil lies in the commonplace person, the unremarkable functionary, ordering genocide. The evil of banality lies not so much or not only in the aesthetic weakness of cultural product today, although there is certainly that; it lies also, and more damagingly, in the self-effacing commonness of it all—a commonness that expunges all traces of a system of production no longer attuned to the needs of its inhabitants, one that expunges those needs themselves as meaningful standards of assessment.

UNIVERSALIZED IMAGINATION: MAKING CONNECTIONS

It would be easy to fall into jeremiad on this topic and leave it at that, but I will not indulge that impulse. What I have argued is this: In part because of tensions within the twinned discourses of individualism and universalism, and in part because of the combined material-economic success of technological capitalism, individualism has become prey to its own aspirations. Evil has become banal, and banality has become evil. The reasons for this, as I have said, lie tangled in the origin of those aspirations themselves, but they have been aided and abetted by less abstract forces: those of technology and money. Now, if you will grant that this picture of our current situation has at least some merit, we still must ask what can be done about it.

I have three things to offer on that score—three things that, each taken alone, may seem insubstantial or ambiguous but that, taken together, I think add up to something powerful. The first is that my earlier scenario of a smooth assimilation of all humans under the rubrics of Mono-Global-Culture-Corp and Compu-Global-Hyper-Mega-Net has to be nuanced and limited by an awareness of the rising tide of defiantly hybrid identities and productively mutating local/global cultures. The world is not in fact surrendering to the global reach of capital with an unbroken sameness, a featureless capitulation to mass culture and market values. Instead, we observe more and more the emergence of wholly new forms of cultural and political identity that incorporate some elements of the dominant story even while preserving many of the distinctive features of the local context. These hybridities, tracked culturally by Homi Bhabha, for example, or politically by Michael Ignatieff are not always forms that we in the industrialized West would consider emancipatory (Bhabha 1994; Ignatieff 1993, 1997). They may preserve practices that are deeply troubling cosmopolitan liberals, especially as it relates to the discourse of rights: blood feuds, religious fundamentalism, female circumcision, widow burning, and so on. These instances, which continue to persist in some countries despite both internal resistance and displays of compliance with international human rights rhetoric, show that the exportation of Western values is a more complicated and less regular matter than optimistic rationalists would like to believe. At the same time, they indicate that pathological versions of exported universalism are as unstable as valid ones when grafted onto distinctive local ways of life. Western democracy does not travel abroad without alteration, and neither does the so-called free market.

The fact of hybrid identities therefore sends a mixed message. It chastens the triumphalism of happy-go-lucky global capitalists, but only at the cost of putting the very idea of the universal into question. We seem to have returned to the impasse between individual and universal with which I began, only on a larger scale. However, the fact of hybrid identities can have another effect that is to make us rethink the notion of universalism in what might prove to be productive—not despite these troubling examples, still less in support of them, but precisely because they are troubling. The second thing I want to highlight here, then, is the possibility of rewriting the discourse of universalism to take account of the far-from-smooth extension of that idea throughout the world. Rather than seeking the goal of a pure universalism of rationality, as Kant did, and finding in the event that the only actual universalism is one of money, and even that one only jagged and mutant, we might shift the focus to another target, what I will call a universalism of imagination. Such a shift may have the ultimate effect of reinvigorating documents such as the Declaration.

This suggestion may strike some as misdirected, if only because the notion that imagination might be universalized is so unfamiliar to us. However, what I mean is not so bizarre as it might sound—and is by no means intended as the last word on the subject, only the first. Imagination is the capacity to see beyond the materials given, including the materials directly given in my necessarily limited personal experience. It is the faculty of the human mind that responds to story and image, that most proximately is excited by the possibilities of art. So it has its acknowledged cultural primacy and its obvious cultural enemy, namely, the evils of banality I tried to articulate a moment ago.

However, imagination also has a political role because it is imagination, not pure practical reason itself, as Kant thought, that responds to the deep pull of justice. The true force of universalism lies not in the act of picking out some dutiful responsibility to the abstract moral law but in the shared capacity of humans to be pained by the pain of others. The human community is not so much a community of reason as it is, at a basic level, a community of feeling. Beyond certain minimalist demands of logic, such as consistency and noncontradiction, it is very likely true that I care about a claim you make or a reason you offer only if I have a prior commitment to care about you. This is something that we can validate not by means of a metaphysical theory that trades in essences but rather by means of describing what Richard Rorty has called "a discursive fact" about us, namely, that we can and do, as matters of uncontroversial fact, respond to the suffering of others. We can all see, without needing any detailed philosophical or anthropological theory, that cruelty is wrong—that, indeed, it might be, as Judith Shklar argued in her book *Ordinary Vices,* the worst thing we do to one another.[9] That is why torture is so abhorrent to us and why declarations of human rights have their place in our imaginations. However, our abhorrence begins with much lower-level sorts of insight: that bullying is unacceptable, that gratuitous insult can have no justification, that suffering humiliation is deeply threatening to our sense of self.

The irony here, of course, is that imagination, like reason, is no proof against cruelty but sometimes, perversely, is its ally. In contrast to Eichmann, who represents the moral evil of absence of imagination, Rorty vividly characterizes O'Brien, the quietly menacing torturer in George Orwell's *1984,* as what happens to a subtle intellectual when he has nothing good left to believe in: the presence of perverted imagination.[10] (I am going beyond the materials given myself in this case: Rorty does not see fit to judge O'Brien as perverse, just bored.[11]) O'Brien is reason's servant, to be sure, and reason appears to be his most effective tool—next only, that is, to imagination. In the end, he is not interested in arguing with Winston and waves away his feeble position-taking and resistance-movement ideology because he has *heard it all before*. What remains then is brutal, penetrating insight. It is O'Brien's capacity to imagine Winston's terror about rats, in other words, that makes him such an effective torturer. The crude tools of physical pain are too blunt for O'Brien: not for him the tooth drill of *Marathon Man* or the testicular shocks of the Khmer Rouge. The deep cruelty of Room 101 is that it is ruled by fearsome imagination—so fearsome, in fact, that its effects are psychological disintegration for its own sake, for the pure exercise of power, not for anything as trite as information or confession. When Winston, in his anguish, says, "Do it to Julia," we know that his destruction as a human being is complete, despite the persistence of his physical body—indeed, wickedly, because of it—for he must then endure the memory of that betrayal and the irremediable pain of seeing her again.

Imagination is not cruelty-proof, in short, as no human capacity is. We must face the possibility that any of us might, under certain circumstances, be an Eichmann—or even an O'Brien. However, despite all this, we must accept that without it we cannot forge even the provisional commitments that bind us one to another. If I cannot *in some sense* see your pain and humiliation as real, then I cannot reliably regard you as worthy of my concern, and if I cannot do that, there is very little reason for us to expect that I will respond meaningfully to a claim that you wish to make. This not to say that *I feel your pain*. Nobody feels anybody else's pain, only his or her own. However, pain has many sources, and the imaginative link of one person to another makes a politically relevant kind of pain—the pain of compassion—possible for us.

Possible, but never guaranteed. There is no transcendental account of human imagination that would lock down these claims, make them foundational in a strong sense. We can rely on our imaginations only provisionally, only contingently. We often fail in imagination: fail to see the effects of an action, fail to see what might be possible that is not yet real, fail to accept the forever failed attempt at creating a perfect human society. However, as often—or so, anyway, it seems to me—we succeed. We succeed in responding to the pain of another, succeed in acting for something good even though we know that it will not change the world from top to bottom, succeed in believing in the forever valid hope of creating a just human society. Thus is imagination sometimes transformed, whether gradually or in explosive moments, from fellow feeling into direct confrontations with power, into the creation of cultural resistance, into more and better-defined claims. Yet, without imagination, I suggest, we can rely on the creation of none of those more frequently defended political actions.

The third thing I want to mention here, and it will be the last thing I say, is that imagination has many sources, some of them unlikely. Popular art and popular culture are not, contrary to knee-jerk dismissiveness, always and necessarily banal. There is much in their production that drives the bulk of words, pictures, and narratives toward banality today, as I mentioned. However, there are moments, not too few either, when human voices seem to speak through the cumbersome and dangerous machinery of that mass production: when a connection is made between the human being who, somewhere, wrote the pop song or penned the line of dialogue that, right now, takes me or you somewhere we had not gone before. At that moment, imagination has snaked through the self-concealing forces of market and money and sounded a note of something better, and no amount of simulacral reproduction or mass commodification can, finally, take that away from us.

I do not wish to overstate the case here. The link between this kind of experience and political action is not unbroken or even always obvious. It is not that popular culture, or culture more generally, necessarily leads to political action. It does not, and cultural acts directed consciously toward prompting a political response are something else, namely, propaganda. Cultural signs are often merely symptomatic of larger, material fault lines that cannot be addressed adequately if we remain at the level of cultural analysis.[12] Of course, it is possible for our imaginative responsiveness itself to be exploited, the way in which radio jingles or compelling high-speed miniature narratives of television ads lodge in our brains, just as much as a good Radiohead riff or a scene from a Hal Hartley film or, for that matter, a Beethoven overture or a line from Shakespeare. Yet the act of consumption, seemingly unavoidable, can itself become—can be made to be—unexpectedly liberating, as we rearrange and appropriate the offered materials for our own purposes and projects.[13] That is no easier now than it has ever been; it is also no less important. The point, as ever, is that seeing beyond ourselves is the only way to begin realizing the complicated project of emancipation. It is no more than the beginning of that task, not an end to it.

As beginnings go, however, it is a good one. Imaginative connections remind us, as nothing else can, that we are, as citizens embedded in cultures, neither entirely free nor entirely imprisoned. We are social and cultural creatures, which means that we are both defined by and defining of the times in which we live. We can never wholly transcend our social contexts, can never fully pass beyond the limits and strictures and distortions of the cultural medium in which we exist. However, we are never completely dominated by those contexts, either, never the robotic cultural dopes of the nihilistic vision. If, ignoring this duality, we continue to believe, as many apparently do today, that there can be no valid action until we *do* transcend our limits—that everything else is falling short, or selling out, or buying in—then we are doomed to leave everything as it is, and I am not quite ready to leave everything as it is. That attitude, in fact, strikes me as the most banal of banal evils.

As for the project of universal human rights, let us say something that is neither banal nor utopian: We are working on it.

NOTES

Earlier versions of this chapter were presented at the Symposium on the Artist and Human Rights (Kingwell 1998), which commemorated the Declaration's fiftieth anniversary; at Innis

College, University of Toronto, in November 1998 as the Harold Innis Memorial Lecture; at the Queen's University Philosophy Colloquium, also in November 1998; and at the Conference on Democracy and Democratic Discourse, University of Colorado, in March 1999. I thank the organizers of all these events for the opportunities they provided. My thanks also to the students of my University of Toronto graduate seminar "Culture and Politics" in the fall of 1998 for their many searching and inspiring comments on these issues.

1. One of the difficulties with the Declaration, from its acceptance at the United Nations, has been the issue of compliance. Many regimes who are signatories to the document have achieved only partial compliance; moreover, sometimes that compliance is cynical or merely for show. Too often, the presence of human rights rhetoric on the political podium has masked the violation of those rights in nearby prisons or detention centers.

2. Compare, on this point, Linda McQuaig (1998), who argues that technology's ability to track market transactions outweighs its tendencies to make them invisibly fast. However, even if true, ability is not reality: There are few encouraging signs that this feature of technological prowess is controlling the blind speed of trading.

3. Alison Jagger accused me of demonstrating "wishful thinking" in using the phrase "late capitalism" here. I take it that this was a comment on what might be thought a presumption that capitalism is on its way out. I presume nothing of the kind; like Mandel, I mean by the phrase simply that form of capitalism that is primarily postindustrial or electronic.

4. It is, for example, the sense that John Ralston Saul gives to banality in his description of Canadian Prime Minister Brian Mulroney in *The Doubter's Companion* (1994, 40).

5. The phrase once again is Jameson's (1991).

6. The classic statement of this position is probably Adorno and Horkheimer's exquisitely pessimistic assessment in "The Culture Industry: Enlightenment as Mass Deception" (1993, 29–43). I discuss some implications of the view in Kingwell (2000, chap. 4).

7. This is a softer version of the postmodernism of, for example, Jean Baudrillard, whose idea of the simulacral, or hyperreal, arises with the death of the representational and real. A representation is always a representation *of* something, something real, whereas a simulacrum is merely one of many equivalent things without need (or possibility) of something they represent, thus the disappearance of reality as a meaningful category (see Baudrillard 1983).

8. For an illuminating discussion of this new form of specifically cultural reification, see Jameson (1991, 314–318). By Jameson's reasoning, even emphatically modern cultural markers that focus on the unique act of production by an artist can be reified via consumption. Compare, on the point, my reading of Munch's *The Scream* in Kingwell (2000, chap. 4).

9. Shklar (1984, chap. 1). For Rorty's discussion of Shklar's insight, see, among others, his *Contingency, Irony, and Solidarity* (1989).

10. Rorty (1989, 169–188). I leave aside for now the question of whether this gloomy characterization of intellectuals is directed toward Rorty's colleagues.

11. I thank David Mapel for sharpening this point for me. The judgment of perversity might suggest that we are once again moving past imagination into another realm of value: What makes an imagination perverse, in other words, except an independent (presumably rational) standard of rightness and wrongness? However, my claim is that the judgment of perversity is not based on an a priori moral standard, even though we might, for various good purposes, tease out such a standard in our articulations and theorizing; it is, instead, based on our terrible ability to identify with the humiliation and betrayal of Winston by his own desires to transfer the threatened harm to Julia.

12. Compare, on this issue, Richard Rorty's denunciation of academic cultural studies in *Achieving Our Country: Leftist Thought in Twentieth-Century America* (1998). I cannot agree with Rorty's straightforward dichotomy between "activist" leftists and "spectatorial" ones: Sometimes accurate cultural diagnosis is the necessary prologue to effective political action. I do agree that the former is not a substitute for the latter. I thank Christine Sypnowich for pressing me on this point.

13. Michel de Certeau is illuminating on the productive possibilities that, paradoxically, seem to reside in consumption: tactical maneuvers of transformation, alteration, and subversion. Using the very systems of representation that stand over against them, resistant consumer–producers can engage in a critique of consumption that "redistributes its space; it creates at least a certain play in that order, a space for maneuvers of unequal forces and for utopian points" (see de Certeau 1984, 18; Jenkins 1992, chap. 6).

12

A Culture of Publicity

Simone Chambers

In this chapter, I tell two optimistic stories. One story takes place in the international world of human rights and the other in the domestic world of democratic
politics. The hero, if you will, of both stories is publicity. By publicity, I first mean
what is commonly meant by publicity, that is, to make public or to bring something
to the attention of the public. I go beyond this ordinary language use, however, and
also mean publicity in a Kantian sense. Here publicity means not only bringing something to the public's attention but also requiring or asking the public to scrutinize
critically the object in question. This introduces a rational component to publicity.
Critical scrutiny also has an ordinary language meaning and then a somewhat more
technical sense. The ordinary-language meaning refers to a scrutiny that is skeptical
or questioning and often seeks out weakness or fault. When I use the term, I mean
all these things, but I also mean "critical" in the more Kantian sense of critical as in
Critique of Pure Reason. Here Kant is trying to find not the fault in reason but rather
the structure of reason through uncovering and unpacking all its components. It is
an attempt to lay open to the philosopher's eye all that is contained in reason, all
that is presupposed by reason, and all that is meant by reason.[1] Publicity, then, when
working at its most critical, attempts to lay open to the public's eye all that is contained in an object, all that is presupposed by the object, and all that is meant by
that object.

The question of concern here is, What role does publicity play in a global rights
culture and democratic political culture? My answer is that in the global rights culture, publicity can furnish a universalization test for global norms by opening up
those norms to the critical scrutiny of a diverse international community. In democracies, which are governed by states in a way that the global environment is not,
publicity has an added and more concrete role. In addition to furnishing a universalization test, publicity is also and ideally a democratic watchdog, overseeing the

actions and policies of the state. I want to suggest that this role is jeopardized when the objects of our scrutiny are trivialized. Furthermore, the media is often complicit in this trivialization. Despite threats to publicity, however, there is evidence, in particular in new social movements, that the public sphere has not been completely colonized by commercialism and "scandalism."

A GLOBAL CULTURE OF PUBLICITY

When writing about the French Revolution and its status as a progressive event, Kant argued that we should not look at "momentous deeds or crimes committed." Indeed, the events themselves were not that important. Instead, to understand the significance of the French Revolution, we must look "at the mode of thinking of the spectators which reveals itself publicly" (Kant 1963, 143). If we take this insight and apply it to the twentieth century and to what arguably is the most significant event of our century, World War II, but more particularly the Holocaust, an interesting picture emerges. The mode of thinking of the spectators (and participants alike) in the aftermath of World War II revealed itself in a public declaration: the Universal Declaration of Human Rights.[2] This declaration was a direct and public response to the racial hierarchies of Nazi Germany.[3]

When historians look back on the twentieth century and attempt to periodize globalization, I am not so sure that they will find that it began with the Internet explosion, the collapse of communism, increased capital mobility, advanced transportation technology, or even in the McWorld movement. It is not improbable that many will see it having begun more than fifty years ago in the Universal Declaration of Human Rights (Held 1993, 33–37). This declaration now represents a global idiom in which all peoples must talk. It is, at a minimum, a rhetoric that is very difficult to escape. Although the principles of this declaration are violated daily, it is surprising how many people from very different cultures, backgrounds, and life worlds publicly endorse it in principle. The amount of diversity that is contained within the list of signatories is astounding. It is very hard to stand up within the international community and publicly declare that human rights are worthless and that one has no intention of respecting them,[4] but how significant or even positive is this fact? Is this just another case of Western moral imperialism? Have non-Western countries been forced to sign this declaration and then give lip service to it just to be allowed into the club, and is it just lip service in the sense that we have a rhetoric of rights but that this rhetoric has no anchor in reality? I want to argue that the existence and indeed persistence of a global rhetoric of human rights is indeed significant. Its significance is found in the fact that that rhetoric has survived in a global culture characterized by publicity. We live in a cynical, critical, pluralistic age. Public principles come under attack from all quarters. The fact that human rights have survived the type of critical scrutiny that modernity imposes on any global universalist claims is quite astounding. I want now to discuss some of the philosophical assumptions at work behind my statement that a global culture of publicity gives us grounds for declaring that the global rhetoric of rights is more than the imposition of Western values on the rest of the world.

Modernity brings with it the breakup of insulated and monolithic worldviews that limit social actors to one unquestioned source of justification. A more common way of describing this development is to say that modernity brings value pluralism. Not only do we see the proliferation of types of justifications for, say, moral positions, but we also see the recognition of such a proliferation. In this sense, even highly homogeneous and traditional societies participate in modernity and pluralism. It is not that they acknowledge the worth or even tolerate other points of view; it is, rather, that they become aware that there are other points of view. Although the Taliban of Afghanistan, for example, do not value pluralism, they are aware of the fact of pluralism. This awareness, in turn, colors and shapes their interpretation of Islamic fundamentalism. It is very difficult even for the most isolated and traditional cultures to hide from the knowledge that there are other ways of life besides their own. It is difficult to deny the fact of pluralism.

How does pluralism contribute to the justification of human rights? In answering this question, I borrow Jürgen Habermas's concept of differentiation (Habermas 1981, 67–70). He argues that the break up of widely shared and taken-for-granted value systems is the result of a process of differentiation. With differentiation, social actors begin to distinguish between different types of situations that call for different types of explanations and meanings. For example, people begin to recognize that the question "how one goes to heaven" is distinct from the question "how heaven goes" and that the latter can be answered independently of the former.[5] This serves to exclude religion as an appropriate reference in explaining the movement of planets. The process of differentiation places a more complex world before our eyes: We see the growing autonomy of the spheres of science, morality, religion, law, and aesthetics. Each of these spheres becomes uncoupled from traditional interpretations and thus requires new interpretations to underpin it.[6]

Differentiation involves rationalization. I mean rationalization not in the sense of instrumentalization but in the sense that more and more things in the world, from moral principles to the revolution of the planets, require their own set of reasons and explanations. Communicative rationality stands at the center of this process. The intuitive idea behind communicative rationality is that an action or statement is rational to the extent that the actor or speaker can give good reasons for the action or statement.[7] Applying this standard of rationality across cultures means that the greater the extent to which a cultural belief system opens up the possibility of searching for the best possible reason—allowing for revision, corrigibility, criticism, and so on—the more rationalized is that culture. What I want to suggest is that modern culture is highly rationalized in this sense. The search for reasons (whether that be the reason the sun rises or the reason I ought to help my neighbor) is a more critical and open process, allowing participants more flexibility in entertaining alternatives, than are comparable searches in premodern cultures. This is not to make a blanket claim about the modern world being better than the premodern world. Rationalization has some costs that we might find quite high, as in the disappearance of certain traditional ways of life and the strong solidarities that accompany those ways of life.[8] I cannot evaluate this question here. I will simply say that, for better or for worse, we now live in a world that holds out the opportunity to critically scrutinize claims to truth and rightness in a way that one does not see prior to the rise of rationalism in the seventeenth century.

Differentiation and rationalization are destabilizing forces that call into question "givens": Less and less of our cultural horizons are simply taken as given. With modernity we see the attempt to penetrate more deeply than ever before into the presuppositions of our worldview and the modern perspective itself. Thus, although we can never fully escape our cultural horizons (there is no view from nowhere), we do try to become aware of the way in which those horizons limit our thinking. For example, we as moderns have become aware, in a way that premoderns were not, that our view of the world is bound by something like a horizon and that our arguments draw on background and hidden assumptions within our culture. The reasons that we offer for our beliefs and principles must be self-critical and deep precisely because we are conscious of all the things (interests, ethnocentricity, cultural bias, unexamined assumptions, socialization, domination, psychological factors, and so on) that can lie hidden behind arguments. Differentiation creates a different and, I will argue, a more demanding context in which to answer questions such as, Why ought I to do that?

In all societies and cultures, in all times and places, individuals have engaged in critical self-reflection and questioned received ideas. Perhaps this is part of human nature. The claim that I want to make is not that modern individuals are necessarily more critical or thoughtful than premodern individuals. Rather, I want to suggest that modernity offers a new context of criticism and self-reflection. Differentiation and rationalization create a more open universe from which to draw criticism. The result is that criticism of received ideas and dominant principles is both deeper and wider in the modern context than the premodern. I call this the ubiquity and universalization of criticism, respectively: Fewer and fewer things are immune from criticism, doubt, dispute, and challenge. One of the defining features of modernity is that nothing is in principle "beyond question." Indeed, the very idea that there are things beyond question invites the modern mind to question it. This will perhaps be disputed by postmodern thinkers who often imply that modernity is characterized by blindness to hidden forms of domination. However, the very fact that people such as Foucault, Derrida, or Homi Bhabha *criticize* the assumptions of modern thinkers is evidence that very few assumptions can lie hidden for long.[9] As William Connolly (1988, 3) has put it, "[T]he aspiration to become post-modern is one of the paradigmatic ways to be modern . . . the aspiration to delineate the frame of modernity is a paradigmatic idea of the modern age." There will, of course, always be unproblematized assumptions at work behind our conversations, but our very concern for the role of hidden assumptions leads us to expose as many as possible. Part of our moral universe is exposing to public scrutiny hidden interests, ethnocentricity, cultural bias, unexamined assumptions, socialization, domination, moral imperialism, and so on. Our deep distrust of one another as moral authorities guarantees that our criticisms go very deep and that our standards of acceptance are very high.

However, it is not only that criticism is deeper within the modern context; it is also that criticism is wider. Moral claims must respond to a wider array of objections from a plurality of points of view. This is particularly true in moral discourse because modernity has brought with it the idea that moral claims cannot be evaluated on the grounds of who makes them. The universalization of morality opens the door to the universalization of criticism.[10] This means that if we are interested in justifying and responding to criticism, then gender, social position, race, religion, ethnicity, geographic location, and so on of the objector are irrelevant. The more inclusive the moral discourse is, the more pressure exists to find arguments and principles that are acceptable to everyone, that is, the more universal is that discourse. The universalization of criticism, although part of the modern context, attempts to transcend context. Take, for example, the inclusion of future generations in the debate about the environment. Here, the reasons we find convincing must also include objections that could possibly be made by those who must live with our decisions down the road. The more varied the perspectives and worldviews are that converge on a moral principle under critical conditions, the closer that principle comes to fulfilling a claim to universality.

One might want to respond to all this by saying that even if what I have said so far is plausible, it still might be the case that all we do in the modern world is criticize. Nothing has been able to pass this high test. The ubiquity and universalization of criticism has simply opened the door to moral skepticism and relativism. I want to suggest that human rights may be a counterexample. Ubiquitous and universal criticism characterize the debate over human rights. One of the central themes of that debate is the question of whether universal human rights in general, and the Universal Declaration of Human Rights in particular, contain an unacceptable Western bias. I cannot survey the voluminous literature on this topic here. I can make a few general points. This is a typically modern debate in that it seeks to unmask hidden and illicit particularism in claims to universalism. Thus, it involves subjecting human rights to a publicity test. This debate attempts to lay out to the public eye all that is contained in human rights, all that is presupposed by human rights, and all that is meant by human rights. The debate forces defenders of human rights to seek arguments and reasons that appeal to non-Western value systems and to answer objections (many of which are well founded) from a wide range of perspectives. This in turn is a stringent test of universality. The debate has indeed changed many assumptions about human rights and the way in which they are understood and applied (Bauer and Bell 1999). As one participant in this debate has noted, "[T]he cross-cultural critique does not invalidate the Declaration of Human Rights, but offers new perspectives for an internal criticism and sets limits of validity of Human Rights, offering at the same time both possibilities for enlarging its realm, if the context changes and mutual fecundity with other conceptions of Man and reality" (Panikar 1982, 92, n. 76).

The ubiquity and universalization of criticism must be understood as potentialities that have been opened up within modernity and not necessarily as fully realized actualities. We often do not exercise the opportunities to criticize that have been extended to us, or we take things for granted, or we are silenced, or we dismiss criticism without fully considering its merit, and so on. In the case of the human rights debate, there are all sorts of ways that debate falls short of an ideal of publicity. A small international elite dominates the debate excluding most ordinary citizens.[11] There is evidence, however, that there are many sources of domestic human rights agitation, particularly when it comes to questions of compliance.[12] Nevertheless, in many parts of the world, there are significant civil and political as well as social and economic barriers to hearing all the relevant voices of the human rights debate. Furthermore, organizations such as the United Nations are dominated by a few big players and fall very short of giving equal critical voice to all participants. Global inequalities of wealth also undermine the critical force of publicity. Nevertheless, the Age of Reason really has turned out to be an "age of criticism." This does not lead, as Nietzsche thought it would, to nihilism. It leads instead to search for reasons that have the widest and deepest support given our horizons.

The point here is that we have good grounds for claiming that beliefs and principles that survive the exacting type of criticism characteristic of modernity are rational. This facet of modernity does not allow us to say that we have arrived at the moral truth, but it does allow us to say that principles that are widely accepted at the same time as being widely debated (e.g., human rights) have a more rational foundation than principles that have not been able to survive critical examination (e.g., racial hierarchies). The foundation is more rational in the sense of rationality that I outlined previously. Rational principles are ones that have the best possible reasons supporting them.

The Universal Declaration of Human Rights is still with us. It has been subject to a fifty-year publicity test. In that time, the rhetoric of rights has grown stronger, not weaker. Domination (cultural, economic, or military) cannot account for the continued *credibility* of the idea of human rights, not only in the West but all over the world. That credibility does not reside in any one comprehensive moral view, although each of us as individuals might find a particular comprehensive view convincing. The credibility resides in the historical fact that so many different people could endorse the idea. It is not the numbers of people that enhances credibility (as if morality were a matter for majorities to establish). It is the diversity of the people, coupled with minimum conditions of freedom to criticize, that can create the confidence that human rights are well founded.

What about the claim that rights talk is mere rhetoric and that in the real world we see vast violations of human rights? The first answer is that even if my argument were persuasive, it says nothing about conformity to agreed-on rules. In Kant's defense of moral progress, he makes it very clear that he is not claiming that there is "an ever growing quantity of morality." My claim is similar. I want to suggest that there are objective grounds for claiming that *human rights* are an improvement on premodern particularism. *Human beings,* on the other hand, are not necessarily getting better. Modern moral agents are not necessarily more moral than premodern agents; rather, only the rules of the game are getting better. Furthermore, that states violate human rights is not necessarily evidence that human rights do not command wide-ranging and sincere agreement among diverse groups.

I would also argue, although space does not permit it here, that there is a growing conformity to human rights sometimes even against the interest of dominant groups who benefit from their violation. Public statements, even when utterly insincere, can sometimes bind the speaker in unforeseeable ways. To engage in the rhetoric of rights makes public officials accountable in the terms of human rights. I will offer an example that is admittedly from the West but that illustrates my point nevertheless. For many years, the Quebec government defended legislation that banned English commercial signs, not by saying that the English have no rights as a minority (an unthinkable public statement in a liberal democracy) but by claiming that the ban on using one's mother tongue in commercial signage was not a violation of an important freedom. They engaged in the rhetoric of rights, and some would say that they were hoisted on their own petard because it became more and more difficult to give a public justification for the legislation in the terms that the rights discourse offered. Public arguments became less and less persuasive even to the government's strongest supporters. The final straw came when the UN Human Rights Commission ruled that the offending clause of the language legislation was indeed a violation of human rights. This put Quebec in some very bad company and in essence shamed the Quebec government into repealing the clause.[13] They were in no danger of losing an election; the English minority had little leverage, economic or otherwise; there were no material costs in refusing to repeal. The "costs" were in credibility. This proved to be quite effective.

Thus, publicity can serve a second and related function. Not only does the global debate on human rights strengthen their rational credibility, but publicity in the sense of exposing violations can play a role in compliance. There is a growing international civil society, populated by nongovernmental organizations (NGOs) such as Amnesty International or Human Rights Watch and dedicated to exposing and publicizing human rights violations.[14] The role of publicity as whistle blower and watchdog is more characteristic of the democratic arena, however, so I now turn to this arena.

A DEMOCRATIC CULTURE OF PUBLICITY

I want to increase the focus somewhat and look at how a culture of publicity functions in a specific political context, namely, in a liberal democratic order. Unlike the global context, the claim that publicity plays an important role in maintaining democracy is hardly controversial. The interesting question in a domestic political context is, What are the major threats to publicity? Here I want to argue that one of the major threats to publicity in highly developed liberal democracies is a cultural trivialization of publicity or, rather, the objects of publicity.[15] As a culture, we are very interested in exposing what is hidden, unmasking what is veiled, and shining a critical light into what lies in the shadows, but what are the objects of our scrutiny? One danger is that publicity becomes depoliticized by focusing on what is salacious, private, and scandalous. This danger highlights the minimum role that the First Amendment or freedom-of-information legislation plays in maintaining publicity. The special role that publicity plays in democracies is safeguarded through the strengthening of a political culture in which citizens are motivated to engage in critical debate about important questions. After outlining the ideal function of publicity, I will develop this argument in more detail.

In Thucydides' *Peloponnesian War,* some of the most riveting and famous passages belong to public discussions of weighty matters of justice, power, and legitimacy. The Mytilenian debate in which Athenian citizens must decide whether to enslave or to put to death a whole population is today still a lesson in the dangers of *raison d'etat.* Although public, the debates in the Athenian Assembly were not an example of publicity as I am using the term here. Publicity is a peculiarly modern concept that is tied to the rise of the public sphere. The modern public sphere must be understood as something distinct from government, indeed a sphere that can limit, challenge, and criticize government. The Athenian Assembly was the government. Citizens debating the fate of Mytilenians represented a public authority, not a public sphere. The public sphere in the sense that I am talking about it first comes on the historical scene as an extension of civil society. Civil society in turn is the space that bourgeois society creates between the family and the state for economic and associational life.[16] The ideas, interests, values, and ideologies formed within the relations of civil society are voiced and made politically efficacious in the public sphere.

The rise of bourgeois civil society is paralleled by the rise of a corresponding public sphere. In this space, private citizens come together to form a public for the first time. The proliferation of political clubs, journals, and pamphlet writing, as well as regular but informal political meetings in coffee houses, salons, and so on, serve as venues for the formation of a public opinion that is not simply the aggregation of private opinions about public matters. Rather, it is an opinion that is itself formed publicly, that is, in critical public debate. Thus, opinion is public in three senses: It is about public matters, it is in the public domain, and it is produced by a public (i.e., private citizens) interacting in the public sphere.

What is new in this situation is that authority and publicity are no longer joined in one sphere as they were in the Athenian Assembly. Political authority and public airing of issues or publicity now confront each other as separate political forces.[17] In describing this development in England, for example, Habermas (1989, 66) notes that "by the turn of the nineteenth century, the public's involvement in critical debate of political issues had become organized to such an extent that in the role of a permanent critical commentator it had definitely broken the exclusiveness of Parliament and evolved into the official discussion partner of the delegate."

At first, the political function of public opinion is simply public criticism. However, as state actors come to heed the voice of public opinion, a new and stronger role is envisioned. "Since the critical public debate of private people convincingly claimed to be in the nature of a noncoercive enquiry into what was at the same time correct and right, a legislation that had recourse to public opinion thus could not be explicitly considered as domination" (Habermas 1989, 82).

Critical debate in the public becomes a test of rationality and right. By making public the grounds for state action and subjecting these grounds to the critical force of public debate, one can ensure that the state has just reasons for its actions as well as that citizens believe that these reasons are just. Following Kant, this has come to be known as the principle of publicity (Kant 1970a, 85; 1970b, 130). Publicity reconciles the requirements of right (justice/general interest) with the requirements of politics (obedience/stability) (Kant 1970b, 130). Kant states the principle in the following way: "[A]ll actions affecting the rights of other human beings are wrong if their maxim is not compatible with their being made public." The idea is that the sovereign is the guardian of the general interest and thus should have no reason to fear public debate on the legitimacy of his actions. Indeed, a sovereign who fears public debate is a sovereign who fears that his actions are not in the general interest and suspects that that fact will be brought to light within public debate. A policy "which cannot be publicly acknowledged without thereby inevitably arousing the resistance of everyone to my plans, can only have stirred up this necessary and general (hence *a priori* foreseeable) opposition against me because it is itself unjust and thus constitutes a threat to everyone" (Kant 1970b, 126).

In addition to serving as a negative test for the justness of laws, publicity also serves as a means of gaining obedience while respecting each citizen as an autonomous moral agent capable of making rational judgments. "There must be a *spirit of freedom,* for in all matters concerning universal human rights, each individual requires to be convinced by reason that the coercion which prevails is lawful, otherwise he would be in contradiction with himself." Thus, by making public the grounds for state action and subjecting these grounds to the critical force of "independent and public thought," one can ensure that the state has just reasons for its actions as well as that citizens believe that these reasons are just (Kant 1970a, 85).

Kant's great faith in publicity was connected to his idea of enlightenment. Opening up a public sphere to critical debate created not only a critical watchdog but also the conditions necessary to get people to think for themselves. Enlightenment involved thinking for oneself, and thinking for oneself involved breaking the bonds of superstitions and the influence of authority and tradition (Kant 1970a, 54–60). It was difficult if not impossible to do this on one's own. The stimulus of exchange and debate in which challenges to one's ideas and values must be answered encouraged and fostered autonomous thinking. Independent thought can be achieved only in critical interaction with others. The creation of an enlightened and active citizenry would in turn set limits on the state. The optimistic assumption at work here is that injustice and domination cannot survive the scrutiny of an enlightened and civic-minded public. As Steven Holmes notes, "Enlightenment theorists in general tended to contrast *publicity* with the obscurantism of priests, the intrigues of courtiers, and the secret cruelties of tyrants, petty or enthroned."[18]

Publicity was to serve two functions. The first was to bring to light and to place under the public eye the action of states. This in itself would create an incentive structure discouraging certain gross violations of justice and honesty. Second, once brought to the public eye, state action would be subject to public reason, that is, critical rational debate that would evaluate whether a policy was in the public interest.

The salutary effects of publicity have often been used as arguments in defense of free speech and the important role that the press has in curbing tyrants and encouraging rational debate. It is not my intention to engage the debate about whether such arguments are the best defense of freedom of the press (Meiklejohn 1960). Instead, I want to suggest that these arguments have tended to distract the eye from a certain lack of connection between publicity and free speech. While it is true that demands for publicity led to demands for freedom of expression, it is not true that demands for free speech necessarily led or lead to demands for publicity. To put this another way, although free speech is a necessary condition of publicity, it is far from being a sufficient condition. Habermas's analysis of what went wrong with the bourgeois public sphere makes this point rather nicely.

In Habermas's earliest discussions of the public sphere, although sympathetic to the ideal of publicity, he nevertheless argued that such a principle inevitably succumbed to the contradictions of the liberal/capitalist order (Habermas 1989, 141–235). Kant's public might have been critical, but it was very bourgeois in the sense that it both was restricted to property owners and pursued primarily economic interests in the public sphere.[19] Inclusiveness, however, brought a degeneration of the quality of discourse. Critical debate was replaced by the consumption of culture and an apolitical sociability. Participation became fatally altered, and the public sphere became an arena of advertising rather than a site of criticism. There is a public sphere, but it is not the home of publicity. Such functions as exposing injustice have been pushed aside, and we see the public sphere being colonized by commercialism. Habermas's earlier work took this pessimistic line. Mass society has been overwhelmed by the mass media, which in turn has been overwhelmed by economic interests. Our desire for publicity is complicit in this transformation: It allows the public sphere to be governed by the sensibilities of *People* magazine. This is surely not what Kant envisioned. One of the things to note about this diagnosis, First

Amendment doctrine, interpretation, or enforcement appears irrelevant to the demise of publicity. Guaranteeing freedom of speech does not guarantee that we will use that freedom of speech in critical ways, indeed, that we will exercise that freedom at all. The First Amendment does not appear to be the right weapon to fight a battle against the trivialization of the public sphere. The arena for this battle is cultural, not legal.

Is this diagnosis fair? Is Kant's optimism to be fully discredited? Habermas's later career has seen the development of a theoretical approach that is much more optimistic about the possibility of rekindling the emancipator potential of the public sphere first identified by Enlightenment thinkers of the eighteenth century. Much of contemporary democratic theory has taken his lead in this matter, finding the possibility of emancipation in a revitalized and democratized principle of publicity.

How can we transform the public sphere into an arena of critical autonomous debate that is insulated from the distorting effects of power and money? The essential Kantian insight is kept intact. Legitimacy is pursued through public accountability. Public and rational scrutiny of state action keeps the state honest. The issue is how to ensure that the public in fact scrutinizes state action and that that scrutiny is rational.

The first components in maintaining a healthy and democratic public sphere are legal and constitutional safeguards. However, as I have noted, although freedom of speech and association are necessary conditions of a strong public sphere, they are far from being sufficient conditions. As Habermas (1996, 369) notes, "[B]asic constitutional guarantees alone cannot preserve the public sphere and civil society from deformations. The communicative structures of the public sphere must rather be kept intact by an energetic civil society." If the public sphere is to perform the function of democratic watchdog, then a high level of critical debate must be maintained. Maintaining this type of debate is not simply a matter of maintaining formal rules of accessibility, equality, and noncoercion. These rules are rules of noninterference. By themselves, they do not require that citizens talk about important things or approach political issues critically and rationally. Indeed, no laws can force citizens to engage in critical debate; they can merely create the opportunities to do so.

Members of civil society, not the state, bear the responsibility of sustaining an effective democratic public sphere. Thus, revitalizing publicity calls for a kind of political activism and not legal activism. It requires encouraging a deliberative political culture in which citizens have a sense that their participation in the public sphere has meaning and significance.

Evidence that the public sphere has not been entirely trivialized and that democracy still has cultural resources can be found in new social movements. Habermas, along with a number of other critical theorists, identify new social movements as the actors who have done the most in keeping the democratic ideals of publicity alive (Cohen and Arato 1992). They have done this through bringing new voices into the public sphere as well as creatively altering the public sphere itself. Habermas (1996, 370) observes that "actors who support the public sphere are distinguished by the *dual orientation* of their political engagement: with their programs, they directly influence the political system, but at the same time they are also reflexively concerned with revitalizing and enlarging civil society and the public sphere as well as with confirming their own identities and capacities to act."

The environmental movement offers a good example of this dual orientation. On the one hand, environmentalists are intent on influencing legislation, shaping public opinion, and containing economic growth. At the same time, however, the environmental movement has consciously contributed to the expansion of associational life, to the encouragement of grassroots participation, to the development of new and innovative forms of involvement, and to the extension of public forums of debate and deliberation. This sort of activity empowers citizens within civil society, helps maintain independent thinking, and expands and strengthens democracy by giving citizens effective means of shaping their world.

The focus on social movements as important democratic actors is meant only to highlight the defining characteristics of publicity-enhancing activity and to show that it is still possible to mobilize citizens for serious causes. Citizens not engaged in activism can also play a significant role in this process. The creation of a healthy culture of publicity is at the heart of theories of deliberative democracy that offer alternatives to liberal, pluralist, or economistic understandings of democracy. Voting-centric democratic theory is being replaced by talk-centric democratic theory (Benhabib 1996; Bohman 1996; Chambers 1996). The voting-centric view sees democracy as the arena in which fixed preferences and interests compete via fair mechanisms of aggregation. In contrast, theories of deliberative democracy focus on the communicative processes of opinion and will formation that precede voting. Theorists are interested in how deliberation can shape preferences, moderate self-interest, maintain conditions of equality, enable dialogic empowerment, and produce reasonable justification for majority decisions. In other words, interest has shifted from what goes on in the voting booth to what goes on in the discursive interactions of civil society. While nineteenth- and early twentieth-century democratization focused on expanding the vote to include everyone, today democratization focuses on expanding the public sphere to give everyone a say. Voice rather than votes is the vehicle of empowerment. A democratized public sphere offers everyone, especially marginalized groups, the opportunity to participate in shaping, influencing, and criticizing public opinion.

Along with the theoretical defense of deliberative democracy, there is a growing discussion of the institutional and structural transformations that can encourage and foster a culture of publicity and create defenses against the colonization of commercialism. In fighting the tendency of the public sphere to become depoliticized, many democratic theorists shun direct regulation. While it is true that some liberal democracies have highly regulated public spheres with such things as "public affairs" content regulation for television and radio, this approach runs up against the twin liberal principles of free speech and antipaternalism. The very minimal and often voluntary attempts to regulate the content of the public sphere (e.g., civic journalism or voluntary ratings systems) often meet stiff opposition from individuals and groups worried about who is making content decisions for the rest of us. There is a final problem with the content regulation approach: It is not realistic. Even if it were possible to regulate the content of the public sphere sufficiently (which seems unlikely), if citizens are uninterested in participating in public debate, then no amount of public affairs programming will make them care about politics.

The health of the public sphere is dependent on the inclinations and interests of citizens; it resides at the level of culture, which is why a great many theorists of deliberative democracy concerned with maintaining the democratic relevance of publicity have turned toward institutions that shape culture. Central among those institutions are the public school system and the network of associational life that surrounds many citizens in their navigation of civil society. It is not a coincidence that many theorists of deliberative democracy are also theorists of civic education (Barber 1992; Gutmann 1987). A healthy and vibrant public sphere requires first that citizens are given the tools, skills, and knowledge to participate effectively in the public sphere. Furthermore, civic education ought to offer young citizens reasons why they might want to participate in the public sphere. From the point of view of democratic citizenship, teaching the lessons of the civil rights movement is not simply about the history of rights; it is also about what citizens can do when they mobilize. There is a procedural lesson, if you will, in the civil rights movement. That lesson is about the power of publicity to change the system when new voices enter the public sphere. A great deal of very interesting work is being done to shape an education system that encourages young adults to harness the power of publicity.

Also relevant is work being done in regard to the resources that civil society offers in building a healthy public sphere. Tocqueville once noted that associations are schools for citizenship. He argued that associational participation could safeguard liberty by being the effective conduit of citizen criticism. In democracies, despotic power grows out of citizen apathy and self-interest. They leave the public weal up to others while pursuing private gain and advancement. Participation in the intermediary associations, from community church organizations to bowling leagues, can teach individuals the skills of cooperation and civility necessary for citizenship. Such participation can also turn attention away from narrow self-interest and toward more general concerns that affect the community. Liberty, according to Tocqueville, will survive only if citizens maintain an interest in public affairs. This insight has been picked up by many interested in the quality of debate and participation (Putnam 1993).

These developments are not doing away with trivialization or commercialization, but they are creating pockets of publicity within the public sphere. These pockets tend to spring up around crisis issues or particularly pressing dilemmas or issues that have direct salience to the community. This is a realistic model of citizen participation. It is not possible to maintain high levels of civic participation at all times and on all topics. However, these pockets can keep alive the ideal of publicity as a democratic watchdog. They can put our natural tendency to want to expose to good uses.

Deliberative forums are springing up all over the country at both the national and the local level. Through the joint efforts of the Kettering Foundation, the Civic Participation Network, Public Agenda, and other organizations, thousands of community-based groups nationwide are engaged in public deliberation about political issues. The National Issues Forums organized by the Kettering Foundation not only include thousands of citizens in weekend-long national deliberative forums but also serve as a model for longer-term "deliberative processes" in various communities grappling with difficult and divisive political issues. A smaller-scale initiative that is being mirrored across the country can be seen in the Boulder (Colorado) Valley School Board's yearlong project of public deliberation about school choice, equity, and resource allocation in the district. The object here is to bring parents, teachers, administrators, state and local officials, and political representatives together in a public forum to air the issues. Rather than asking citizens to deliberate in the rushed environment of an election campaign, this initiative hopes to bring out the full rational potential of publicity by having a long-term conversation.[20]

This view of democracy requires strong constitutional protections for public speech, but it is clear that it requires much more than this as well. If publicity is to do its job in keeping power in check, then citizens need to be given the spaces, as the Boulder Valley school district is doing, to engage in critical debate. This calls for a more robust vision of protecting the public sphere than a marketplace of ideas where opportunity is understood as no legal barrier to entering the debate. We must evaluate the public sphere from the point of view not only of formal freedoms but also of substantive content. Here there is an obligation to furnish and fund forums where citizens can exercise critical scrutiny and talk about the things they care about.

NOTES

1. The more technical version of this must acknowledge that Kant's critique was a transcendental critique. Transcendental arguments are arguments that seek the conditions of possibility for some given phenomenon. At the most rudimentary level, they are transcendental in the obvious sense that they "transcend," or go beyond, the phenomenon to uncover what must be presupposed if we are to make any sense of the phenomenon whatsoever. Thus, for example, Kant, in his most famous transcendental argument, asked the question, How is experience possible? Kant set out to discover what must be presupposed if we were even to conceive of human knowledge and science as possible (Kant 1956).

2. In 1948, fifty of fifty-eight participating states signed the Universal Declaration of Human Rights. The United Nations now has 188 members, the vast majority of which have signed the major UN human rights instruments, such as the International Covenant on Civil and Political Rights. These instruments are legally binding treaties spawned by the original Declaration.

3. I am not alone in making this argument. See, for example, Habermas (1999, 268).

4. The "Asian Values" debate, which has seen some political leaders in Asia claim that human rights criticism of their regimes is an indefensible imposition of Western values, comes

the closest to such a stand perhaps. However, even here there is no rejection of universal principles of dignity and humanitarian treatment. See Bauer and Bell (1999).

5. In "Letter to the Grand Duchess Christina," Galileo, appealing to Cardinal Baronies in his defense of science, cites the Cardinal as saying that "the intention of the Holy Ghost is to teach us how one goes to heaven, not how heaven goes" (Drake 1957, 186).

6. It is important to remember that although a differentiated life world can be described as more complex than an undifferentiated life world, this does not mean that centered worldviews are not multifarious and intricate in the sense of accounting for a countless number of interconnected factors of life in a coherent way. Primitive and premodern worldviews can indeed be very complex; however, it is a different type of complexity.

7. "Thus assertions and goal-directed actions are the more rational the better the claim (to propositional truth or to efficiency) that is connected with them can be defended against criticism. Correspondingly, we use the expression 'rational' as a disposition predicate for persons from whom such expressions can be expected, especially in difficult situations" (Habermas 1981, 9–10).

8. Many have noted the price we pay for modernization. I have already mentioned Clifford Geertz, but Max Weber probably has one of the most famous versions of this argument when he talks about the disenchantment that accompanies rationalization. See Weber (1978).

9. I would like to add that all three of these writers endorse human rights despite their criticisms of modernity.

10. Although there are huge disputes about the content, form, and justification of moral principles, there is one characteristic that all modern moral theory shares: Moral agency is universalized in the sense that it is no longer tied to specific group membership or natural attributes. If it is wrong for me to do x in a certain situation, then it is wrong for anyone to do x in this situation.

11. For example, Habermas (1999, 268) suggests that the United Nations needs a "'second level' of representation for global citizens as a supplement to the General Assembly of governmental representatives." See also Held (1995).

12. Michael Ignatieff (1999, 59–60) recently wrote, "In Pakistan, it is local human rights groups, not international agencies, who are leading the fight to defend poor country women from being burned alive when they disobey their husbands."

13. For a more detailed account of this case, see Chambers (1996, chap. 14).

14. Korey (1989). Korey argues that the global spread of human rights has more to do with NGOs than with the United Nations or governments.

15. This is one of the many examples of what Habermas has called the Janus face of modern rationalization. For each new possibility opened up by modernity, there is a corresponding "pathology" that is peculiarly modern.

16. Some conception of civil society exclude economic relations, see Chambers (in press).

17. Of course, debates in Parliament are often part of the public sphere. The distinction between publicity and authority is sometimes blurred in practice. However, we can think of debates in Parliament from the point of view of contributions (e.g., through reporting and media coverage) to the formation of public opinion. By contrast, we can also think about such debates as procedural steps in the enactment of enforceable legislation.

18. Holmes (1990, 26).

19. There are a number of very good feminist critiques of the bourgeois conception of the public sphere. Some feminists argue that despite Habermas's efforts to overcome the

limitations of the Kantian conception, his view still contains residues of bourgeois exclusions. See Meehan (1995), especially the essays by Joan Landes and Nancy Fraser.

20. For a more in-depth discussion of the Boulder case as well as a general discussion of deliberative initiatives across the country, see Abu-Haidar (2000).

Bibliography

Abu-Haidar, Sumaya. 2000. "Talking Power: Diversity and Inclusion in Public Deliberation." Doctoral diss., University of Colorado at Boulder.

Adorno, Theodor W., and Max Horkheimer. 1993. "The Culture Industry: Enlightenment as Mass Deception." In *The Cultural Studies Reader,* edited by Simon During. London: Routledge.

Advisory Committee, Public Interest Obligations of Digital Television Broadcasters. 1998. *Charting the Digital Broadcasting Future.* Washington, D.C.: National Telecommunications and Information Administration, U.S. Department of Commerce.

Alcoff, Linda. 1991–1992. "The Problem of Speaking for Others." *Cultural Critique* 20: 5–32.

Altheide, David L., and Robert P. Gilmore. 1972. "The Credibility of Protest." *American Sociological Review* 37 (1): 99–108.

Althusser, Louis. 1971. *Lenin and Philosophy and Other Essays.* Translated by Ben Brewster. New York: Monthly Review Press.

Amenta, Edwin, and Yvonne Zylan. 1991. "It happened Here: Political Opportunity, the New Institutionalism, and the Townsend Movement." *American Sociological Review* 56 (2): 250–265.

Anderson, Benedict. 1983. *Imagined Communities: Reflections on the Origins and Spread of Nationalism.* London: New Left Books.

Ansolabehere, Stephen, Roy Behr, and Shanto Iyengar. 1991. "Mass Media and Elections: An Overview." *American Politics Quarterly* 19 (1): 109–139.

———. 1993. *The Media Game: American Politics in the Television Age.* New York: Macmillan.

Anzaldua, Gloria. 1990. "La Concienca de la Mestiza: Towards a New Consciousness." In *Making Face, Making Soul: Haciendo Caras: Creative and Critical Perspectives by Women of Color,* edited by Gloria Anzaldua. San Francisco: Aunt Lute Foundation Books.

Arendt, Hannah. 1958. *The Human Condition.* Chicago: University of Chicago Press.

Aristotle. 1991. *On Rhetoric: A Theory of Civil Discourse.* Translated by George Kennedy. New York: Oxford University Press.

Arrow, Kenneth. 1985. "The Economics of Agency." In *Principals and Agents: The Structure of Business,* edited by John W. Pratt and Richard Zeckhauser. Boston: Harvard Business School Press.

Athanasiou, Tom. 1985. "High-Tech Alternativism: The Case of the Community Memory Project." In *Radical Science 16: Making Waves: The Politics of Communication,* edited by Radical Science Collective. London: Free Association Books.

Balkin, J. M. 1996. "Media Filters, the V-Chip, and the Foundations of Broadcast Television." *Duke Law Journal* 45: 1131.

Barber, Benjamin. 1992. *An Aristocracy of Everyone: The Politics of Education and the Future of America.* New York: Ballantine.

Barnhurst, Kevin G., and Diana Mutz. 1997. "American Journalism and the Decline in Event-Centered Reporting." *Journal of Communication* 47 (4): 27–53.

Barnhurst, Kevin G., and Catherine A. Steele. 1997. "Image-Bite News: The Visual Coverage of Elections on U.S. Television, 1968–1992." *Harvard International Journal of Press/Politics* 2 (1): 40–58.

Barron, Jerome A. 1967. "Access to the Press—a New First Amendment Right." *Harvard Law Review* 80: 1641.

Bartels, Larry M. 1993. "Messages Received: The Political Impact of Media Exposure." *American Political Science Review* 87 (2): 267–285.

———. 1997. "Campaign Quality: Standards for Evaluation, Benchmarks for Reform." Paper presented at the annual meeting of the American Political Science Association, Washington, D.C.

Baudrillard, Jean. 1983. *Simulations.* New York: Semiotext(e).

Bauer, Joanne R., and Daniel A. Bell, eds. 1999. *The East Asian Challenge for Human Rights.* New York: Cambridge University Press.

Bazelon, David L. 1979. "The First Amendment and the 'New Media'—New Directions in Regulating Telecommunications." *Federal Communications Law Journal* 31: 201.

Beck, Ulrich. 1992. *The Risk Society: Towards a New Modernity.* Translated by Mark Ritter. London: Sage.

Beck, Ulrich, Anthony Giddens, and Scott Lash. 1994. *Reflexive Modernization: Politics, Tradition and Aesthetics in the Modern Social Order.* Stanford, Calif.: Stanford University Press.

Benhabib, Seyla. 1996. "Toward a Deliberative Model of Democratic Legitimacy." In *Democracy and Difference: Contesting the Boundaries of the Political,* edited by Seyla Benhabib. Princeton, N.J.: Princeton University Press.

Benkler, Yochai. 1999. "Free as the Air to Common Use: First Amendment Constraints on Enclosure of the Public Domain." *New York University Law Review* 74: 354.

Bennett, Lerone. 1966. *Confrontation: Black and White.* Baltimore: Penguin.

Beresford, David. 1987. *Ten Men Dead: The Story of the 1981 Irish Hunger Strike.* London: Grafton.

Berry, Jeffrey M. 1989. *The Interest Group Society.* 2nd ed. Glenview, Ill.: Scott, Foresman.

BeVier, Lillian R. 1998. *Is Free TV for Federal Candidates Constitutional?* Washington, D.C.: AEI Press.

Bhabha, Homi K. 1994. *The Location of Culture.* London: Routledge.

Bobbio, Norberto. 1989. *Democracy and Dictatorship: The Nature and Limits of State Power.* Translated by Peter Kennealy. Minneapolis: University of Minnesota Press.

Bodin, Jean. 1962. *The Six Books of a Commonweal.* Translated by Richard Knolles and edited by K. D. McRae. Cambridge, Mass.: Harvard University Press.

Bohman, James. 1991. *New Philosophy of Social Science: Problems of Indeterminacy.* Cambridge: MIT Press.

———. 1995. "Modernization and Impediments to Democracy: Hypercomplexity and Hyperrationality." *Theoria* 86: 1–20.

———. 1996. *Public Deliberation: Pluralism, Complexity, and Democracy.* Cambridge: MIT Press.

———. 1999a. "Citizenship and Norms of Publicity: Wide Public Reason in Cosmopolitan Societies." *Political Theory* 27 (2): 176–202.

———. 1999b. "Democracy as Inquiry, Inquiry as Democracy: Pragmatism, Social Science and the Division of Labor." *American Journal of Political Science* 43 (2): 590–607.

Bohman, James, and William Rehg. 1997. *Deliberative Democracy: Essays on Reason and Politics.* Cambridge: MIT Press.

Bonner, Elena. 1986. *Alone Together.* Translated by Alexander Cook. New York: Knopf.

Braidotti, Rosi. 1992. "The Exile, the Nomad, and the Migrant." *Women's Studies International Forum* 15 (1): 7–10.

Branch, Taylor. 1988. *Parting the Waters: America in the King Years 1954–1963.* New York: Simon & Schuster.

Buchanan, Bruce. 1996. *Renewing Presidential Politics: Campaigns, Media, and the Public Interest.* Lanham, Md.: Rowman & Littlefield.

Bullock, Henry A. 1971. "Urbanism and Race Relations." In *The Urban South,* edited by Rupert B. Vance and Nicholas J. Demerath. Freeport, N.Y.: Books for Libraries Press.

Bulmer, Martin, and Anthony M. Rees, eds. 1996. *Citizenship Today: The Contemporary Relevance of T. H. Marshall.* London: UCL Press.

Calabrese, Andrew. 1997. "Creative Destruction? From the Welfare State to the Global Information Society. *Javnost/The Public* 4 (4): 7–24.

———. 1999a. "The Information Age According to Manuel Castells." *Journal of Communication* 49 (summer).

———. 1999b. "The Welfare State, the Information Society, and the Ambivalence of Social Movements." In *Communication, Citizenship, and Social Policy: Re-Thinking the Limits of the Welfare State,* edited by Andrew Calabrese and Jean-Claude Burgelman. Lanham, Md.: Rowman & Littlefield.

Calabrese, Andrew, and Mark Borchert. 1996. "Prospects for Electronic Democracy in the United States: Re-Thinking Communication and Social Policy." *Media, Culture and Society* 18: 249–268.

Calabrese, Andrew, and Barbara R. Burke. 1992. "American Identities: Nationalism, Media, and the Public Sphere." *Journal of Communication Inquiry* 16 (2): 52–73.

Carden, Maren Lockwood. 1974. *The New Feminist Movement.* New York: Russell Sage Foundation.

Castells, Manuel. 1996. *The Rise of the Network Society. Vol. 1: The Information Age: Economy, Society, and Culture.* Cambridge, Mass.: Blackwell.

———. 1997. *The Power of Identity. Vol. 2: The Information Age: Economy, Society, and Culture.* Malden, Mass.: Blackwell.

———. 1998. *End of Millenium. Vol. 3: The Information Age: Economy, Society, and Culture.* Malden, Mass.: Blackwell.

Censer, Jack R., and Jeremy D. Popkin, eds. 1987. *Press and Politics in Pre-Revolutionary France.* Berkeley and Los Angeles: University of California Press.

Chaffee, Steven, and Stacey Frank. 1996. "How Americans Get Political Information: Print versus Broadcast News." *Annals of the American Academy of Political and Social Science* 546 (July): 48–58.

Chambers, Simone. 1996. *Reasonable Democracy: Jürgen Habermas and the Politics of Discourse.* Ithaca, N.Y.: Cornell University Press.

———. In press. "A Critical Theory of Civil Society." In *Alternative Conceptions of Civil Society,* edited by Will Kymlicka and Simone Chambers. Princeton, N.J.: Princeton University Press.

Clark, Kenneth B. 1970. "The Civil Rights Movement: Momentum and Organization." In *Roots of Rebellion,* edited by Richard P. Young. New York: Harper & Row.

Cohen, Jean L., and Andrew Arato. 1992. *Civil Society and Political Theory.* Cambridge: MIT Press.

Cohn, Carol. 1993. "Wars, Wimps and Women: Talking Gender and Thinking War." In *Gendering War Talk,* edited by Miriam Cooke and Angela Willacott. Princeton, N.J.: Princeton University Press.

Collins, Patricia Hill. 1990. *Black Feminist Thought: Knowledge, Consciousness and the Politics of Empowerment.* New York: Unwin Hyman.

Committee of Concerned Journalists. 1999. "The Clinton Crisis and the Press: A New Standard of American Journalism?" September 8. Available at <http://www.journalism.org/Clintonreport.htm>.

Connolly, William. 1988. *Political Theory and Modernity.* Oxford: Blackwell.

Cook, Timothy E. 1998. *Governing with the News: The News Media as a Political Institution.* Chicago: University of Chicago Press.

Costain, Anne. 1978. "Eliminating Sex Discrimination in Education: Lobbying for Implementation of Title IX." *Policy Studies Journal* 7: 189–195.

———. 1979. "Lobbying for Equal Credit." In *Women Organizing,* edited by Bernice Cummings and Victoria Schuck. Metuchen, N.J.: Scarecrow Press.

———. 1981. "Representing Women: The Transition from Social Movement to Interest Group." *Western Political Quarterly* 34: 100–115.

———. 1983. "The Women's Lobby: Impact of a Movement on Congress." In *Interest Group Politics,* edited by Allan Cigler and Burdett Loomis. Washington, D.C.: Congressional Quarterly Press.

———. 1992. *Inviting Women's Rebellion: A Political Process Interpretation of the Women's Movement.* Baltimore: Johns Hopkins University Press.

———. 1998. "Women Lobby Congress." In *Social Movements and American Political Institutions,* edited by Anne Costain and Andrew McFarland. Lanham, Md.: Rowman & Littlefield.

de Certeau, Michel. 1984. *The Practice of Everyday Life.* Translated by Steven Rendall. Berkeley and Los Angeles: University of California Press.

de Sola Pool, Ithiel. 1990. *Technologies without Boundaries: On Telecommunications in a Global Age.* Cambridge, Mass.: Harvard University Press.

Dewey, John. 1988. *The Public and its Problems. Vol. 2: The Later Works, 1925–1953.* Carbondale: Southern Illinois University Press.

Didion, Joan. 1991. "New York: Sentimental Journeys." *New York Review of Books* 38 (1–2): 45–56.

Downing, John. 1984. *Radical Media: The Political Experience of Alternative Communication.* Boston: South End Press.

Dryzek, John S. 1999. "Transnational Democracy." *Journal of Political Philosophy* 7 (1): 30–51.

Duhacek, Gordana (Dasa). In press. "How We Didn't Survive Nationalism, Which Is No Laughing Matter, or Gender Perspectives on Political Identities in Yugoslavia." In *Gender and Citizenship: Contentions and Controversies in East-West Debates,* edited by Joanna Regulska.

Duyvendak, Jan W. 1992. "The Power of Politics: New Social Movements in an Old Polity, France 1965–1989. Doctoral diss., University of Amsterdam.

Eberly, Rosa A. 1993. "Andrea Dworkin's Mercy: Pain, *Ad Personam,* and Silence in the 'War Zone.'" *Pre/Text: A Journal of Rhetorical Theory* 14 (3–4): 273–304.

———. 2000. *Citizen Critics: Literary Public Spheres.* Urbana: University of Illinois Press.

Efron, Edith. 1971. *The News Twisters.* Los Angeles: Nash.

Eisenstein, Elizabeth. 1968. "Some Conjectures about the Impact of Printing on Western Society and Thought: A Preliminary Report." *Journal of Modern History* 40 (1): 1–56.

———. 1986. *Print Culture and Enlightenment Thought.* Chapel Hill: Hanes Foundation, Rare Book Collection/University of North Carolina at Chapel Hill.

Ellmann, Maud. 1993. *The Hunger Artists: Starving, Writing, and Imprisonment.* Cambridge, Mass.: Harvard University Press.

Entman, Robert M. 1992. "Blacks in the News: Television, Modern Racism, and Cultural Change." *Journalism Quarterly* 69 (2): 341–361.

Epstein, Steven. 1996. *Impure Science: AIDS, Activism and the Politics of Knowledge.* Berkeley and Los Angeles: University of California Press.

Erbring, Lutz, Edie N. Goldenberg, and Arthur H. Miller. 1980. "Front-Page News and Real-World Cues: A New Look at Agenda-Setting by the Media." *American Journal of Political Science* 24 (1): 16–49.

Farnsworth, S. J. 1997. "Media Use and Political Support: The Implications for Political Participation." Paper presented at the annual meeting of the Midwest Political Science Association, Chicago.

Febvre, Lucien Paul Victor, and Henri-Jean Martin. 1976. *The Coming of the Book: The Impact of Printing, 1450–1800.* Translated by David Gerard. London: New Left Books.

Ferris, Charles D., and Terrence J. Leahy. 1989. "Red Lions, Tigers and Bears: Broadcast Content Regulation and the First Amendment." *Catholic University Law Review* 38: 299.

Foucault, Michel. 1973. *Madness and Civilization.* Translated by Richard Howard. New York: Vintage.

———. 1975. *The Birth of the Clinic.* Translated by Alan M. Sheridan. New York: Vintage.

———. 1979. *Discipline and Punish.* Translated by Alan M. Sheridan. New York: Vintage.

———. 1980. *The History of Sexuality.* Vol. 1. Translated by Robert Hurley. New York: Vintage.

———. 1991. "Governmentality." In *The Foucault Effect: Studies in Governmentality,* edited by Graham Burchell, Colin Gordon, and Peter Miller. Chicago: University of Chicago Press.

Fraser, Nancy. 1986. "Toward a Discourse Ethic of Solidarity." *Praxis International* 5 (4): 425–429.

———. 1997. *Justice Interruptus: Critical Reflections on the "Postsocialist" Condition.* New York: Routledge.

Friedan, Betty. 1963. *The Feminine Mystique.* New York: Dell.

Gagnon, Valeve P. 1997. "Imagined Frontiers: Notions of Borders and Groupness." In *Frontiers: The Challenge of Interculturality,* edited by Bozidar Jaksic. Belgrade. Originally published in *Erasmus* (Zagreb), fall 1996.

Galileo. 1957. *Discoveries and Opinions of Galileo.* Translated by Stillman Drake. New York: Doubleday Anchor.

Gallup, George H. 1972. *The Gallup Poll: Public Opinion, 1935–1971.* Vol. 3. New York: Random House.

Gamson, William. 1988. "Political Discourses and Collective Action." *International Social Movement Research* 1: 219–244.

———. 1990. *The Strategy of Social Protest.* 2nd ed. Belmont, Calif.: Wadsworth.

———. 1992. *Talking Politics.* Cambridge: Cambridge University Press.

Garnham, Nicholas. 1992. "The Media and the Public Sphere." In *Habermas and the Public Sphere,* edited by Craig Calhoun. Cambridge: MIT Press.

Garrow, David J. 1978. *Protest at Selma.* New Haven, Conn.: Yale University Press.

———. 1986. *Bearing the Cross: Martin Luther King, Jr., and the Southern Christian Leadership Conference.* New York: Morrow.

Geertz, Clifford. 1986. "The Uses of Diversity." *Michigan Quarterly* 25: 105–123.

Gelb, Joyce. 1995. "Feminist Organization Success and the Politics of Engagement." In *Feminist Organizations,* edited by Myra Marx Ferree and Patricia Yancey Martin. Philadelphia: Temple University Press.

Gelb, Joyce, and Marian Lief Palley. 1977. "Women and Interest Group Politics." *American Politics Quarterly* 5: 331–352.

———. 1982. *Women and Public Policies.* Princeton, N.J.: Princeton University Press.

———. 1987. *Women and Public Policies.* Rev. ed. Princeton, N.J.: Princeton University Press.

Gerhards, Jurgen, and Dieter Rucht. 1992. "Mesomobilization: Organizing and Framing in Two Protest Campaigns in West Germany." *American Journal of Sociology* 98 (3): 555–595.

Giddens, Anthony. 1990. *The Consequences of Modernity.* Stanford, Calif.: Stanford University Press.

Gilliam, Franklin D., Jr., and Shanto Iyengar. 1997. "Prime Suspects: The Effects of Local News on the Viewing Audience." Paper presented at the annual meeting of the Western Political Science Association, Tucson, Arizona.

———. 1998. "The Corrosive Influence of Local Television News on Racial Beliefs." Paper presented at the annual meeting of the Association for Education in Journalism and Mass Communications.

———. forthcoming. "The Crime Script in Local News." Unpublished paper. Department of Political Science, University of California, Los Angeles.

Gitlin, Todd. 1980. *The Whole World Is Watching: Mass Media in the Making and Unmaking of the New Left.* Berkeley and Los Angeles: University of California Press.

Godek, S. G. 1997. "Effects of Network Television News and Newspapers on Political Trust and the Sense of Political Efficacy in the 1972–1974 American National Election Study Panel." Paper presented at the annual meeting of the Midwest Political Science Association, Chicago.

Goldhaber, Michael. 1983. "Microelectronic Networks: A New Workers' Culture in Formation?" In *The Critical Communications Review. Vol. 1: Labor, the Working Class, and the Media,* edited by Vincent Mosco and Janet Wasko. Norwood, N.J.: Ablex.

Goodman, Ellen. 1997. "Digital Television and the Allure of Auctions: The Birth and Stillbirth of DTV Legislation." *Federal Communications Law Journal* 49: 517.

Gould, Roger V. 1991. "Multiple Networks and Mobilization in the Paris Commune, 1871." *American Sociological Review* 56 (6): 716–729.

———. 1993. "Collective Action and Network Structure." *American Sociological Review* 58 (2): 182–196.

Grossman, Lawrence. 1995. *The Electronic Republic.* New York: Viking.

Guéhenno, Jean-Marie. 1995. *The End of the Nation-State.* Translated by Victoria Elliott. Minneapolis: University of Minnesota Press.

Gurevitch, Michael, and Jay G. Blumler. 1990. "Political Communication Systems and Democratic Values." In *Democracy and the Mass Media,* edited by Judith Lichtenberg. Cambridge: Cambridge University Press.

Gusfield, Joseph R. 1981. *The Culture of Public Problems: Drinking-Driving and the Symbolic Order.* Chicago: University of Chicago Press.

Gutmann, Amy. 1987. *Democratic Education.* Princeton, N.J.: Princeton University Press.

Habermas, Jürgen. 1970. *Toward a Rational Society.* Boston: Beacon.

———. 1973. *Theory and Practice.* Boston: Beacon.

———. 1981. *The Theory of Communicative Action.* Vol. 1. Translated by Thomas McCarthy. Boston: Beacon.

———. 1989. *The Structural Transformation of the Public Sphere: An Inquiry into a Category of Bourgeois Society.* Translated by Thomas Burger. Cambridge: MIT Press.

———. 1996. *Between Facts and Norms: Contributions to a Discourse Theory of Law and Democracy.* Cambridge: MIT Press.

———. 1998. *The Inclusion of the Other.* Edited by Ciaran Cronin and Pablo DeGrieff. Cambridge: MIT Press.

———. 1999. "The War in Kosovo: Bestiality and Humanity: A War on the Border between Legality and Morality." *Constellations* 6 (3): 263–272.

Haight, Timothy, Robert Rubinyi, and Anna L. Zornosa. 1983. "Uses of Computer and Communication Technologies by Grass-Roots Community Organizations." In *Proceedings from the Tenth Annual Telecommunications Policy Research Conference,* edited by Oscar H. Gandy Jr., Paul Espinosa, and Janusz A. Ordover. Norwood, N.J.: Ablex.

Hall, Stuart. 1997. "The Centrality of Culture: Notes on the Cultural Revolutions of Our Time." In *Media and Cultural Regulation,* edited by Kenneth Thompson. London: Sage.

Hart, Roderick P. 1997. *DICTION: The Text-Analysis Program.* Thousand Oaks, Calif.: Sage/Scolari.

———. 2000. *Campaign Talk: Why Elections Are Good for Us.* Princeton, N.J.: Princeton University Press.

———. In press. "Redeveloping DICTION: Theoretical Considerations." In *New Directions in Computer Content Analysis,* edited by M. West. New York: Ablex.

Hart, Roderick P., D. Smith-Howell, and J. Llewellyn. 1996. "News, Psychology, and Presidential Politics." In *The Psychology of Political Communication,* edited by Ann N. Crigler. Ann Arbor: University of Michigan Press.

Harvey, David. 1989. *The Condition of Postmodernity.* Oxford: Blackwell.

Hauser, Gerard A. 1968. "The Example in Aristotle's Rhetoric: Bifurcation or Contradiction?" *Philosophy and Rhetoric* 1 (1): 78–90.

———. 1985. "Aristotle's Example Revisited." *Philosophy and Rhetoric* 18 (3): 171–180.

———. 1999. *Vernacular Voices: The Rhetoric of Publics and Public Spheres.* Columbia: University of South Carolina Press.

Havel, Václav. 1989. *Letters to Olga: June 1979–September 1982.* Translated by Paul Wilson. New York: Henry Holt.

Hazlett, Thomas W. 1990. "The Rationality of U.S. Regulation of the Broadcast Spectrum." *Journal of Law and Economics* 33: 133.

Headrick, Daniel R. 1991. *The Invisible Weapon: Telecommunications and International Politics, 1851–1945.* New York: Oxford University Press.

Heater, Derek B. 1990. *Citizenship: The Civic Ideal in World History, Politics, and Education.* London: Longman.

Held, David. 1993. "Democracy: From City-States to a Cosmopolitan Order?" In *Prospects for Democracy: North, South, East, West,* edited by David Held. Stanford, Calif.: Stanford University Press.

———. 1995. *Democracy and the Global Order: From the Modern State to Cosmopolitan Governance.* Stanford, Calif.: Stanford University Press.

Hempel, Carl G. 1965. *Aspects of Scientific Explanation, and Other Essays in the Philosophy of Science.* New York: Free Press.

Herod, Andrew, Gearóid Ó Tuathail, and Susan M. Roberts. 1998. *An Unruly World? Globalization, Governance, and Geography.* London: Routledge.

Hess, Stephen. 1991. *Live from Capitol Hill: Studies of Congress and the Media.* Washington, D.C.: Brookings Institution.

Hibbing, John R., and Elizabeth Theiss-Morse. 1998. "The Media's Role in Public Negativity toward Congress: Distinguishing Emotional Reactions and Cognitive Evaluations." *American Journal of Political Science* 42 (2): 475–498.

Holmes, Steven. 1990. "Liberal Constraints on Private Power?: Reflections on the Origins and Rational of Access Regulation." In *Democracy and the Mass Media,* edited by Judith Lichtenberg. Cambridge: Cambridge University Press.

Homer. 1990. *The Iliad.* Translated by Robert Fagles. New York: Viking.

Honneth, Axel. 1992. "Integrity and Disrespect: Principles of a Conception of Morality Based on the Theory of Recognition." *Political Theory* 20: 2.

———. 1997. *The Struggle for Recognition: The Moral Grammar of Social Conflict.* Translated by Joel Anderson. Cambridge, Mass.: Polity Press.

Horwitz, Robert B. 1989. *The Irony of Regulatory Reform: The Deregulation of American Telecommunications.* New York: Oxford University Press.

Hubbard, Howard. 1968. "Five Long Hot Summers and How They Grew." *Public Interest* 12: 3–24.

Huber, Peter. 1996. "Cyber Power." *Forbes* 158 (December 2): 142–147.

Hundt, Reed E. 1996. "A New Paradigm for Broadcast Regulation." *Journal of Law and Communications* 15: 527.

Ignatieff, Michael. 1993. *Blood and Belonging: Journeys into the New Nationalism.* Toronto: Viking.

———. 1997. *The Warrior's Honor.* Toronto: Viking.

———. 1999. " Human Rights: The Midlife Crisis." *New York Review of Books,* May 20, 59–60.

Iyengar, Shanto. 1991. *Is Anyone Responsible? How Television Frames Political Issues.* Chicago: University of Chicago Press.

———. 1996. "Framing Responsibility for Political Issues." *Annals of the American Academy of Political and Social Science* 546: 59–70.

Iyengar, Shanto, and Donald R. Kinder. 1987. *News that Matters: Television and American Opinion.* Chicago: University of Chicago Press.

Iyengar, Shanto, Mark D. Peters, and Donald R. Kinder. 1982. "Experimental Demonstrations of the 'Not-So-Minimal' Consequences of Television News Programs." *American Political Science Review* 76: 848–858.

Iyengar, Shanto, and Adam Simon. 1993. "News Coverage of the Gulf Crisis and Public Opinion: A Study of Agenda-Setting, Priming, and Framing." *Communication Research* 20: 365–383.

Jaggar, Alison. 1989. "Love and Knowledge: Emotion in Feminist Epistemology." *Inquiry: An Interdisciplinary Journal of Philosophy* 32 (June): 51–76.

———. 1993. "Taking Consent Seriously: Feminist Practical Ethics and Actual Moral Dialogue." In *Applied Ethics: A Reader,* edited by Earl R. Winkler and Jerrold R. Coombs. Oxford: Blackwell.

———. 1998a. "Globalizing Feminist Ethics. *Hypatia: A Journal of Feminist Philosophy* 13 (2): 7–31.

———. 1998b. "Sexual Equality as Parity of Effective Voice." *Journal of Contemporary Legal Issues* 9 (spring): 179–202.

Jameson, Fredric. 1991. *Postmodernism, or, the Cultural Logic of Late Capitalism.* Durham, N.C.: Duke University Press.

Jenkins, Henry. 1992. *Textual Poachers: Television Fans and Participatory Culture.* New York: Routledge.

Johnstone, Henry W., Jr. 1990. "Rhetoric as a Wedge: A Reformulation." *Rhetoric Society Quarterly* 20 (4): 333–338.

Kant, Immanuel. 1956. *Critique of Pure Reason.* Translated by L. W. Beck. Indianapolis: Bobbs-Merrill.

———. 1963. "An Old Question Raised Again: Is the Human Race Constantly Progressing?" In *On History,* by Immanuel Kant. Indianapolis: Library of Liberal Arts.

———. 1970a. "On the Common Saying: 'This May Be True in Theory, but It Does Not Apply in Practice.'" In *Kant: Political Writings,* edited by Hans Reiss. Cambridge: Cambridge University Press.

———. 1970b. "Perpetual Peace." In *Kant: Political Writings,* edited by Hans Reiss. Cambridge: Cambridge University Press.

———. 1983. *Perpetual Peace and Other Essays.* Translated by Ted Humphrey. Indianapolis: Hackett.

Katzenstein, Mary Fainsod. 1987. "Comparing the Feminist Movements of the United States and Western Europe: An Overview." In *The Women's Movements of the United States and Western Europe: Consciousness, Political Opportunity, and Public Policy,* edited by Mary Fainsod Katzenstein and Carol McClurg Mueller. Philadelphia: Temple University Press.

———. 1990. "Feminism within American Institutions: Unobtrusive Mobilization in the 1980s." *Signs* 16: 27–54.

———. 1995. "Discursive Politics and Feminist Activism in the Catholic Church." In *Feminist Organizations,* edited by Myra Marx Ferree and Patricia Yancey Martin. Philadelphia: Temple University Press.

Keane, John. 1991. *The Media and Democracy*. Cambridge: Polity Press.

Kerbel, M. 1994. "Covering the Coverage: The Self-Referential Nature of Television Reporting of the 1992 Presidential Campaign." Paper presented at the annual meeting of the Midwest Political Science Association, Chicago.

Khor, Martin. 1998. "NGOs Mount Protests against MAI." August 22. Available at <http://www.globalpolicy.org/socecon/bwi-wto/indexmai.htm>.

King, Martin Luther, Jr. 1963. *Why We Can't Wait*. New York: Harper & Row.

Kingwell, Mark. 1998. "The Banality of Evil, the Evil of Banality." Paper presented at the Symposium on the Artist and Human Rights, Ottawa.

———. 2000. *Better Living: In Pursuit of Happiness from Plato to Prozac*. New York: Crown.

Klite, Paul, Robert A. Bardwell, and Jason Salzman. 1997. "Local TV News: Getting Away with Murder." *Press/Politics* 2 (2): 102–112.

Koopmans, Ruud. 1992. "Democracy from Below: New Social Movements and the Political System in West Germany." Doctoral diss., University of Amsterdam.

Korey, William. 1998. *NGOs and the Universal Declaration of Human Rights: A Curious Grapevine*. New York: St. Martin's.

Krattenmaker, Thomas G. 1998. *Telecommunications Law and Policy*. 2nd ed. Durham, N.C.: Carolina Academic Press.

Krattenmaker, Thomas G., and L. A. Powe Jr. 1995. "Converging First Amendment Principles for Converging Communications Media." *Yale Law Journal* 104: 1719.

Krosnick, Jon A., and Laura A. Brannon. 1993. "The Impact of the Gulf War on the Ingredients of Presidential Evaluations: Multidimensional Effects of Political Involvement." *American Political Science Review* 87: 963–975.

———. 1995. "New Evidence on News Media Priming." Paper presented at the annual Meeting of the American Association for Public Opinion Research.

Kuhn, Thomas S. 1970. *The Structure of Scientific Revolutions*. 2nd ed. Chicago: University of Chicago Press.

Kuron, Jacek. 1968. *Revolutionary Marxist Students in Poland Speak Out, 1964–1968*. New York: Merit Press.

Kymlicka, Will. 1997. "The Sources of Nationalism: A Commentary on Taylor." In *The Morality of Nationalism,* edited by Robert McKim and Jeff McMahan. New York: Oxford University Press.

Latour, Bruno. 1987. *Science in Action: How to Follow Scientists and Engineers through Society*. Cambridge, Mass: Harvard University Press.

Lee, Eric. 1997. *The Labour Movement and the Internet: The New Internationalism*. London: Pluto Press.

Lichtenberg, Judith. 1997. "Nationalism: For and (Mainly) Against." In *The Morality of Nationalism,* edited by Robert McKim and Jeff McMahan, 158–175. New York: Oxford University Press.

Lichter, Robert, and Ted Smith. 1996. "Why Elections Are Bad News: Media and Candidate Discourse in the 1996 Presidential Primaries." *Harvard International Journal of Press and Politics* 1 (4): 15–35.

Lipovetsky, Gilles. 1994. *The Empire of Fashion: Dressing Modern Democracy*. Translated by Catherine Porter. Princeton, N.J.: Princeton University Press.

Lipsky, Michael. 1970. *Protest in City Politics*. Chicago: Rand McNally.

Logan, Charles W. 1997. "Getting beyond Scarcity: A New Paradigm for Assessing the Constitutionality of Broadcast Regulation." *California Law Review* 85: 1687.

Lorde, Audre. 1984. *Sister Outsider*. Freedom, Calif.: Crossing Press.

Lowry, Dennis T., and Jon A. Shidler. 1995. "The Sound Bites, the Biters, and the Bitten: An Analysis of Network TV News Bias in Campaign '92." *Journalism and Mass Communication Quarterly* 72 (1): 33–44.

Lugones, Maria C., and Elizabeth V. Spelman. 1983. "Have We Got a Theory for You! Feminist Theory, Cultural Imperialism and the Demand for 'the Woman's Voice.'" *Hypatia: A Journal of Feminist Philosophy* 1 (1): 573–581.

Luke, Tim. 1978. "Culture and Politics in the Age of Artificial Negativity. *Telos* 35 (spring): 55–72.

Mansbridge, Jane. 1986. *Why We Lost the ERA*. Chicago: University of Chicago Press.

Marwell, Gerald, Pamela E. Oliver, and Ralph Prahl. 1988. "Social Networks and Collective Action: A Theory of the Critical Mass." *American Journal of Sociology* 94 (3): 502–534.

Marx, Gary T. 1974. "Thoughts on a Neglected Category of Social Movement Participant: The Agent Provocateur and the Informant." *American Journal of Sociology* 80 (2): 402–442.

———. 1979. "External Efforts to Damage or Facilitate Social Movements: Some Patterns, Explanations, Outcomes, and Complications." In *The Dynamics of Social Movements*, edited by Mayer N. Zald and John D. McCarthy. Cambridge, Mass.: Winthrop.

McAdam, Doug. 1982. *Political Process and the Development of Black Insurgency, 1930–1970*. Chicago: University of Chicago Press.

———. 1986. "Recruitment to High-Risk Activism: The Case of Freedom Summer." *American Journal of Sociology* 92 (July): 64–90.

———. 1996. "Movement Strategy and Dramaturgic Framing in Democratic States: The Case of the American Civil Rights Movement." *Research on Democracy and Society* 3: 155–176.

McAdam, Doug, and Ronnelle Paulsen. 1993. "Specifying the Relationship between Social Ties and Activism." *American Journal of Sociology* 99 (November): 640–667.

McCarthy, John D., and Mayer N. Zald. 1973. *The Trend of Social Movements in America: Professionalization and Resource Mobilization*. Morristown, N.J.: General Learning Press.

McCombs, Maxwell, and Donald Shaw. 1972. "The Agenda Setting Function of the Mass Media." *Public Opinion Quarterly* 36: 176–187.

McFall, Lynne. 1991. "What's Wrong with Bitterness?" In *Feminist Ethics*, edited by Claudia Card. Lawrence: University Press of Kansas.

McQuaig, Linda. 1998. *The Cult of Impotence: Selling the Myth of Powerlessness in the Global Economy*. Toronto: Viking.

Meehan, Johanna, ed. 1995. *Feminists Read Habermas: Gendering the Subject of Discourse*. London: Routledge.

Meiklejohn, Alexander. 1948. *Free Speech and its Relation to Self-Government*. New York: Harper & Row.

———. 1960. *Political Freedom: The Constitutional Powers of the People*. New York: Harper.

Melucci, Alberto. 1996. *Challenging Codes: Collective Action in the Information Age*. Cambridge: Cambridge University Press.

Mendelberg, T. 1997. "Executing Hortons: Racial Crime in the 1988 Presidential Campaign." *Public Opinion Quarterly* 61 (1): 134–157.

Mendelsohn, Matthew. 1998. "The Construction of Electoral Mandates: Media Coverage of Election Results in Canada." *Political Communication* 15 (2): 239–253.

Meyers, Diana Tietjens. 1997. "Emotion and Heterodox Moral Perception: An Essay in Moral Social Psychology." In *Feminists Rethink the Self,* edited by Diana Tietjens Meyers. Boulder, Colo.: Westview.

Michnik, Adam. 1985. *Letters from Prison and Other Essays.* Translated by Maya Latynski. Berkeley and Los Angeles: University of California Press.

Milburn, Michael A., and Anne B. McGrail. 1992. "The Dramatic Presentation of News and Its Effects on Cognitive Complexity. *Political Psychology* 13 (4): 613–632.

Miller, J. M., and J. A. Krosnick. 1997. "Anatomy of News Media Priming." In *Do the Media Govern?: Politicians, Voters, and Reporters in America,* edited by Shanto Iyengar and Richard Reeves. Thousand Oaks, Calif.: Sage.

Miller, Toby. 1998. *Technologies of Truth: Cultural Citizenship and the Popular Media.* Minneapolis: University of Minnesota Press.

Minkoff, Debra. 1993. "Shaping Contemporary Organizational Action: Women's and Minority Social Change Strategies, 1955–85." Paper presented at the annual meeting of the American Sociological Association, Miami.

Montgomery, Kathryn C. 1989. *Target, Prime Time: Advocacy Groups and the Struggle over Entertainment Television.* New York: Oxford University Press.

Moraga, Cherrie. 1983. *Loving in the War Years: Lo que nunca paso por sus labios.* Boston: South End Press.

Narayan, Uma. 1997. *Dislocating Cultures: Identities, Traditions, and Third-World Feminism.* New York: Routledge.

Natanson, Maurice. 1978. "The Arts of Indirection." In *Rhetoric, Philosophy, and Literature: An Exploration,* edited by Don M. Burks. West Lafayette, Ind.: Purdue University Press.

Nickel, James W. 1999. "Economic Liberties." In *The Idea of Political Liberalism,* edited by Victoria Davion and Clark Wolf. Lanham, Md.: Rowman & Littlefield.

Noyes, Richard E., S. Robert Lichter, and Daniel Amundson. 1993. "'Was TV Election News Better This Time?' A Content Analysis of 1988 and 1992 Campaign Coverage." *Journal of Political Science* 21: 3–25.

Offe, Claus. 1985. *Contradictions of the Welfare State.* Cambridge: MIT Press.

O'Malley, Padraig. 1990. *Biting at the Grave: The Irish Hunger Strikes and the Politics of Despair.* Boston: Beacon.

Page, Benjamin I. 1996. *Who Deliberates? Mass Media in Modern Democracy.* Chicago: University of Chicago Press.

Page, Benjamin, and Robert Shapiro. 1989. "Educating and Manipulating the Public." In *Manipulating Public Opinion: Essays on Public Opinion as a Dependent Variable,* edited by Michael Margolis and Gary Mauser. Pacific Grove, Calif.: Brooks/Cole.

Panikar, R. 1982. "Is the Notion of Human Rights a Western Concept?" *Diogenes* 120.

Paterson, Randi, and Gail Corning. 1997. "Researching the Body: An Annotated Bibliography for Rhetoric." *Rhetoric Society Quarterly* 27: 5–29.

Perelman, Chaïm, and Lucie Olbrechts-Tyteca. 1969. *The New Rhetoric: A Treatise on Argumentation.* Translated by John Wilkinson and Purcell Weaver. Notre Dame, Ind.: University of Notre Dame Press.

Pew Research Center for the People and the Press, 1997. "Press Unfair, Inaccurate, and Pushy," Pew Research Center for the People and the Press. September 8. Available at <http://www.people-press.org/content.htm>.

Phelan, Shane. 1994. *Getting Specific: Postmodern Lesbian Politics.* Minneapolis: University of Minnesota Press.

Pierson, Christopher. 1998. *Beyond the Welfare State? The New Political Economy of Welfare.* 2nd ed. University Park: Pennsylvania State University Press.

Piven, Frances F., and Richard A. Cloward. 1979. *Poor People's Movements.* New York: Vintage.

Popkin, Jeremy D. 1990. *Revolutionary News: The Press in France, 1789–1799.* Durham, N.C.: Duke University Press.

Powell, Michael K. 1998. "The Public Interest Standard: A New Regulator's Search for Enlightenment." September 16. Available at <http://www.fcc.gov/commissioners/powell>.

Price, Monroe E., and John F. Duffy. 1997. "Technological Change and Doctrinal Persistence: Telecommunications Reform in Congress and the Court." *Columbia Law Review* 97: 976.

Price, Vincent, and Edward J. Czilli. 1996. "Modeling Patterns of News Recognition and Recall." *Journal of Communication* 46 (2): 55–78.

Public Citizen, Friends of the Earth, Sierra Club. 1999. "International Coalition Launches Campaign against the MAI: A New Stealth Investment Agreement." August 19. Available at <http://www.citizen.org/press/pr-mai1htm>.

Putnam, Hilary. 1994. "Pragmatism and Moral Objectivity." In *Words and life,* edited by James Conant. Cambridge, Mass.: Harvard University Press.

Putnam, Robert. 1993. *Making Democracy Work: Civic Traditions in Modern Italy.* Princeton, N.J.: Princeton University Press.

Quadagno, Jill. 1992. "Social Movements and State Transformation: Labor Unions and Racial Conflict in the War on Poverty." *American Sociological Review* 57 (5): 616–634.

Ratushinskaya, Irina. 1989. *Grey Is the Color of Hope.* Translated by Alyona Kojevnikov. New York: Vintage International.

Rawls, John. 1993. *Political Liberalism.* New York: Columbia University Press.

Reuters. 1999. "Gates Backs 'Fast Track' Power for Clinton." August 22. Available at Lexis-Nexis Academic Universe.

Rochon, Thomas. 1998. *Culture Moves: Ideas, Activism, and Changing Values.* Princeton, N.J.: Princeton University Press.

Rockefeller, Steven C. 1992. "Comment." In *Multiculturalism and "The Politics of Recognition,"* edited by Charles Taylor et al. Princeton, N.J.: Princeton University Press.

Rorty, Richard. 1989. *Contingency, Irony, and Solidarity.* Cambridge: Cambridge University Press.

———. 1998. *Achieving Our Country: Leftist Thought in Twentieth-Century America.* Cambridge, Mass.: Harvard University Press.

Rosenberg, Gerald N. 1991. *The Hollow Hope.* Chicago: University of Chicago Press.

Rosenthal, Naomi, Meryl Fingrutd, Michele Ethier, Roberta Karant, and David McDonald. 1985. "Social Movements and Network Analysis: A Case Study of Nineteenth Century Women's Reform in New York State." *American Journal of Sociology* 90 (5): 1022–1054.

Rosston, Gregory L., and Jeffrey S. Steinberg. 1997. "Using Market-Based Spectrum Policy to Promote the Public Interest. *Federal Communications Law Journal* 50: 87.

Rubin, Gretchen C. 1998. "Quid Pro Quo: What Broadcasters Really Want." *George Washington Law Review* 66: 686.

Ryan, Amy F. 1998. "Don't Touch That V-Chip: A Constitutional Defense of the Television Program Rating Provisions of the Telecommunications Act of 1996." *George Washington Law Review* 87: 823.

Ryan, Charlotte. 1991. *Prime Time Activism.* Boston: South End Press.

Saul, John R. 1994. *The Doubter's Companion.* New York: Free Press.

Scarry, Elaine. 1985. *The Body in Pain: The Making and Unmaking of the World.* New York: Oxford University Press.

Schiller, Herbert I. 1989. *Culture, Inc.: The Corporate Takeover of Public Expression.* New York: Oxford University Press.

Schlozman, Kay. 1990. "Representing Women in Washington: Sisterhood and Pressure Politics." In *Women, Politics, and Change,* edited by Louise Tilly and Patricia Gurin. New York: Russell Sage Foundation.

Seago, K. S. 1994. "The 'New' Political Sophistication: News That Doesn't Matter." Paper presented at the annual meeting of the Midwest Political Science Association, Chicago.

Sennett, Richard. 1994. *Flesh and Stone: The Body and the City in Western Civilization.* New York: Norton.

Sforza, Michelle, Scott Nova, and Mark Weisbrot. 1999. "Writing the Constitution of a Single Global Economy: A Concise Guide to the Multilateral Agreement on Investment." August 19. Available at <http://www.preamble.org/MAI/maioverv.html>.

Shapiro, Susan. 1987. "The Social Control of Impersonal Trust." *American Journal of Sociology* 93: 623–658.

Shcharansky, Anatoly. 1988. *Fear No Evil.* Translated by Stefani Hoffman. New York: Random House.

Shklar, Judith N. 1984. *Ordinary Vices.* Cambridge, Mass.: Harvard University Press.

Slavin, Sarah. 1995. "National Organization for Women (NOW)." In *U.S. Women's Interest Groups,* edited by Sarah Slavin. Westport, Conn.: Greenwood.

Snow, David A., and Robert D. Benford. 1988. "Ideology, Frame Resonance, and Participant Mobilization." In *From Structure to Action: Social Movement Participation across Cultures,* edited by Bert Klandermans, Hanspeter Kriesi, and Sidney Tarrow. Greenwich, Conn.: JAI Press.

———. 1992. "Master Frames and Cycles of Protest." In *Frontiers in Social Movement Theory,* edited by Aldon D. Morris and Carol M. Mueller. New Haven, Conn.: Yale University Press.

Snow, David A., Jr., E. Burke Rochford, Steven K. Worden, and Robert D. Benford. 1986. "Frame Alignment Processes, Micromobilization, and Movement Participation." *American Sociological Review* 51 (4): 464–481.

Snow, David A., Jr., Louis A. Zurcher, and Sheldon Ekland-Olson. 1980. "Social Networks and Social Movements: A Microstructural Approach to Differential Recruitment." *American Sociological Review* 45 (5): 787–801.

Spalter-Roth, Roberta, and Ronnee Schreiber. 1995. "Outsider Issues and Insider Tactics: Strategic Tensions in the Women's Policy Network during the 1980s." In *Feminist Organizations: Harvest of the New Women's Movement,* edited by Myra Marx Ferree and Patricia Yancey Martin. New York: Russell Sage Foundation.

Spiller, Pablo T., and Carlo Cardilli. 1999. "Towards a Property Rights Approach to Communications Regulation." *Yale Journal on Regulation* 16: 53.

Stanley, Harold W., and Richard G. Niemi. 1998. *Vital Statistics on American Politics: 1997–1998.* Washington, D.C.: Congressional Quarterly Press.

Steele, Catherine A., and Kevin G. Barnhurst. 1996. "The Journalism of Opinion: Network News Coverage of U.S. Presidential Campaigns, 1968–1988." *Critical Studies in Mass Communication* 13 (3): 187–209.

Stumberg, Robert. 1998. "Sovereignty for Sale." Testimony before the House International Relations Subcommittee of International Economic Policy and Trade, March 5, 1998. August 19. Available at <http://www.stelling.nl/mai/nievws/5-3.html>.

Sullivan, Kathleen M. 1989. "Unconstitutional Conditions." *Harvard Law Review* 102: 1413.

Sunstein, Cass R. 1993. *Democracy and the Problem of Free Speech.* New York: Free Press.

Taglieri, Joe. 1999. "Pressure from Citizens' Groups Kills Trade Treaty for Now." *National Catholic Reporter,* January 29.

Tajfel, Henri, and J. Turner. 1986. "An Integrative Theory of Intergroup Conflict." In *The Psychology of Intergroup Relations,* edited by William G. Austin and Stephen Worchel. Chicago: Nelson-Hall.

Tamir, Yael. 1993. *Liberal Nationalism.* Princeton, N.J.: Princeton University Press.

Tarrow, Sidney. 1994. *Power in Movement: Social Movements, Collective Action and Politics.* New York: Cambridge University Press.

Taylor, Charles. 1992. *Multiculturalism and "The Politics of Recognition": An Essay by Charles Taylor.* Edited by Amy Gutmann. Princeton, N.J.: Princeton University Press.

———. 1997. "Nationalism and Modernity." In *The Morality of Nationalism,* edited by Robert McKim and Jeff McMahan. New York: Oxford University Press.

Teeple, Gary. 1995. *Globalization and the Decline of Social Reform.* Toronto: Garamond Press.

Tesanovic, Jasmina. 2000. *Normality: A Moral Opera by a Political Idiot.* San Francisco: Cleis.

Thomas, Laurence. 1992–1993. "Moral Deference." *Philosophical Forum* 14 (1–3): 233–250.

Thompson, John B. 1995. *The Media and Modernity: A Social Theory of the Media.* Stanford, Calif.: Stanford University Press.

Timerman, Jacobo. 1981. *Prisoner without a Name, Cell without a Number.* Translated by Toby Talbot. New York: Knopf.

Tindemans, Léo. 1996. *Unfinished Peace: Report of the International Commission on the Balkans.* Washington, D.C.: Carnegie Endowment.

Tisdale, Sallie. 1994. *Talk Dirty to Me: An Intimate Philosophy of Sex.* New York: Doubleday.

Tomlinson, John. 1991. *Cultural Imperialism: A Critical Introduction.* Baltimore: Johns Hopkins University Press.

Tönnies, Ferdinand. 1957. *Community and Society (Gemeinschaft und Gesellschaft).* Translated by Charles P. Loomis. New York: Harper & Row.

Trujillo, Carla. 1991. "Chicana Lesbians: Fear and Loathing in the Chicano Community." In *Chicana Lesbians: The Girls Our Mothers Warned Us About,* edited by Carla Trujillo. Berkeley, Calif.: Third Woman Press.

Turner, Ralph H. 1969. "The Public Perception of Protest." *American Sociological Review* 34 (6): 815–830.

United Nations General Assembly. 1949. *Universal Declaration of Human Rights.* Lake Success, N.Y.: United Nations Department of Public Information.

United States Attorney General's Commission, Pornography. 1986. *Attorney General's Commission on Pornography: Final Report.* 2 vols. Washington, D.C.: U.S. Department of Justice.

Vance, Carole S. 1986. "The Meese Commission on the Road." *The Nation* 243 (August 2): 65, 76–82.

Wallach, Lori. 1998a. "Multilateral Agreement on Investment: Win, Lose or Draw for the United States?" Written testimony presented before the House Committee on International Relations Subcommittee of International Economic Policy and Trade, March 5, 1998. August 19. Available on Lexis-Nexis Academic Universe.

———. 1998b. "Multinational Madness." *Tikkun,* May 15. Available on Lexis-Nexis Academic Universe.

Walzer, Michael. 1991. "The Idea of Civil Society: A Path to Social Reconstruction (Part of a Symposium on the Social Breakdown of the United States)." *Dissent* 38 (spring): 293–304.

———. 1992. "Comment." In *Multiculturalism and "The Politics of Recognition,"* edited by Charles Taylor, et al. Princeton, N.J.: Princeton University Press.

———. 1995. "The Concept of Civil Society." In *Toward a Global Civil Society,* edited by Michael Walzer. Providence, R.I.: Berghahn Books.

Warren, Mark. 1996. "Deliberative Democracy and Authority." *American Political Science Review* 90: 46–60.

Waterman, Peter. 1996. "A New World View: Globalization, Civil Society, and Solidarity." In *Globalization, Communication and Transnational Civil Society,* edited by Sandra Braman and Annabelle Sreberny-Mohammadi. Cresskill, N.J.: Hampton Press.

———. 1998. *Globalization, Social Movements and the New Internationalisms.* Washington, D.C.: Mansell.

Watters, Pat. 1971. *Down to Now: Reflections on the Southern Civil Rights Movement.* New York: Pantheon.

Waugh, Thomas, ed. 1984. *"Show Us Life": Toward a History and Aesthetics of the Committed Documentary.* Metuchen, N.J.: Scarecrow Press.

Weaver, Richard M. 1965. *The Ethics of Rhetoric.* Chicago: Regnery.

Weber, Max. 1978. *Economy and Society.* Berkeley and Los Angeles: University of California Press.

Weiser, Philip J. 1993. "Ackerman's Proposal for Popular Constitutional Lawmaking: Can It Realize His Aspirations for Dualist Democracy?" *New York University Law Review* 68: 907.

West, Lois A. 1997. *Feminist Nationalism.* New York: Routledge.

Westbrook, Robert B. 1991. *John Dewey and American Democracy.* Ithaca, N.Y.: Cornell University Press.

Wilcox, Michelle. 1997. "Preferring Women in Politics." Unpublished paper.

Williams, Bernard. 1988. "Formal Structures and Social Reality." In *Trust: Making and Breaking Cooperative Relations,* edited by Diego Gambetta. Cambridge: Blackwell.

Williams, Raymond. 1976. *Keywords: A Vocabulary of Culture and Society.* London: Fontana.

Woodward, J. D. 1994. "Coverage of Elections on Evening Television News Shows: 1972–1992." In *Presidential Campaigns and American Self-Images,* edited by Arthur H. Miller and Bruce E. Gronbeck. Boulder, Colo.: Westview.

Woolf, Virginia. 1938. *Three Guineas.* San Diego: Harcourt Brace.

Wriston, Walter B. 1992. *The Twilight of Sovereignty.* New York: Scribner.

Young, Iris Marion. 1990. *Justice and the Politics of Difference.* Princeton, N.J.: Princeton University Press.

———. 1997. *Intersecting Voices: Dilemmas of Gender, Political Philosophy, and Policy.* Princeton, N.J.: Princeton University Press.

———. 2000. *Inclusion and Democracy.* Oxford: Oxford University Press.

Zack, Naomi. 1993. *Race and Mixed Race.* Philadelphia: Temple University Press.

Zajovic, Stasa. 1994. "I Am Disloyal." In *What Can We Do for Ourselves?* Proceedings of the East European Feminist Conference. Belgrade: Centre for Women's Studies, Research and Communication.

Zaller, John R. 1992. *The Nature and Origins of Mass Opinion*. Cambridge: Cambridge University Press.

———. 1996. "The Myth of Massive Media Impact Revived: New Support for a Discredited Idea" In *Political Persuasion and Attitude Change,* edited by D. Muntz. Ann Arbor: University of Michigan Press.

Zatz, Noah D. 1998. "Sidewalks in Cyberspace: Making Space for Public Forums in the Electronic Environment." *Harvard Journal of Law and Technology* 12: 149.

Zolo, Danilo. 1997. *Cosmopolis: Prospects for World Government*. Translated by David McKie. Cambridge: Polity Press.

Index

Tariffs and Trade; Multilateral
Agreement on Investment; North
American Free Trade Agreement
transnational corporations, 76, 77–78.
See also globalization
Trujillo, Carla, 39
trust, 51, 54
Turner, J., 113
Turner, Ralph H., 125
Turner Broadcasting v. FCC, 14, 16–17

UN Charter model of sovereignty, 67
United Nations, 67, 177, 194, 198,
206n2, 207n11. *See also* Universal
Declaration of Human Rights
United States Constitution, 4. *See also*
Equal Rights Amendment; freedom of
speech
Universal Declaration of Human Rights,
177–79, 180, 181, 188, 191n1, 194,
197–98, 206n2
universalism: globalized market culture,
182–86, 187, 191nn2–3; and hybrid
identities, 187–88; of imagination,
188–90; and individualism, 180–82,
184; universal human rights (*see*
human rights); universalization of
morality, 197, 207n10

Vance, Carole S., 149–50
Voting Rights Act of 1965, 130

Walesa, Lech, 142
Wallach, Lori, 77
Walzer, Michael, 29, 76
Warren, Mark, 53
Washington Post, 87, 93–94, 96, 145, 149
Waterman, Peter, 74
Weaver, Richard M., 95
Weber, Max, 207n8
Webster, Daniel, 100
Webster v. Reproductive Health Services,
165, 168, 174
welfare state, 69–70, 71, 74
West, Harry, 144
Westphalian model of sovereignty, 67
Wilcox, Michelle, 32

Williams, Bernard, 51
Williams, Raymond, 28, 45n1
Willie Horton ad, 59, 112–13
WIPO. *See* World Intellectual Property
Organization
Wittgenstein, Ludwig, 35
women: discursive style, 46n10; diversity
in social identities, 32, 45n4;
domestic violence, 169, 171, 207n12;
and the family, 171–72; Hispana-
white/Anglo communication, 41–42;
media coverage of women's issues,
159, 159–63, **160**, **161**, **162**, **171**,
171–74, **172**, **173**; and national
militism, 39–40; sexual violence
against, 138, 147–51, 152; U.S.
events affecting, 165–71. *See also*
feminists and feminism; *and specific
women's groups*
Women's Equity Action League (WEAL),
163, 174n4
Woodward, J. D., 100
Woolf, Virginia, 40
Worden, Steven K., 126
world government. *See* international
governance
World Intellectual Property Organization
(WIPO), 76, 82n14
World Trade Organization (WTO), 76,
77, 79
Wriston, Walter B., 70
WTO. *See* World Trade Organization

Young, Iris Marion, 31–33, 36, 45n3
Yugoslavia, 39–40, 45n1. *See also* Bosnia;
Serbia

Zack, Naomi, 32
Zajovic, Stasa, 40
Zald, Mayer N., 123
Zaller, John R., 156
Zatz, Noah D., 21–22n24
Zolo, Danilo, 75, 81n11
Zornosa, Anna L., 74
Zurcher, Louis A., 120
Zylan, Yvonne, 132

About the Contributors

James Bohman is Danforth Professor of Philosophy at Saint Louis University. He is the author of *Public Deliberation: Pluralism, Complexity and Democracy* (MIT Press, 1996) and *New Philosophy of Social Science: Problems of Indeterminacy* (MIT Press, 1991). He has also recently edited books on *Deliberative Democracy* (with William Rehg) and *Perpetual Peace: Essays on Kant's Cosmopolitan Ideal* (with Matthias Lutz-Bachmann), both with MIT Press. He is currently writing a book on cosmopolitan democracy.

Andrew Calabrese teaches media studies in the School of Journalism and Mass Communication at the University of Colorado at Boulder. He has published many research articles on communication politics and policy and is editor of *Information Society and Civil Society* with Slavko Splichal and Colin Sparks (Purdue University Press, 1994) and *Communication, Citizenship and Social Policy* with Jean-Claude Burgelman (Rowman & Littlefield, 1999). His current research is focused on the end of citizenship as a theme in contemporary discourse about media and globalization.

Simone Chambers is associate professor of political science at the University of Colorado at Boulder. She is the author of the prize-winning book *Reasonable Democracy: Jürgen Habermas and the Politics of Discourse* (Cornell University Press, 1996). She has published numerous articles and book chapters on democratic theory and discourse analysis.

Anne N. Costain is director of the LeRoy Keller Center for Study of the First Amendment, professor of political science, and associate vice president, University of Colorado. She is the author of *Inviting Women's Rebellion: A Political Process Interpretation of the Women's Movement* (Johns Hopkins University Press, 1992) and editor of *Social*

Movements and American Political Institutions along with Andrew S. McFarland (Rowman & Littlefield, 1998).

Heather Fraizer is a doctoral student in comparative politics at the University of Colorado at Boulder. Her dissertation examines the social movement outcomes of environmental groups in Chile. Her previous work has included research on: women's political participation in the former Soviet Union, repression and democratization, and U.S. riots.

Roderick P. Hart holds the Shivers Chair in Communication and Government at the University of Texas at Austin. He serves as director of the Strauss Institute for Civic Participation. He is the author of ten books, including *Campaign Talk: Why Elections Are Good for Us* (Princeton University Press, 2000).

Jerry Hauser is professor of communication and department chair at the University of Colorado, Boulder. He is the author of *Vernacular Voices: The Rhetoric of Publics and Public Spheres* (South Carolina Press, 1999) and *Introduction to Rhetorical Theory* (Harper and Row, 1986 and Waveland Press, 1991), as well as numerous articles in scholarly journals.

Shanto Iyengar is professor of communication and political science at Stanford University. He holds a Ph.D. from the University of Iowa and taught previously at the University of California, Los Angeles and the State University of New York at Stony Brook. His areas of interest include mass media and politics, public opinion, and political psychology. His principal publications include *Do the Media Govern?* co-edited with Richard Reeves (Sage, 1997), *Going Negative* co-authored with Stephen Ansolabehere (Free Press, 1995), and *Is Anyone Responsible?* (University of Chicago Press, 1991).

Alison M. Jaggar is professor of philosophy and women's studies at the University of Colorado at Boulder. She is the author or editor of several books on feminist theory, ethics, and politics, including, most recently, *A Companion to Feminist Philosophy* with Iris Young (Blackwell, 1999). She is currently working on a feminist theory of moral reason. Jaggar was a founding member of the Society for Women in Philosophy and is past chair of the American Philosophical Association Committee on the Status of Women.

Mark Kingwell is associate professor of philosophy at the University of Toronto. He is the author of four books in political and cultural theory, including *A Civil Tongue: Justice, Dialogue and the Politics of Pluralism* (Pennsylvania State University Press, 1995), which won the Spitz Prize in political theory. His work has appeared in many academic journals as well as in *Harper's*, the *New York Times Magazine*, and the *Utne Reader*. His work has been translated into eight languages. He has just published a new book, *The World We Want: Virtue, Vice, and the Good Citizen* (Viking, 2000).

Doug McAdam is professor of sociology at Stanford University. He is the author of numerous books and articles on social movements and the dynamics of contention.

Among his best-known works are: *Political Process and the Development of Black Insurgency, 1930–1970*, a new edition of which was published in 1999 by the University of Chicago Press, and *Freedom Summer* (Oxford University Press, 1988), which was a finalist for the American Sociological Association's Best Book Award for 1991. He is co-author, with Sidney Tarrow and Charles Tilly, of *Dynamics of Contention* (Cambridge University Press, forthcoming 2001).

James W. Nickel is professor of philosophy at the University of Colorado at Boulder, where he has taught since 1982. Nickel specializes in ethics, political philosophy, and philosophy of law. He is the author of *Making Sense of Human Rights* (University of California Press, 1987). Recent publications include "Group Agency and Group Rights," in *Ethnicity and Group Rights*, edited by Will Kymlicka and Ian Shapiro (New York University Press, 1997), and "Economic Liberties," in *The Idea of Political Liberalism*, edited by Victoria Davion and Clark Wolf (Rowman & Littlefield, 2000).

Phil Weiser is a professor at the University of Colorado at Boulder, where he holds a joint appointment at the School of Law and the Interdisciplinary Telecommunications Program. He received his B.A. with high honors from Swarthmore College and his J.D. with high honors from New York University. Before joining the University of Colorado, he worked at the Justice Department's Antitrust Division, where he served as special counsel on telecommunications policy to the assistant attorney general.